BEATLES

MYTHS AND LEGENDS

NEIL NIXON

Typeset by Jonathan Downes,
Cover and Layout by SPiderKaT for CFZ Communications
Using Microsoft Word 2000, Microsoft Publisher 2000, Adobe Photoshop CS.

First published in Great Britain by Gonzo Multimedia

c/o Brooks City,
6th Floor New Baltic House
65 Fenchurch Street,
London EC3M 4BE
Fax: +44 (0)191 5121104
Tel: +44 (0) 191 5849144
International Numbers:
Germany: Freephone 08000 825 699
USA: Freephone 18666 747 289

© Gonzo Multimedia MMXVI

ISBN: 978-1-908728-55-5

Dedication

To my longtime work colleague, friend and Beatles obsessive Michael Ellis who has been known to greet me with such cheery missives as; 'Honestly Neil, you're the only person on earth listening to that rubbish this morning, nobody else alive takes Atomic Rooster seriously.'

This one's for you Michael

The Beatles: Myths and Legends

Contents

Introduction - Let Me Take You Down

The Beatles remain the best-selling, most critically praised popular music act in history. Beyond that, the band and their works probably form the most inspirational force ever produced by one act in the popular music industry. In cultural terms only the power of Elvis comes close. Many acts, and many styles of music have brought changes to the music world but it takes an exceptional musical act to bring about the monumental shifts that have attended the work of The Beatles. There is very little Beatle ephemera left unrecorded. You will find books chronicling the activities of the band on a day by day basis, detailed considerations of every track and every musician appearing on every track. Elsewhere a range of detailed biography and investigation attempts to achieve the last word in explaining the nuances of the individual Beatle lives. No band in popular music history has ever been so studied, argued over or dreamed about. The range of meanings arising from the individual actions and recorded works of The Beatles continue to expand.

Which is where this niche investigation comes in. There have been urban legends and rumours about the band since they first became famous. Some of the stories in this book go back that far, notably the wrong-headed wonder that never ceases claiming Ringo Starr to be Jewish. The Beatles' drummer was the subject of a 1964 death threat because of that. No amount of evidence to the contrary appears to have completely strangled the Jewish rumour. Indeed, no amount of provable evidence appears to be able to kill off the best Beatle rumours and legends. So this book celebrates and explores these stories. To the best of our knowledge it is the first book to do so by focussing on the band. There are separate works providing more detail on the alleged death of Paul McCartney in late 1966, and on the alleged role of U.S. security services in the killing of John Lennon in 1980. These works are cited when their research has informed what is written here. But the present book sets out to do a slightly different job to those tomes, and to the many other Beatle related books, websites and articles which have been trawled in the search for information to make this book.

Broadly speaking the intention of this book is to mix the best known Beatle legends with others of a lower profile and – therefore – provide a readable and entertaining overview of the whole bizarre world of Beatle beliefs. This is not an academic book in the traditional sense, it lacks footnotes and copious referencing and doesn't set out to promote a specific theory about its contents. That is intentional. I wanted the book to be read and enjoyed rather than studied.

However, following up any of the threads mentioned here is easily achieved by Googling the websites quoted, finding the books cited or simply setting off into cyberspace to hang around with those who have already explored these stories. Similarly, this is not a book about urban legends, though some of the stories explored here count conclusively as well established legends. Beyond presenting and discussing the various stories in the book the real point of this work is to collect the strangest and most sublime Beatle stories between one set of covers and celebrate the extraordinary array of beliefs arising from one rock band. In doing so this book deliberately heads into very esoteric territory. The point of this meander from the main conspiracy theories and rumours is to show the full range of Beatle strangeness so far as stories relating to the Fab Four are concerned. Along with the tried and tested death rumours *The Beatles: Myths and Legends* revives a little remembered and utterly strange death rumour relating to George Harrison and trawls a selection of Ringo related stories before providing a digest of the very margins of Beatle releases, looking into the music widely attributed to the band and occasionally bootlegged as genuine output when it is nothing of the sort. I hope the collection of chapters, each with its own identity, works like a good Beatle album, showcasing the four individuals who made up the most successful popular music combo the world is ever likely to see, and also celebrating the unique chemistry that made the band much more than the sum of four significant talents (five if you count George Martin's considerable input).

It struck me in the writing of the book that each Beatle has the rumour or legend he deserves. John is commemorated in terms of his importance as an activist and his power to influence others, Paul's death rumour celebrates the minutiae of creative elements in Beatle songs and artwork, George's rumour grows directly from his ability to inspire others to seek spirituality and the varied Ringo rumours celebrate the man's understated ability to amaze the unwary by achieving things they never believed he could. The varied rumours about Beatle songs that were never recorded by any of the band cover everything from Beatle-alike beat music – "Lies" by Knickerbockers – to cutting edge musical creativity – like *Meet The Residents* – and the sheer diversity of material included in the final chapter speaks volumes about the music people believe The Beatles to have been capable of creating.

So this book is a celebration of the band, albeit a strange celebration and not one The Beatles would ever have sought or approved of. It might be useful to imagine it as an "all round to mine" get together at which you turn up and find yourself wondering; "where the hell do these people go the rest of the time, I've never met them?" That's pretty much how I felt every time I turned up to a Motörhead gig, but it never stopped me going to the gigs or looking for the next one. When the various Beatles have commented on any of the rumours here it has tended to be negatively. It is possible that the band were to some extent complicit in encouraging the early moments of Paul is dead rumours because these were provably driving record sales during a period when the band were not playing live. But, that novelty soon wore off for The Beatles, and pretty much every other rumour or legend in this collection has been ignored by the various Beatles or actively discouraged. The point of this book isn't so much to revive belief in any of this, but to collect and present a part of Beatle history that is always likely to remain on the margins of why they matter. So this is a book for die-hards and the open minded, and one Beatle book with a market well outside of Beatle fans. Very little of what you read as the mainstay of a rumour or legend here is true. Where you encounter truth – like the fact the FBI most certainly kept files on John Lennon – it doesn't prove a subsequent story; like the FBI being complicit in his murder.

Ultimately what you believe is down to you. This book is a guide to the greatest hits of a strange canon of stories. There is so much more of this online that only the truly rabid could keep up with all developments. I've tried to be objective where most of the material is concerned, though I'll readily admit that my main interest here is collecting and collating this stuff. My fascination is focussed on why these stories emerge and why people believe them. Personally I don't believe any of the rumours or legends here are true; though I do stand by the list of reasons why The Beatles were lucky to recruit Ringo.

More than anything else I hope the combination of challenging ideas and entertainment on offer here makes you glad you gave this book your time and effort to read it. At their best – which is for most of their recorded output – The Beatles produced work that repaid repeated listening and inspired others in many ways. They may be long gone, but their story carries on for as long as people continue to be inspired by the band.

Finally, the usual disclaimer; the facts here are as accurate as I could get them. Though the business of investigating conspiracies and their online supporters is fraught with difficulty. Things I claim you can find and quote in my arguments may have changed or vanished by the time you go looking. Similarly, there are inconsistencies in things cited here, up to and including the way names are written. For example, those conspiracy theorists most pedantic about their work typically write "MK-ULTRA" whilst some official documents of the time have it as "MKULTRA." When quoting an original source I've gone with their spellings of names and other specifics. When discussing the same items in my own words I've gone with the spellings I thought most reputable. All I can say is I've done my best to keep it clear and plain. It wasn't easy to start with, hopefully your enjoyment of the stories will not be greatly spoiled.

Chapter 1

John Lennon: Was Killed in an Authorised CIA 'Hit'

The Beatle myth with crossover appeal and the strongest ongoing legend of all the Beatles' conspiracy and legend stories. The gist of this story suggests the CIA were behind the brainwashing of Mark David Chapman and the man (almost) universally agreed to be the sole murderer of John Lennon was, in fact, a programmed assassin activated when his handlers decided he should go into action. The decision to unleash Chapman occurred after Lennon had ended his self-imposed exile from the music business and, crucially, a few days before Lennon was due to take to the streets in a protest march in support of Japanese American workers in San Francisco. Seen in these terms Lennon's killing amounts to a political assassination carried out on someone best known as a rock musician. The reason for the deed – according to most of the conspiracy theory material available in books and online – was specifically to neuter Lennon's campaigning and political agitation. The general aim of taking out the spokesman for a generation was also useful. Conspiracy theories generally see the timing of all of this as significant both because Lennon was in the process of re-launching his music and activism and also because Lennon was assassinated after the U.S. had elected Ronald Reagan to his first term as president, but before Reagan had taken office. In general, the theorists considering the killing of Lennon in this context don't suggest Reagan had any knowledge of the plot, or would have approved it if he had. Some theories link Reagan's impending presidency to the event because they see CIA motivation being driven by the knowledge that American foreign and domestic policy was preparing to veer strongly to the right; making it less tolerant of activism and the kind of outspoken championing of the downtrodden which had been a feature of John Lennon's most significant period as a campaigner. As a final twist to the main argument about Lennon's alleged assassination it should be noted that the man's fight for permanent citizenship in the USA would – in all likelihood – have ended successfully in 1981 had he lived. His fight for the right to remain in the country was consistent news in the early seventies. The difference between someone whose presence is acknowledged and tolerated (i.e. John Lennon in December 1980) and a permanent resident (i.e. Lennon as he may well have been in December 1981) is considered central to Lennon's death by many of those who believe the fatal shooting to be an act of political assassination. The argument runs that Lennon's receipt of full U.S. citizenship would have heralded a period when he ceased to fear deportation and would have become as active and radical as he had in the late sixties, making him a potent and persistent critic of the policies Reagan and his administration were planning to implement.

Before we dive headlong into a morass of mind-bending Fab Four fables, a word of warning is in order. The paragraph above, though complex and teasing out a few threads, is about as simple as any of this gets. Each Beatle tale will demand its own style of telling, some will take flights of fancy likely to make your jaw drop, even if you thought you knew the story before reading it. Beatle myth and legend is not a place for the literal thinker or anyone intolerant of a vivid claim lacking hard evidence. In 1977 The Grateful Dead once gleefully titled a compilation of their best weed-steeped anthems with the title *What a Long Strange Trip It's Been.* With all due respects to some of the most successful stoners ever to fumble with a fingerpick, I'd suggest the labyrinthine lunacy of the most outrageous tales offered as explanations for Beatle activity leave strange trips behind and exist somewhere on the outer fringes of human reasoning. Lennon provides us with the best entry into this peculiar world attaching itself to the most successful pop group this planet is ever likely to see, because his story is the sanest and best evidenced. Not – for one second – that I'm suggesting it's true. It's also, probably, the easiest to tell because it has already been exhaustively researched and the best researchers in this area have written coherent books. Some of the loose ends are tied up by their efforts, some gaps in the official record are also clearly exposed. Therefore, we'll begin our consideration of the "assassination" of John Lennon by recounting the research and writing of those who got to the original witnesses and first sought out and digested the pertinent documents.

Foremost amongst these was Fenton Bresler (1929-2003) a British barrister and journalist. Whatever its merits as a convincing work in support of most of the claims in the first paragraph of this chapter Bresler's *Who Killed John Lennon?* (1989) is easily the single best researched investigation of the alleged CIA plot behind the killing. More significantly it is the work that under-pins the vast majority of subsequent investigation and theory in this area. Finally, from the point of view of someone who has spent a significant amount of man hours reading all manner of Beatle related conspiracy arguments, Bresler's book is refreshingly well written and erudite. So, the outline of the main arguments which follows acknowledges Fenton Bresler's work in compiling a case suggesting John Lennon was assassinated to order. However, in reading this we should consider what a glowing and characterful *Daily Telegraph* obituary for Bresler stated: "Among Bresler's own admitted weaknesses was one for conspiracy theories." The *Daily Telegraph* further noted Bresler was "invariably good company," a fact that goes some way to explaining the popularity and accessibility of *Who Killed John Lennon?* Literary critics were prone to being sniffy about Bresler's prose style, but his various conspiracy related works sold well and, on the evidence of the websites contributing to this book, continue to be influential.

Who Killed John Lennon? never claims to prove its case. It does, however, dig so deeply in the circumstantial evidence that the argument relating to Mark Chapman's status as a Manchurian candidate assassin is rooted in as many provable facts as the practiced barrister can muster. Bresler's unease at the conviction of Mark Chapman grew from things he already knew to be true with regard to activity in the U.S. secret services. His conviction that he was right strengthened when he managed to prove significant gaps in the understanding of the police officers who investigated the death of John Lennon. The strongest test of Bresler's argument never came to pass because Chapman's guilty plea effectively ensured that the bulk of the evidence relating to the killing of Lennon would never be tested in court. The legal hearings were mainly limited to a consideration of any mitigation regarding Chapman's mental state at the time of the killing. The claims about the motive behind the crime and the means by which he achieved them made in Chapman's statements to police remained on file, and untested in cross examination.

The foundation of Bresler's case is certainly strong, because he makes it so. From the outset Bresler accepts that 40 years of practice at the London Bar and a concurrent journalistic career have made him suspicious of easy explanations of murder. He admits Chapman may have been a "'lone nut'" but doesn't find the notion convincing. Bresler made it his business to accrue "the largest number of documents" hitherto released under America's Freedom of Information Act on the killing, though the majority of the file remained closed to researchers at the end of the eighties whilst Bresler was doing his research.

Bresler's initial suspicions surround the killer himself. Much of the work he had previously done in court and in newsrooms meant he was alarmed when Chapman – apparently hell bent on becoming notorious as the man who killed John Lennon – spurned his day in court by pleading guilty. Bresler soon became more convinced the case wasn't as presented because he sought out key players who had not previously been interviewed in press coverage. Notable amongst these was police lieutenant Arthur O' Connor, retired by the time Bresler found him but – on 8 December 1980 – the man commanding the duty force of detectives in New York's twentieth precinct who responded to the initial emergency call and arrested Mark David Chapman. The basis for what follows the opening chapter in *Who Killed John Lennon?* revolves largely around Bresler's ability to weave plausibility into an arrangement of the known facts that adds them up to support the case that Lennon was assassinated for America's national good. Perhaps more accurately that Lennon was assassinated for the national good as a group of covert operatives perceived it. In that regard Bresler struggles to find the hard evidence to extend his knowledge of brainwashing experiments, or other covert operations to prove beyond any reasonable doubt that Mark Chapman fits the models he presents. However, the basis of almost all the robust arguments subsequently presented with regard to the killing of John Lennon comes from Bresler's organisation of the arguments and from the consistent nuggets he personally unearthed through his own investigations. The first conspicuous gem in this collection occurs on page 17 of his book when he quotes Arthur O' Connor stating "He [Chapman] looked as if he could have been programmed" on the night of the killing.

Conspiracy theories by their very nature are fuelled by believers who gather and interpret the facts. So, it makes sense to break up the main planks of the argument from Bresler's book to present undisputed facts, and point out the interpretations others have found. The CIA – who are the agency most often implicated in any conspiracy to "assassinate" Lennon – was founded in 1947. Legislation, in the form America's National Security Act of July 1947 brought the agency into being and tasked them with replacement of the CIG (Central Intelligence Group) which had always been seen as a temporary organisation. In the aftermath of World War Two the nation needed a strong agency, capable of gathering and assessing intelligence to identify and neutralise threats to America's national security. Technically speaking, both then and now, the CIA functions as an "external" agency, focussed on gathering information from around the world. The FBI (Federal Bureau of Investigation), established in 1908, is the domestic agency investigating home grown threats. Whilst the various domains appear to have clear boundaries, set specifically with regard to being on and off American soil, the realities have never been that clear. There is copious documentation, and much evidence easily found online, of exposure of the CIA's domestic activity. Some of this evidence concerns investigations and hearings; notably regarding the infamous "Family Jewels" (specific U.S.-based CIA investigations from the early fifties to mid-seventies). Some of the CIA's U.S.-based activities broke all the major boundaries by using the agency's resources for purposes never intended when it was brought into being. However, much of what has been proven since clearly made sense to those authorising everything from occasional wire taps to widespread investigations. Finally, it should be remembered that the CIA, the FBI and their various associated organisations are in the business of security, and sometimes this means employing the experts, wherever they might be found in the world, because the job demands levels of talent and expertise that are hard to source. In this regard, covert assassination of targets posing a threat to U.S. national security has – according to conspiracy theory at least – become one area in which the CIA are world leaders. One strength the agency offers is a network of contacts and expertise second to none. Much of the information exposed and leaked over the years has presented a picture of agencies like the CIA operating in full awareness that everything from the rendition of suspects to some surveillance was best done in overseas territories where the less savoury elements of the work could be completed a long way from the watchful eyes of journalists and campaigners. However, sometimes an agency, like the CIA, intent on taking out a foreign target posing a threat to their national security, might find their best opportunity arrives when that target visits their country. So, the best way for the CIA to deal with dangerous foreigners might be to shoot them in the USA.

Defectors including Edward Snowden in recent years, and Philip Agee who wrote *Inside the Company: CIA Diary* (1974), have been able to expose covert operations hidden from public view. Agee's book has a relevance to the killing of John Lennon because Agee names the YMCA (with whom Mark Chapman worked around the world) as an organisation providing cover (not necessarily on a voluntary basis) for CIA activity. Snowden's work in exposing the way U.S. intelligence work revealed a lot about security links between the U.S. National Security Agency (NSA), and other organisations including the CIA and Britain's GCHQ. Whilst a lot of the material revealed by Snowden related to general data harvesting there were other revelations about the extent of subterfuge employed by the security agencies and some of the tactics used that confirmed suspicions held by many. Snowden revealed the NSA, CIA and GCHQ had infiltrated online gaming and spied on users of *Second Life* and *World of Warcraft*. The infiltrations included the creation of make-believe characters as a way to interact with other gamers. The security services also monitored the sexual activity of a number of targets online with a view to using the information gathered to discredit them. A particular focus of this work was to target people they regarded as "radicalizers."

Foremost amongst the exposure of the infamous CIA "Family Jewels" in the seventies was a *New York Times* front page report by Seymour Hersh in December 1974. This blew the lid on the way the agency had directly violated its charter through conducting a domestic intelligence gathering operation on an industrial scale during the Nixon administration. The target of the operation was the anti-war movement who sought to get the U.S. forces out of Vietnam. When much of the material relating to the illegal activity finally became public in 2007 there were details of a range of illegal surveillance operations along with specific plans relating to assassinations and experimentation on human subjects. None of which proves anti-war John Lennon was a specific target of CIA assassination – either planned or completed – but it does present a picture of security organisations ostensibly pursuing their official agendas but frequently tempted away, or instructed to engage in other operations deemed important for security reasons. In this culture much effort is employed to ensure that others who might well be horrified at the work done in their name never find out what is going on. For every whistle blower willing – like Edward Snowden – to sacrifice a career there are countless other employees who continue with their work and leave their careers in the security services without ever revealing what crossed their desks. As a finale to this diversion from the main business of considering the killing of John Lennon it is worth noting that the National Security Archive pages relating to the CIA Family Jewels give Lennon one top ten entry he never sought. An inset box listing ten of the most viewed and interesting jewels places a "Document describing John Lennon funding anti-war activists" at #8 in their chart, two places below a "Plan to poison Congo leader Patrice Lumumba." All the documents remain online as of this writing.

If Fenton Bresler was prepared to admit a weakness for conspiracy theories ahead of his investigation into the killing of John Lennon, he was hardly alone. To his generation of journalists the reality of government conspiracies, usually with the aid of an official security agency, was a given. In the decade leading up to the killing of John Lennon many covert operations had come to light and the Watergate scandal had shown that the most cynical operations could be carried on with involvement at the highest level. Leaving aside whatever Richard Nixon did, or didn't, know about the Watergate break-in; that story in particular changed the world with regard to the way conspiracy theories were viewed. By the time the beleaguered president Nixon resigned in 1974 the machinery of government had been tested to near destruction, the world knew that the most powerful man on the planet was distrustful to the point he routinely taped office conversations and the credibility of his office had been shredded by repeated denials about involvement and assertions that he could ride out the crisis. To put in crudely, his resignation could be viewed as a small victory in an ongoing war between a government and its people. The irony in this being that these events occurred in a nation fond of promoting itself as the leading defender of freedom for individuals and human rights. Bresler was one of many journalists believing that a wealth of secrets lay hidden in documents produced by the U.S. government and its security agencies.

It is still a mighty leap of logic to go from hard evidence that the U.S. security agencies operated beyond their remit and frequently at odds with their public to proving they were involved in the killing of a rock musician. However, the various foundations of a case are built solidly by Bresler. Firstly, the notion that a "Manchurian Candidate" assassin could be employed in such an operation is argued with copious detail. Manchuria, a region in Northeast Asia, is irrelevant to this story. So, to a large extent, is the Richard Condon novel that details the kidnap of soldiers in the Korean War who are held prisoner in Manchuria, and finally released back to the USA. Through a series of recurring nightmares some of the group finally realise that they have been brainwashed into believing Sergeant Raymond Shaw is a hero who saved them. In reality Shaw is a programmed assassin who can be triggered into action when he sees the Queen of Diamonds playing card. After being activated in this way he will forget his killing work and go back to being a military hero. The story, of course, is fiction. But the elements under-pinning the fiction are pertinent here.

It is beyond dispute that both cold war superpowers were interested in the potential of mind manipulation to programme individuals. Some appalling cases of coercion and worse have come to light, notably the deaths of Harold Blauer and Frank Olson. Blauer's death in January 1953 was subsequently proven to have been linked to a dosage of a mescaline derivative. Blauer – a former tennis professional – had inadvertently become part of an experiment carried out with the involvement of the U.S. Army Chemical Corps, and – in 1987 – his estate received over $700,000 in damages. The case of scientist Frank Olson revolves around the cause of his fatal fall (or leap) from a New York hotel window in 1953. Despite an out of court settlement in 1975 some details of the case still remain secret and the case has become a staple of conspiracy theories. What is not in dispute is that Olson was administered LSD without his knowledge. The involvement of the CIA in the death of Olson is widely reported and there are cases of experts in the black arts of mind control going public with some details of their work. Lt Commander Thomas Narut spoke about "Dimensions of Stress and Anxiety" at a NATO conference in Oslo. As Jim Keith reports in his book *Mind Control, World Control* "One thing [Narut] mentioned was that there was no shortage of enlisted men who could be studied…he talked about his work with 'combat readiness units,' whose participants included commandos and undercover operatives at U.S. embassies worldwide, including hitmen and assassins." Narut's apparent gaffe in being so willing to reveal these details is one of a series that feed the standard accounts of covert operations in this area. It is now widely known and reported that operation MK-ULTRA investigated the use of mind-control in the context of its potential use by the U.S. security services. The Church Committee Report is widely available online and it exposes much of what went on and – in a statement that will surprise nobody who has read this far into the chapter – the report notes: "Some MKULTRA activities raise questions of legality implicit in the original charter."

All of this information proves beyond doubt that the U.S. had an interest in being able to force people to act against their will to do the bidding of the security services. It doesn't specifically implicate Mark Chapman or identify John Lennon as an agreed target of assassination.

If Lennon was ever considered a serious candidate to be taken down in the interests of U.S. national security then the motives were linked to his fame, and outspokenness in support of a number of civil rights causes. Lennon's various campaigns for peace are well known. Lines from his songs, particularly "Imagine" are quoted in support of peace campaigns to this day. Less well remembered now are the specific political campaigns and causes to which he leant his support. On 11 December 1971 Lennon was onstage in Ann Arbor, Michigan at the John Sinclair Freedom Rally; specifically there to support four of the "Chicago Seven" who had been convicted of a conspiracy to use violence to disrupt the 1968 Democratic Presidential Convention. Prominent amongst the defendants – all of whom were later cleared on appeal – was Jerry Rubin. Rubin – a Berkeley dropout and serial campaigner for a range of social justice causes – was just the kind of counter-culture idealist hated by right wingers for his ability to whip up support for all manner of issues. Lennon's fame and ability to be heard was far greater than that of Rubin. But Rubin's heat-seeking ability to put himself at the centre of a range of campaigns, combined with Lennon's ability to sloganize and market such ideas soon raised the level of activity as the FBI continued to record Lennon's activities in the U.S. There were even CIA agents in the crowd for the gig in Ann Arbor, whether they went out and bought the works of a stellar line up of the usual left wing suspects and a sprinkling of those not usually seen in such company isn't recorded, but it was one hell of a show, boasting: John and Yoko, Phil Ochs, David Peel, Stevie Wonder sax legend Archie Shepp and Bob Seger alongside a few less well remembered acts: Joy of Cooking, The Up and Teegarden and Van Winkle.

Lennon's presence in the USA was only possible because an earlier embargo on his presence there, imposed because of a drugs conviction in Britain, had been lifted in August 1971. John and Yoko duly moved to New York City, the place he would call home until the end of his life. By the time Lennon arrived in New York he already had an active FBI file. A flavour of the attitude J Edgar Hoover's organisation held toward The Beatles in general is seen in a report on Lennon and George Harrison's journey, with their respective wives, to the U.S. in 1970. FBI agents were sent a memo from Hoover which stated, in part: "While Lennon and the Harrisons have shown no propensity to become involved in violent antiwar demonstrations… [the FBI should] remain alert for any information of such activity on their part or information [about] their using narcotics." So, basically, keep a watching brief and nail them the second they step out of line. A number of writers, including Bresler and University of California professor of History Jon Wiener would subsequently use FBI documentation retrieved under Freedom of Information legislation to tell stories about Lennon. Wiener's *Come Together: John Lennon in his Own Time* (1984) chronicles the activism and beliefs that made Lennon such a potent cultural spokesman.

The Bureau were concerned enough by the end of May 1972 to be referring to Lennon's campaigning and support for marginalized groups as "Revolutionary Activities." Lennon for his part was aware of the interest and surveillance and once told author, journalist, comedian and former Merry Prankster Paul Krassner that if anything happened to him and Yoko "it was not an accident." From the perspective of the security agencies tailing Lennon the concerns were real enough. The anti-war campaign in the USA was impacting directly on politics. With an election due in late 1972 and Nixon campaigning hard and likely to win, both the FBI and CIA were digging deep into the financing and organisation of those opposed to continued U.S. involvement in Vietnam. Lennon was playing an active part. In October 1972, with the election imminent, an anonymous CIA agent reported: "John LENNON, a British subject, has provided financial support to Project "Yes", which in turn paid the travel expenses to the World Assembly of a representative of leading antiwar activist Rennie DAVIS." In this period and beyond Lennon and those phoning him were used to hearing clicks on the line and well aware he was a subject of interest for U.S. internal security.

The attention directed at Lennon during this time wasn't simply down to his anti-war activism. From the day he arrived in New York and took up temporary residence it was obvious he wanted to make a permanent home in the country. The tensions on both sides were high. Lennon may have been outspoken and unrepentantly left wing in many of his ideas and attitudes, but he was also an international celebrity and a serious artist with a highly influential body of work to his name. His views posed problems for a country intent on stifling a protest movement, especially one as powerful and effective as that against the war in Vietnam. There were various groups, both organised and sporadic, intent on protesting against the war. Collectively they represented a constant source of news items and arguments against official U.S. policy. Lennon's agreement with their cause made him an annoyance to right wing Americans in general. On the other hand the U.S. authorities could look like hypocrites if a man so synonymous with the cause of personal freedom was barred from taking up residence in the United States. From Lennon's point of view the U.S. offered opportunities, both personal and professional, and a chance to be taken seriously in a range of roles; artist, activist, musician. It also offered a chance for himself and Yoko to start over in the country where her daughter, Kyoko, lived and for them to build a closer relationship with her. Lennon was well aware the FBI were taking an interest in his movements. He was also trapped by his inclination to support causes like the case of the Chicago Seven, and the knowledge that such activism was likely to work against his attempts to become a fully-fledged U.S. citizen.

Jon Wiener, writing an article for the *Los Angeles Times* on 8 October 2010, summarised some of the key events as Lennon fought a deportation order that stayed in place for years. "In 1972, John Lennon had a problem. He and his wife, Yoko Ono, had been living in New York for a year, and they wanted to stay. But it happened also to be the year President Nixon was running for reelection...Lennon and Ono often showed up at antiwar rallies to sing "Give Peace a Chance" — and to tell their fans that the best way to give peace a chance was to vote against Nixon.

The Nixon White House responded by ordering Lennon deported." The order was issued on 23 March 1973, several weeks after a dejected and increasingly drunk John Lennon had made a boorish spectacle of himself as he sat with a party of those opposed to Richard Nixon to watch the incoming election results on television. With state after state falling to the Republicans the planned party soon took on the grim dynamics of a wake.

Lennon's guilty plea to the charge of cannabis possession in 1968 effectively ruled out his immigration to the U.S. because anyone convicted of any drugs offence was banned. So, the White House had the perfect argument in claiming this case wasn't personal, it was simply a matter of U.S. policy.

But, as Wiener notes: "Lennon and Ono had powerful friends who petitioned the Immigration and Naturalization Service on their behalf." These friends organised a campaign on behalf on John and Yoko's right to remain and those petitioning on their behalf were a list of the great and the good in cutting edge arts in the USA at the time, along with some of the usual suspects. The material is now online, showing letters from – amongst others - Joan Baez, Beat poet Gregory Corso, novelists John Updike and Joseph (*Catch 22*) Heller, journalist Joyce Carol Oates, painter Jasper Johns and composers John Cage and Leonard Bernstein of "West Side Story." One of the more singular offerings is a hand written missive from Bob Dylan stating: "John and Yoko inspire and transcend and stimulate…[and] help put an end to this mild dull taste of petty commercialism which is being passed off as artist art by the overpowering mass media…Let John and Yoko stay!"

The bulk of the material was from east coast and left wing types, though Tony Curtis was notable as a high profile Hollywood contributor, arguing: "The presence of John Lennon and Yoko Ono is of cultural advantage to our country." Even New York mayor John Lindsay wrote that the talents of the pair were "among the greatest of our time," adding the deportation proceedings were "a grave injustice."

John and Yoko's political activism gradually spiralled down, though the occasional event – like a protest in June 1973 at the South Vietnamese Embassy in Washington DC supporting an imprisoned female Buddhist peace activist – still made headlines. Perhaps of more interest to the security forces was the couple's attendance the day after the demonstration at the Watergate hearings that were gradually eroding the power base Nixon had schemed to maintain.

The two sides were trapped in a public battle that went on for years. The majority of the breaks fell Lennon's way. Watergate, his own behaviour and the ongoing unpopularity of a losing war in Asia all contributed to the downfall of Richard Nixon in 1974. On 27 July 1976, with Nixon's successor Gerald Ford firmly ensconced in the White House, Lennon finally got his Green Card (though as with most residency permits issued during this period the card was actually blue). Ford, facing a presidential election himself in 1976, seemed to hold a different opinion on The Beatles to his predecessor. He even met George Harrison in 1975, or possibly the imposter claiming to be George Harrison (assuming the real George did die early in 1974). But that is, literally, another chapter. Lennon's full citizenship – with all its attendant benefits – should have followed in due course in 1981.

The hearing at the New York Immigration Bureau was something of a media circus, with speakers in support of Lennon including Gloria Swanson (who had encountered him in a health food store and testified to the potential he held to encourage young Americans to eat healthily). Norman Mailer showboated superbly by lauding Lennon's standing as an artist and throwing in a typically pugilistic and competitive aside: "We lost TS Elliot to England and only got Auden back." For his part Lennon confirmed he had never been a member of the Communist Party, had no intention of becoming involved in attempts to overthrow the U.S. government and fully intended to make his long term home in the country. After 90 minutes of hearings Judge Ira Fieldsteel ruled in Lennon's favour, the courtroom erupted into applause, the first round of audience appreciation Lennon had enjoyed at a live event since striding onstage with Elton John in front of 20,000 people at Madison Square Garden in October 1974 to play his number one "Whatever Gets you thru the Night" and two Beatles' songs.

Lennon slowly went into self-imposed exile from the end of 1975. That year he fulfilled his contract with Apple, albeit with very little in the way of new creative ideas to show. The *Rock 'n' Roll* album released in February of that year was a Phil Spector produced revisiting of the music that inspired the young Lennon; complete with a cover photograph taken in Hamburg of

Lennon in a doorway, dressed in jeans and leather jacket. Three blurry figures in the foreground are so indistinct as to appear ghostly, an effect created with the simple trick of a long exposure and getting Lennon to remain static whilst the figures walked quickly. The three figures are Paul McCartney, George Harrison and Stu Sutcliffe. The album went to #6 in both the U.S. and UK. The frequently acrimonious goings on in the recording sessions are chronicled in May Pang's book *Loving John.* The album presented standards done with a Spectoresque wall of sound and Lennon's vocals alternating a cynical snarl and soulful touches. The standout track, a soul filled reworking of the Ben E King hit "Stand by Me" was the lead single, and the only single from the album to make any significant dent in charts around the world. Critically reviews were mixed, though most could see the value of the work, the main critical gripe revolved around the singer's choice to follow the U.S. chart topper *Walls and Bridges* with a covers record.

Rock 'n' Roll's worst moments are jump about medleys, ripping rapidly through the best known moments of songs, "Rip It Up/ Ready Teddy" is there and gone in just over one and a half minutes. "Bring It On Home/ Send Me Some Lovin'" is slightly more respectful to the originals, mashing the pair in just over three and half minutes. The usual excuse for the inclusion of such blatant filler tracks suggests an artist re-connecting with a muse or simply taking the time out to have fun. Eye-witness accounts, including that of May Pang point out the making of this album was anything but enjoyable but its best moments do channel an infectious energy and Lennon gets over the grief of working with Spector and inside the music far enough to show he was always a natural rock 'n' roller, with one of the best white voices ever employed in performing such music.

The *Shaved Fish* compilation followed towards the end of October 1975, a little over two weeks after Lennon's 35th birthday. Lennon's 35th birthday on 9 October that year was a major watershed in his life for another reason. The birth of Sean, the child he and Yoko had longed for since the late sixties, brought new chances to the pair. Both were at a distance from children born earlier in their lives and both were desperate to make parenthood work. The release of *Shaved Fish* and – five years after it was originally released as the title track to his best-selling solo album – the UK release of "Imagine" as a single allowed Lennon to sign off his Apple contract (which officially expired in 1976) and make a statement about his solo achievements. It also allowed him to take control of his life and plan to make fatherhood his focus for the next few years. *Shaved Fish* proved to be a steady seller, becoming one of the first albums to achieve the new platinum status, required because massive selling albums were making a mockery of the old limits. In the U.S. gold records typically marked $1 dollars of business, meaning 250,000 units shipped was generally enough. The 1976 redefinition gave albums shifting a million units a platinum rating, with half that earning a gold record. Amongst the first platinum albums *Shaved Fish* offered a glimpse of the key elements in Lennon's creative vision. Almost a chronological trawl of his finest singles, *Shaved Fish* showed an angrier, cantankerous and reactive Lennon turning out a perfect concoction of rocking polemics and playful missives on side one, "Instant Karma" and "Power to the People" sit agreeably alongside each other at the centre of the side before the searing "Mother" changes the mood abruptly and "Woman Is The Nigger of the World" ends the side on an unrepentant note.

"Imagine" is pulled out of chronological order to open a more reflective and resigned series of songs on side two, leading a perfectly sequenced quartet including "Whatever Gets you thru The Night," "Mind Games" and "#9 Dream." Aside from sequencing the songs out of chronological order the one creative liberty taken on the album is the relegation of "Give Peace a Chance" to fragments of song opening and closing the album.

The FBI were monitoring Lennon throughout 1975 but it is debateable what those sifting the intelligence were concluding. If the two albums that signed off Lennon's account gave any coherent message it revealed an increasingly reflective man, aware of his past but focussed closer to home than had previously been the case. Lennon was reunited with Yoko and their commitment was shown in their new-born son. *Rock 'n' Roll* showed a man in touch with his musical roots and in charge of his performing skills, *Shaved Fish* told a story of revolutionary increasingly looking inward to calm the emotions fuelling the earlier outbursts. By entering the longest silence of his creative life John Lennon made the most significant statement of all about his ongoing war with injustice. For the next five years the battles he fought were personal, revolving around holding the demons about his own upbringing in check and providing unconditional love and security to a young child with no comprehension of the way others saw his father. Lennon's time as a house husband is chronicled in detail in the controversial *The Lives of John Lennon* by Albert Goldman. Goldman's scathing portrayal of a drug-addled, lethargic, self-hating and infantile man, prone to violent rages and ferocious collisions with those closest to him is at odds with some other accounts. And, as with Goldman's similarly infamous account of the life of Elvis Presley, it devotes the vast majority of its considerable wordage to savaging the myth of the man, often ignoring established views of the artistic achievements that created the myth. If any statement gives us licence to ignore Goldman's book here it is the one made by Sean Lennon. Faced with Goldman's claim that Lennon was so disengaged he would turn the infant Sean "facing away from him so that the boy will not have the opportunity to paint a wet, smacky kiss on his father's face," Sean was adamant that Goldman was wrong, very wrong in fact. Sean told Elliot Mintz in a radio interview: "I'd kiss him, I'd sit on his lap – all the time, any way I wanted to. What he [Goldman] writes is just stupid. Dad was a great person as a father. He did twenty years of fathering in the five years that I knew him."

From the point of the alleged conspiracy amongst America's security services to kill Lennon the debate about the accuracy of the lengthiest account of Lennon's house husband years reveals one important truth. Whatever the man was doing inside the Dakota, and wandering out to enjoy his favourite cappuccino coffee in the afternoon, it didn't involve day to day contact with revolutionary groups or, indeed, much active politics at all. The accounts from those closest to Lennon describe a man immersed in simpler activities including walks in Central Park, holidays, baking bread and snuggling his growing son. Lennon was involved in business and aware of the deals, mainly handled by Yoko that consolidated a significant fortune in well-chosen investments including property and other assets, like rare and valuable cattle. But it was Yoko, more than he, who put in the work to build a secure financial foundation for their future. Lennon was working, at his own pace, and some of the music made in that period eventually emerged to be turned into Beatle records by his former bandmates. But there were no contractual obligations for a set number of albums in a specified period of time and – whatever his state of mind and health – Lennon's engagement with his family was greater than his engagement with the music business or social activism.

He also stayed close to home in New York for much of the time. There were no tours or live gigs, though the Lennons did head to Japan, Bermuda and a few other destinations during this period. Monitoring him from a security point of view got easier, and there was less to report and nothing – apparently – about which to get hugely concerned. Lennon's new contract with Geffen Records in 1980 brought this period to an abrupt end. *Double Fantasy* is widely, and wrongly, believed to be the first album release on David Geffen's new label. In fact Donna Summer's *The Wanderer* was four weeks ahead of it. But *Double Fantasy* certainly earned the world wide headlines because securing the first new music from Lennon, ten years after The Beatles' disbandment was unquestionably a major coup. The concept for the album had already been developed by John and Yoko, who also paid their own money for the sessions at the Record Plant in New York, only going public when they were satisfied with the quality of what was being produced. The couple's publicist, Bruce Replogle, was then charged with circulating the news, and samples of the work, to major record labels. The response was immediate and positive with the couple finding offers from all the usual suspects, and a few high-aiming candidates from smaller companies. David Geffen, a noted shrewd operator, is widely reported to have signed the couple because he insisted on speaking to Yoko first and was mindful of the clear intent for *Double Fantasy* to highlight each of the Lennons as equal contributors.

Some crucial facts are largely lost now in the face of the outpouring of love that followed Lennon's killing. But, there was a period between 17 November 1980 and 8 December in which *Double Fantasy* and its lead single "(Just Like) Starting Over" were given an honest critical assessment from a press and public expecting that these offerings marked a new phase of a lengthy career. The single reached the top ten on both sides of the Atlantic, but didn't reach the top five in either of those territories during Lennon's lifetime. After the killing the declining sales suddenly took an about turn. Critical reaction to *Double Fantasy* was respectful rather than gushing. The major rock music publications were glad to see John back, and intrigued and sympathetic by a concept that put the Lennons' relationship at the heart of the album and alternated their songs. But in Lennon's absence from releasing new material punk had come and begun to disappear in the UK, leaving in its wake a new generation of post punks who took their inspiration from obscure European films and doom-laden electronic music as much as The Beatles. Where The Beatles were a clear inspiration, in the emerging jangle pop of a host of British independent labels the valued tracks were the early beat pop and three chord wonder concoctions from the days when John and Paul were within touching distance as they wrote. His homeland in particular damned John's part in *Double Fantasy* with faint praise and hoped earnestly his mojo would return with more fire in future. Yoko, by contrast, got some of the most sympathetic attention she ever enjoyed during her husband's lifetime. Indeed, Yoko was a clear inspiration to some of those in the forefront of British punk; The Slits, X-Ray Spex and Essential Logic in particular owed a debt to Yoko's sound and vocal style.

In the USA things were slightly more positive. Lennon's value as a cultural icon in that territory was so high that more reviewers were prepared to regard his half of *Double Fantasy* as a reckoning and consolidation, more positive in this regard than Bob Dylan's headlong sprint for God around the same time or the increasingly predictable offerings of others mired in mid-career. Punk had meant less in America with bands like The Cars and The Knack, who would have been consigned as power-pop in Britain, leading punk's sales.

But nothing in Lennon's *Double Fantasy* work presented a clear threat to U.S. security interests, either internal or external and very few reviewers were seriously exploring a possible future in which the man would become a musical spokesman for a massive community of activists. Lennon's lyrics suggested quite clearly he had lost interest in such a move. "Beautiful Boy" was where he was at now, loving fatherhood and pouring his wonderment into a love song easily understood by besotted parents everywhere. "Woman" and "Dear Yoko" joined "(Just Like) Starting Over" in exposing the private love the Lennons held for each other to public view. When John did address his former life it was to place it firmly in the past and identify himself as a different person to the public image. "Cleanup Time" for all its goodtime boogie roll is a statement about the Lennons cleaning up everything from their finances to recreational drug use and "Watching the Wheels" finds a contented Lennon aware of the same worries he agitated against years before, but choosing to sit out the fight. He's "no longer riding on the merry-go-round" and enjoying the distance and disconnection because when it comes to the endless turning of the wheels he "really love[s] to watch them roll." "Watching the Wheels" is the nearest thing to a political statement Lennon makes on the album and represents a companion piece to the earlier "primal scream" statements in "God" on the *Plastic Ono Band* album. Both songs reject a series of options to peel away Lennon's position, and both eventually come down to the only contentment appearing in connection with others and in the moment. But "Watching the Wheels" lacks urgency and – crucially – lacks raw pain and anger. By *Double Fantasy* Lennon was clearly rejecting the notion that he had to compete with anyone, that staying "on the ball" mattered or that anything other than "doing what I'm doing" would improve his life. If the song doesn't offer the specific of just believing in "Yoko and me" that forms the hope in "God" it still makes the same statement because everything else on *Double Fantasy* makes it clear that "doing what I'm doing" amounts to living a contented family life in New York where "watching shadows on the wall" is a simple joy.

If a fevered FBI meeting was called to consider Lennon's return and the contents of *Double Fantasy* surely it disbanded in a less frenzied state than it started. To give the FBI, or indeed any of the major security organisations in America, their due, they'd doubtless contrived some means of hearing the whole of the sessions for *Double Fantasy* soon after 22 September when the main work was done. So they would have known what it took the public years to discover; the discarded tracks from the album did display more diverse styles and some slightly edgier efforts from Lennon, notably "Nobody Told Me" with its references to "UFOs over New York" and "a little yellow idol to the north of Kathmandu." But if American security were investigating every detail of Lennon's new work they – surely – would have been reassured by a few things. His stranger and more experimental work was still massively tame compared to the material produced by much younger performers in 1980. Even the trips into previously uncharted territory, like the reggaefied "Borrowed Time" still drew heavily on the idea that

Lennon's security came from his domestic contentment and his happiness grew when freeing himself from cares about the future. "Borrowed Time," incidentally, was inspired by an incident on a yachting holiday (not a place radical activists hell bent on smashing the state are normally found) and its lyric focusses on the feelings that grew when Lennon had to take the wheel of his yacht in a storm because the raging weather had fatigued the crew and/or laid them low with seasickness. Ironically Lennon reckoned his recovery from heroin addiction chronicled in "Cold Turkey" had left a lingering side-effect of rendering him immune to seasickness. "Borrowed Time" might borrow stylistically from Bunny Wailer, but it packs the same message as "Watching the Wheels." "Nobody Told Me" might suggest UFOs traverse the skies of a major American city but it told nobody in 1980 anything Lennon hadn't already told them in a scribbled note on the *Walls and Bridges* cover where he dates his own UFO sighting in 1974. The conversational aside of "and I ain't surprised" that follows the UFO reference and the general sense of staggering bemusement at everything happening to the singer is totally misplaced when we consider the real intent of this outtake from the *Double Fantasy* sessions. Lennon recorded a rough version with the *Double Fantasy* band but the song was never meant for a John and Yoko album. Lennon was responding to Ringo's need for new material for the album that would eventually be released as *Stop and Smell the Roses* (1981). So, it makes sense to listen to the version on *Milk and Honey* but stretch your listening imagination to hear the down-to-earth Ringo wrapping his lugubrious larynx around the strange events. Had Lennon lived into 1981 then, in all likelihood, he and Ringo would have recorded the song with Ringo on lead vocals in a session already scheduled when Lennon was killed.

Aside from the two discarded *Double Fantasy* tracks that made posthumous single release, the rest of Lennon's *Milk and Honey* efforts are contented love songs very much in keeping with the *Double Fantasy* vibe. What – frankly – did the security forces have to fear from the music Lennon was making in 1980?

And, if they were genuinely worried about immigrant singers preaching revolution and packing albums with un-American broadsides why the hell was Neil Young still breathing as the eighties dawned? He'd embraced punk's fury with a willingness that suggested it was the shot in the arm his generation needed. A response written large over the blistering electric second side of *Rust Never Sleeps* (1979) wherein he opens the four tracks with "Powerfinger" a 1975 song written from the point of a desperate young man killed in a futile attempt to defend his family against an oncoming gun boat. The characters might have English names but the allusions to the Vietnam War, or any conflict promoted by remote politicians and suffered by powerless people trying to do their best, are obvious. The two middle songs following "Powerfinger" – "Welfare Mothers" and "Sedan Delivery" – are rattling punk-styled rockers trawling their stories from sleaze and cynicism, in the first the narrator extols the virtues of the freely available sex offered by unemployed single mothers and in the second the driver only specifies one delivery made; of "chemicals and sacred roots," so we might usefully assume the job he so clearly loves means making deliveries by sedan, not delivering the cars themselves. "Hey Hey, My My (Into the Black)" closes *Rust Never Sleeps* with a crunching riff and Young stating "it's better to burn out than it is to rust." Young clearly saw the dawn of punk as his own opportunity to cut an album as stark and uncompromising as Lennon's *Plastic Ono Band* and "Hey Hey, My My (Into the Black)" sees a man a little under five years younger than John

Lennon heading as far away from "Watching the Wheels" as he can. Young's next studio album, *Hawks and Doves,* was released in the same month as *Double Fantasy.* With one folk side and one country side *Hawks and Doves* has the same brand of easy melodies as Lennon presented at the time but even at his most conservative Young couldn't resist the choppy polemics of "Union Man" (praising the strength in numbers of musicians and – by implication - any skilled trade) or "Comin' Apart at Every Nail" in which the fences across rural America become a metaphor for the social fabric of a country "Comin' apart at every nail." *Hawks and Doves* ends on the title track which, lyrically at least, is in the same area Lennon explored in the bulk of his *Double Fantasy* session songs. The outside world is threatening because "Hawks and doves are circling in the rain" but Young is "ready to go, willing to stay and play" so his "sweet love can dance another free day." In this version of America in limbo between Carter and Reagan a contented home life is the goal but an engagement with life's political realities is a must, and the ironic reference to "play" is Young proving he is practicing what he preaches as he plasters both cynicism and passion over the country side of the album.

Spokesmen for a generation singer songwriters looked like an endangered species as monetarism and MTV hovered just over the horizon. But Neil Young's work in the period shows John and Yoko had options a long way beyond the material recorded in the *Double Fantasy* tracks and those eventually used on *Milk and Honey.*

In fact, John and Yoko had re-emerged publicly for a high profile day in 1979. On 27 May that year they took out a page in the *New York Times* to issue a public statement about what they were doing, and why. The dreamy link it forges between wishes and realities in life is a world away from the angry and agitated polemics that marked their public outbursts at the start of the same decade. All told, the *New York Times* takes the sentiments of "Watching the Wheels" and turns them into a mystic missive more fitting for the end of the decade before:

"Love Letter From John And Yoko To People Who Ask Us What, When And Why".

The past ten years we noticed everything we wished came true in its own time, good or bad, one way or the other. We kept telling each other that one of these days we would have to get organized and wish for only good things. Then our baby arrived! We were overjoyed and at the same time felt very responsible. Now our wishes would also affect him. We felt it was time for us to stop discussing and do something about our wishing process: The Spring Cleaning of our minds! It was a lot of work. We kept finding things in those old closets in our minds that we hadn't realized were still there, things we wished we hadn't found. As we did our cleaning, we also started to notice many wrong things in our house: there was a shelf which should never have been there in the first place, a painting we grew to dislike, and there were the two dingy rooms, which became light and breezy when we broke the walls between them. We started to love the plants, which one of us originally through were robbing the air from us! We began to enjoy the drum beat of the city which used to annoy us. We made a lot of mistakes and still do. In the past we spent lots of energy in trying to get something we thought we wanted, wondered why we didn't get it, only to find out that one or both of us didn't really want it. One day, we received a sudden rain of chocolates from people around the world. "Hey, what's this! We're not eating sugar stuff, are we?" "Who's wishing it?" We both laughed. We discovered that when two of us wished in unison, it happened faster. As the Good Book says — Where two are gathered together — It's true. Two is plenty. A New Clear Seed.

More and more we are starting to wish and pray. The things we have tried to achieve in the past by flashing a V sign, we try now through wishing. We are not doing this because it is simpler. Wishing is more effective than waving flags. It works. It's like magic. Magic is simple. Magic is real. The secret of it is to know that it is simple, and not kill it with an elaborate ritual which is a sign of insecurity. When somebody is angry with us, we draw a halo around his or her head in our minds. Does the person stop being angry then? Well, we don't know! We know, though, that when we draw a halo around a person, suddenly the person starts to look like an angel to us. This helps us feel warm towards the person, reminds us that everyone has goodness inside, and that all people who come to us are angels in disguise, carrying messages and gifts to us from the Universe. Magic is logical. Try it sometime.

We still have a long way to go. It seems the more we get into cleaning, the faster the wishing and receiving process gets. The house is getting very comfortable now. Sean is beautiful. The plants are growing. The cats are purring. The town is shining, sun, rain or snow. We live in a beautiful universe. We are thankful every day for the plentifulness of our life. This is not a euphemism. We understand that we, the city, the country, the earth are facing very hard times, and there is panic in the air. Still the sun is shining and we are here together, and there is love between us, our city, the country, the earth. If two people like us can do what we are doing with our lives, any miracle is possible! It's true we can do with a few big miracles right now. The thing is to recognize them when they come to you and to be thankful. First they come in a small way, in every day life, then they come in rivers, and in oceans. It's goin' to be alright! The future of the earth is up to all of us.

Many people are sending us vibes every day in letters, telegrams, taps on the gate, or just flowers and nice thoughts. We thank them all and appreciate them for respecting our quiet space, which we need. Thank you for all the love you send us. We feel it every day. We love you, too. We know you are concerned about us. That is nice. That's why you want to know what we are doing. That's why everybody is asking us What, When and Why. We understand. Well, this is what we've been doing. We hope that you have the same quiet space in your mind to make your own wishes come true.

If you think of us next time, remember, our silence is a silence of love and not of indifference. Remember, we are writing in the sky instead of on paper — that's our song. Lift your eyes and look up in the sky. There's our message. Lift your eyes again and look around you, and you will see that you are walking in the sky, which extends to the ground. We are all part of the sky, more so than of the ground. Remember, we love you.

John Lennon and Yoko Ono
New York City
PS. We noticed that three angels were looking over our shoulders when we wrote this!

The middle-aged contentment of *Double Fantasy* and the "hello trees, hello sky" (almost literally) sentiments John and Yoko had taken it upon themselves to share with any New Yorker willing to buy the paper that day help us form quite a picture of Lennon's mindset in the months before he was killed. The FBI documents released since his death don't identify the album or letter in the paper as cause of concern. In fact, on the available documentary evidence it seems rock journalists and long-term fans were much more concerned about the musical direction being taken. Apart from anything else, Lennon's new laid back approach of simply letting things happen was at odds with the wilful experimentation and knee-jerk passions that marked his highest art. John and Yoko had trusted in others to put together a session band and oversee the production to a return that was always likely to be measured against the very highest standards. Nobody was seriously suggesting Lennon himself was a spent creative force but the manner in which he had gone about this return almost guaranteed a blander, more formulaic sound than anything he had previously produced. *Shaved Fish* told a story of sonic changes and the carving of sounds to support every song. Lennon's particular genius frequently revolved around creating aspects of danger and anger in the sound and deploying minimal musical weaponry to powerful effect. The *Plastic Ono Band* and *Imagine* albums had both achieved this. So, the clean but solid sounds of *Double Fantasy* were a surprise both in their middle-of-the-road precision and in their willingness to resemble some of Lennon's least regarded solo work. Yoko's contributions were notably edgier, at least in her vocal style. The main change from the past and plan for the future clearly revolved around the pair being as integral to the music as were the members of other notable duos of the time, like The Carpenters. John and Yoko were the act, and were doing things together. On the day he was shot Lennon was carrying tapes from a recording session; he'd been producing Yoko's song "Walking on Thin Ice" and this was likely to be the couple's next stab at a hit once the singles off *Double Fantasy* had been exhausted.

One minor variation on the theme of John and Yoko being a team was scheduled for the week beginning Monday 15 December 1980. John, Yoko and Sean were all planning to be in action as part of a demonstration in San Francisco, and tickets were already booked for the family to fly there. From 13 November Japanese-American workers employed by the Japan Foods Corporation (JFC) had been in active dispute with their management. Superficially the dispute was a simple campaign about wage inequality. Japanese-American workers in three companies, JFC and two subsidiaries, were paid less on average than their white American counterparts. The Lennons had already written to the strikers stating:

> We are with you in spirit. Both of us are subjected to prejudice and abuse as an Oriental family in the Western world.
>
> In this beautiful country where democracy is the very foundation of its Constitution, it is sad that we still have to fight for equal rights and equal pay for the citizens.
>
> Boycott it must be, if it is the only way to bring justice and restore the dignity of the Constitution for the sake of all citizens of the US and their children.

Peace and love,
John Lennon and Yoko Ono

New York City
December 1980

The dispute and the projected boycott had potentially wide reaching consequences for JFC, its subsidiaries and the United States. JFC were a massive concern, their business network accounting for around 90% of all the Japanese food imported and distributed around the United States. Ironically, the company tended to have Japanese-American managers and these people were presiding over an employment regime that was – by the end of 1980 – inciting a massive dispute amongst their fellow Japanese-Americans in the company's ranks. A similar disparity in payment existed in other major Japanese companies with a strong presence in the U.S., so – as Fenton Bresler notes: "corporations like Sumitomo and Mitsubishi were watching the dispute anxiously while supporting the three companies [JFC and its subsidiaries] in every way they could."

The impact John, Yoko and Sean would have had on the dispute will never be known, but the timing of the dispute and the march was carefully considered by the Teamsters Union. After rejecting an offer of annual 3 per cent wage increases for three years (a deal that wouldn't have guaranteed their wages kept pace with inflation) the JFC workers continued their pressure during the biggest sales period of the year for their employers.

John Lennon's involvement in the dispute is cited by most conspiracy theorists as the turning point for the CIA and their monitoring of his activities. Fenton Bresler and most of those following in the wake of the arguments presented in *Who Killed John Lennon?* see a perfect storm precipitating the planned assassination. The incoming Reagan presidency with its stated aims to free America from regulation and free up businesses to trade in a greatly streamlined market is part of this picture, along with Lennon's – apparent – willingness to return to front-line activism. The argument goes on to speculate that with Lennon's full citizenship, available from 1981, likely to be little more than a formality the singer would have become more vocal and directly involved in U.S. politics than ever before.

There is some logic to the line-up of contributory causes to the decision to assassinate an entertainer, but also some major facts missing from this crude consolidation of points. These omissions particularly concern the projected protest march. One of the main reasons the Lennons agreed to this particular dispute was a personal approach from one of the main organisers. Specifically, an approach from Shinya Ono, an activist with a lengthy pedigree in this area including membership of the radical Weathermen group who had carried out subversion, up to and including involvement in bombings and jailbreaks. Most of the group's activities were considerably less spectacular but the loose conglomeration had been a breeding ground for inventive subversion and the group remained active for almost twenty years from the late sixties. Shinya Ono was a radical but also an intellectual who had edited *Studies on the Left,* a publication compiling major articles on a range of leftist ideas and achievements. Shinya Ono was a careerist in this area, with much direct activism writing and research to his credit. At the time he approached the Lennons for their support Shinya was 42 years old and enjoyed a reputation for success in his campaigns. All of this might well have motivated the family to book their plane tickets to San Francisco but there was one other appeal Shinya Ono could make to the couple that other activitists would struggle to make; Shinya was family. Specifically, he was Yoko's cousin.

At which point it might be worth taking a small and slightly grim diversion to ask a pertinent question with regard to the alleged assassination of John Lennon. If the FBI were watching Lennon so closely, and if their paranoia about his potential to ignite all range of subversion by his involvement was so great, why were they just focussing on him? Any significant investigation into his life and work in the five years since his last high profile involvement in public life would have revealed the details outlined here. To have considered those details with regard to what was driving the return to public life would have made one thing obvious. Lennon might still be the name people knew but the significant developments in his career from 1975 to 1980 were hugely down to Yoko's actions. If anything, she was the more significant player in the duo. Their massive gain in their financial fortune accrued over five years was mainly down to business dealings she managed. David Geffen had secured the sought after record deal because he had the sense to talk to Yoko and embrace (at least for the purposes of signing the duo) the notion that she was artistically as important as John in their music, and the one piece of protest the Lennons had agreed to on the back of their re-emergence into public life was a dispute in which Yoko's cousin was a major player. If an assassination was thought necessary for the purposes of protecting national security, why not aim for the driving force of the whole operation; Yoko? A hit on Lennon was certain to have major, ongoing resonance and create a martyr. His words, and songs, had the potential to inform and inspire future generations in this direction. But, he had reappeared in comfortable middle age singing love songs to his wife and son, even the unreleased music from the *Double Fantasy* sessions wasn't all that challenging. Left to his own devices Lennon appeared capable of leading his massive fan base into a more contented place than they had occupied a decade before. With regard to their 1980 output Yoko was the avant-garde artist with the more off-the-wall ideas. Lennon without Yoko might have been inclined to return to fatherhood and seclusion. Yoko had a different legacy to John, and would be a much less likely martyr. This is uncomfortable speculation for sure, but worth considering if only because it raises some significant flaws in the simple logic that suggests the killing on 8 December 1980 was the most obvious means of ridding the world of a potent and battle-ready radical.

If Lennon was assassinated to order then Mark David Chapman is more than a lonely and desperately confused individual. Whatever psychiatric history he presents and whatever he says about the reasons for his actions the conspiracy theories generally present him as a "Manchurian Candidate" killer, brainwashed and programmed far from anyone he knew well, and left as a sleeper to be employed by the security services as and when he was needed. Chapman's history has been poured over in a number of books. In addition to Fenton Bresler's argument some of the leading chroniclers of Chapman's story include Jon Wiener's in *John Lennon in his Own Time, John Lennon and the FBI Files* by Phil Strongman and Alan Parker and *Let Me Take You Down: Inside the Mind of Mark David Chapman – Man Who Shot John Lennon*; credited to Jack Jones but culled from two hundred hours of interviews and largely made up of Chapman talking directly to the reader. There is, as we will see, another line of argument presenting Chapman as an unwitting participant in events, on the scene and willing to offer himself as the guilty party as someone else shot Lennon. We'll arrive at that conspiratorial cul-de-sac presently.

The various studies of Mark David Chapman dispute certain key facts within the alleged conspiracy. In particular it is debateable to what extent Chapman was a major fan of either Lennon or The Beatles. It is certainly the case that Chapman's entire collection of solo Lennon records on 8 December 1980 amounted to one newly bought and newly autographed copy of *Double Fantasy.* A copy he bought only after others hanging around outside the Dakota had suggested he do so. Most die-hard Lennon fans, eager with anticipation had snagged the album a few weeks earlier. At the time of his death, Lennon's sales of both his newly released album and single were falling after the initial rush.

Mark David Chapman was born on 10 May 1955 in Fort Worth, Texas. He arrived into a military family, the son of Staff Sergeant David Curtis Chapman of the United States Air Force. Chapman's mother – Diane- was a nurse. Most of those writing about Chapman chronicle a long and unhappy family history in which Chapman's abusive father inflicted a regime of physical and mental cruelty on both the boy and his mother. In *Let Me Take You Down* Chapman is quoted at length describing an escape into a complex fantasy world which started in his early years and continued up to the point at which he shot John Lennon. Foremost in the strange dynamics of his mental empire was his own central character, capable of exercising an omnipotent power over a vast army of minions. In the equally complex family dynamics Chapman was facing in the real world his feelings towards his parents were confused by the fact his mother would climb into his bed after violent conflicts with his father. Mark was soon trapped – both mentally and physically – in the position of forming a barrier between the two, his feelings further churned up by his inability to fight off his father and his love for his mother and simultaneous resentment at her neediness and leaning on him. The situation is a proven recipe for major mental trauma in later life. It certainly compromised Mark's abilities to form lasting and successful relationships. He has never been close to his sister, Susan.

For all the problems at home Chapman spent much of his life as a young man displaying the ability to be cheerful, positive, an effective worker and a figure of some empathy, especially when working with those younger than himself. His career was chequered, with periods of unemployment and a consistent pattern of failing to rise to positions of responsibility because he was unable to earn the college degree necessary to satisfy his employers at the YMCA.

A similar pattern of consistency and inconsistency appears in Chapman's life choices up to the killing of John Lennon. A rebel and outcast from the mainstream at school, Chapman experimented with drugs and was part of a group of friends who saw obsessive involvement in rock culture as a reasonable alternative to studying. Chapman flipped completely from these values to Born Again Christianity and active involvement in the YMCA. The consistent feature of both of these polar opposites is a need to belong and the presence within each group of a means of explaining most of life's complexities. Broadly speaking, *Let Me Take You*

Down... recounts this story from the perspective of hindsight, allowing Chapman to explain his increasing isolation and the realisation that none of the solutions, easy or otherwise, to his malaise stopped him spiralling down into a seething pit of unfocussed anger and confusion. As Chapman argues his case this anger and confusion eventually found its release in committing murder.

We'll consider the claims that this story is a cover tale from a programmed assassin in due course. But, Chapman tells it vividly in *Let Me Take You Down...* a book written in a journalistic creative nonfiction style; strong on dialogue and cinematic description. It beggars belief that so many conversations could be remembered accurately so long after the event but the point of *Let Me Take You Down...* is the direct engagement with Chapman's mind, and his voice, as his story unfolds to the point of committing murder, and coming to terms with what he has done. In this tale, the murder is almost an act of self-destruction, after which Chapman struggles to make sense of how this act could form part of any plan God might have for his life. Were this a novel, centred on Chapman rather than Lennon, the black moment, when the darkness overwhelms our protagonist comes with the dark altar Chapman creates in his hotel room before stepping out to become "the Catcher in the Rye of my generation." He loads five hollow point bullets into the .38 calibre revolver knowing these bullets will cause maximum devastation as they enter Lennon's body. As Jones describes it: "As he closed the door behind him and walked down the hall...he reflected to himself 'It's almost like something a person who was going to commit suicide would do...lay out the things that mean most to them."

The strange assembly of meaningful things Chapman chose to display, knowing that they would be found whether or not he personally survived after shooting Lennon, included his passport, a small Bible open at the New Testament book of John (which he had amended by adding the word "Lennon"), a glowing letter of support for Chapman from a former YMCA colleague, photographs of himself surrounded by laughing Vietnamese children he had supported and helped, a small poster of the *Wizard of Oz* characters Dorothy and the Cowardly Lion and an eight track tape by Todd Rundgren. Another key exhibit in the tokens of a fragmented mind appeared with Chapman at the scene of the killing. A copy of J.D. Salinger's *The Catcher in the Rye* occupied Mark Chapman between his shooting of Lennon and the arrival of the police. In full view of witnesses he remained on the scene outside the Dakota building and read the book before police driver Steve Spiro took him into custody a few minutes after Lennon had been shot.

Conspiracy theories see the strange assembly of items, the obsession with Salinger's novel and Chapman's bizarre behaviour after the shooting as explicable because Chapman was programmed to act in this way. A more prosaic look at the things he chose to give the act meaning consign them to a sadder story. Another reading of the little assembly suggests it amounts to the usual cry for help/ confused coming together of narrative strands from those bringing about the end of their life. A few bits and pieces – like the letter of recommendation – suggesting the person did amount to something, even if very few others recognised the fact, a selection of deep and meaningful art – like the Rundgren tape and Salinger novel – and some crude statements showing the confused individual could intervene and make simple meanings; like the amendment in the Bible and the selection of the Cowardly Lion picture. Taken in that context Chapman was portraying himself as a person with some depth, apparently in control of his actions however hideous they were to others, and someone who had done good work and made a difference to the lives of others.

Having made this statement about who he was and what he had achieved, Chapman described a strange calm feeling at the moment he met Lennon for the second time that day. Having got Lennon's signature on a newly acquired copy of *Double Fantasy* in the afternoon Chapman was now the sole "fan" still waiting outside the Dakota. His purpose, as far as the staff on duty were concerned, was to get Yoko's autograph on the same album. The time was almost 11pm as John and Yoko returned from working on "Walking on Thin Ice" at the Record Plant. Chapman, faced with the pair emerging from their limo, describes his feelings: "There was no emotion in my blood…no anger…it was dead silence in my brain…[Lennon] looked at me… then I heard in my head. It said 'Do it, do it…over and over…'"

Chapman claims to have heard his own voice, as in the audible voice he recognised as his own, saying these words and also describes some lapses of memory with regard to the shooting. Specifically; "I don't remember aiming, I don't remember pulling the bead or whatever you call it. I just pulled the trigger steady five times."

The Charter Undercover .38 Special revolver and five hollow point bullets, designed to collapse on impact and tumble into a body rather than pass through leaving an exit wound, did their job. In all probability one direct hit, at most two, would have been enough. Chapman landed four of the five shots on target. Although Lennon lingered long enough to grunt a few more words to the doorman and the police who drove him to the emergency room, he was as good as dead once the shooting was over.

Lennon would become – in death – a martyr like figure. The words of his songs took on a reverence and depth apparent only to his most loyal fans during his lifetime. Record sales boomed and his 1980 recordings became the only case in his career when his current album and single topped the charts on both sides of the Atlantic. Lennon's image became more than that of a rock star, taking on the broad meanings of an Einstein or Marilyn Monroe. His name was used on everything from a rock festival celebrating his work to the re-naming of Liverpool's Speke airport in his honour. Since his death the iconic status of Lennon has continued to be powerful and widely recognised. So much so that Paul McCartney, as recently as 2015 in an *Esquire* interview said: "When John got shot, aside from the pure horror of it, the lingering thing was, OK, well now John's a martyr. A JFK… I started to get frustrated because people started to say, 'Well, he was The Beatles.

"And me, George and Ringo would go: 'er, hang on, it's only a year ago, and we were all equal-ish'…

"Now the fact that he's now martyred has elevated him to a James Dean, and beyond."

The shooting also transformed Chapman, from a nobody to a notorious killer known around the world. But, in his own mind, Chapman saw the transformation differently. The event was intended to make him "True and pure and real. Not phoney." In other words, his killing of Lennon ridded the world of a phoney who had sold out principles for a comfortable and unchallenging approach to life. By contrast Chapman became "the star in his own movie. One of the rare children who was destined to become what he had idolized years before." In this context Chapman became the Catcher in the Rye, and declared the novel of the same name to be a seminal text, a way for others to follow. In ridding the world of Lennon he had both drawn attention to himself and made a significant gesture against phoniness.

Because Chapman filed a guilty plea the prosecution were denied the chance to fully interrogate his claims to have been influenced by Salinger's novel. However, Chapman was assertive with regard to the power of the book and its relevance to his actions. In February 1981, whilst preparing an insanity plea, he wrote to the *New York Times*.

> "It is my sincere belief that presenting this written statement will not only stimulate the reading of J. D. Salinger's 'The Catcher in the Rye' but will also help many to understand what has happened.
>
> "If you were able to view the actual copy of 'The Catcher in the Rye' that was taken from me on the night of Dec. 8, you would find in it the handwritten words 'This is my statement.'
>
> "Unfortunately I was unable to continue this stance and have since spoken openly with the police, doctors and others involved in this case. I now fully realize that this should not have been done for it removed the emphasis that I wanted to place on the book.
>
> "My wish is for all of you to someday read 'The Catcher in the Rye.' All of my efforts will now be devoted toward this goal, for this extraordinary book holds many answers. My true hope is that in wanting to find these answers you will read 'The Catcher in the Rye.'
>
> Thank you.
> Mark David Chapman
> The Catcher in the Rye

Read specifically the statement equates Chapman and Holden Caulfield, and identifies Chapman as "The" Catcher in the Rye, in other words the person Holden Caulfield dreams of becoming. The significant passage explaining this in the novel occurs when Holden is talking to his sister, Phoebe. She is the only person he loves unconditionally and the conversation concerns his ambitions. It is significant because Phoebe also looks up to Holden and – to some extent – his struggle to find his purpose is also his struggle to mean something in her eyes. By implication, it can be read as all of our struggles to achieve something of meaning without selling out our principles. Holden's fantasy is of a strange, but meaningful, act.

"Anyway, I keep picturing all these little kids playing some game in this big field of rye and all. Thousands of little kids, and nobody's around - nobody big, I mean - except me. And I'm standing on the edge of some crazy cliff. What I have to do, I have to catch everybody if they start to go over the cliff - I mean if they're running and they don't look where they're going I have to come out from somewhere and catch them. That's all I do all day. I'd just be the catcher in the rye and all. I know it's crazy, but that's the only thing I'd really like to be."

Superficially it is a really strange ambition. At odds in the book with Phoebe's suggestion that he follow their father into being a lawyer. Effectively being "the" (singular) Catcher in the Rye amounts to being a secular messiah. The higher power driving the catching of the straying kids is simply the act of knowing what is right and wrong, and directing the lesser beings – in this context the "kids" – away from danger. Holden Caulfield is repelled by anything phoney and, as he struggles to make any sense of life, the fantasy of omnipotence as the Catcher makes appealing sense. If the book was Chapman's "statement" in the aftermath of his shooting of John Lennon then the statement is that he (Chapman) is there to guide us because he can help us separate the real and the phoney, and he can lead us to read the book that will make sense of this divide, and the killing he carried out.

The power of Salinger's novel was evident long before Chapman was discovered with a copy in his hand as Lennon lay dying a few yards away. The book – then and now – remains one of the most controversial novels in the history of American literature. A staple of English classes for decades, it also boasts a history of bans from libraries. During the lengthy silence of Salinger (1919 – 2010) no film adaptation was possible, though *The Catcher in the Rye* has inspired a range of other works and movies. Chillingly, it is also a feature of other shootings. After John Hinckley Jr. shot president Ronald Reagan in 1981 a copy of the novel was found in the would-be assassin's hotel room and Robert John Bardo, a stalker who finally succeeded in murdering actress and model Rebecca Schaeffer, took a copy of *The Catcher in the Rye* to Schaeffer's Hollywood apartment when he shot her dead in July 1989. Bardo – like Chapman – used a newly purchased gun for the killing and even argued he had come to "rescue" Schaeffer.

The extent to which Mark Chapman was certifiably insane at the time of the killing, and in the years leading up to that act, continue to tax conspiracy theorists. With the benefit of hindsight in *Let Me Take You Down...* Chapman is very articulate on the confused feelings overwhelming him. The book also chronicles his dealings with Dr Naomi Goldstein of Bellvue Hospital, New York City. Dr Goldstein was on duty to receive Mark Chapman in the aftermath of the shooting, her testimony is significant to the conspiracy issue because she is one of only two doctors to encounter Chapman in the aftermath of the event who was duty bound only to be impartial. He was subsequently assessed on behalf of both the prosecution and defence as legal debate raged about his fitness to plead, and his actions in the dying hours of 8 December 1980. Dr Goldstein found Chapman to be lucid, capable of detailed recollection and to be aware of the worldwide implication of what he had just done. There was a distinct sense of detachment from the emotional and physical pain he had inflicted, especially with regard to the pain he inflicted on John Lennon. Dr Goldstein and her colleagues noted that Chapman had – if anything – a higher sense of moral justice and social issues than most people. Not that any of this had prevented him gunning down an unarmed man. The lucidity extended to a frank admission by Chapman that he had no idea when he killed John Lennon of whether he would face the death penalty, or merely a prison sentence. Despite being yelled at after the shooting to get out of the area Chapman had remained on site, and offered no resistance when arrested.

He has explained his behaviour since as an act of becoming somebody, an act that necessitated both the extreme act of killing John Lennon and also remaining to be arrested. The roots of the confusion and rage that drove him to kill are explained by Chapman himself in *Let Me Take You Down...* as going back to childhood. He appears to have had the capacity to hate, focus and scheme from a very early age. Along with a strong awareness of death and sin Chapman describes a "preternaturally vengeful grudge" against a playmate. The playmate's name was Borden and Chapman drew up wanted posters against him. Having struggled to feel comfortable within his own skin, and gradually become aware of the hatred he had for his own violent and unfeeling father Chapman took a predictable route into drug use and escaping into both his own fantasy world, and an obsession with rock music. Chapman's memories of these vivid internal fantasies haven't impressed those believing the killing of Lennon to be a programmed hit, but Chapman himself has described a surreal alternative reality created within his own head. A reality populated by his own "Little People." This compliant version of Lilliput allowed Chapman to lord it over minions, creatures both small in stature and possessing the capacity for independent thought. As Chapman hit his formative years with regard to independence the Beatles stopped touring and morphed into a psychedelic assault on the senses. Chapman cites their *Magical Mystery Tour* album, released when he was 12, as the record that first aroused his curiosity about drugs. The album wasn't given a full UK release until a cassette version – entitled *Magical Mystery Tour and Other Hits* – was put out in 1973. The U.S. release lined up a first side of the original psychedelic music from the *Magical Mystery Tour* film, the same songs released on two EP singles in the UK, and backed it with a side of tracks released on single in 1967. To an impressionable 12 year old, the songs offered up their own fantasy world populated with creatures conjured up in the imagination, validating his own grip on reality. The album currently stands at six times platinum sales in the U.S. alone. Its climb to the top of the American charts in the same year that *Sgt Pepper* dominated the same list marked a monumental shift in sounds and styles. For better or worse the time and budget offered to The Beatles to create soundscapes and songs fit to withstand repeated listening without revealing all their secrets marked a watershed. Other artists, notably Bob Dylan and Frank Zappa had released double albums and already combined complex work with significant sales but the quality control of The Beatles and the monumental scale of their sales marked a shift the record industry had to take on board. From the late sixties it was a given that some acts could exist without too much concern about the singles charts and that acts could usefully be contracted for a number of albums. From this point onwards lawyers and businessmen replaced the chancers and music obsessives who had – thus far – driven the music industry. From the point of the industry, this was a golden era with classic and ground-breaking product, built to last. From the point of view of fans like Mark Chapman this was an explosive and exciting time to be a music fan. Listeners knew that no era like this had existed before and the fact their parents' generation were visibly frightened by some of the new developments, notably the blatant reliance on drugs exhibited by some acts, was an added thrill. The Beatles were a massive presence in this change. To American listeners their sometimes parochial references to places in their past – Penny Lane and Strawberry Fields –

could also add an *Alice Through the Looking Glass* magic to the messages in the songs. *Magical Mystery Tour* as released on the original Capitol album lines up

Side one:
1. Magical Mystery Tour
2. The Fool on the Hill
3. Flying
4. Blue Jay Way
5. Your Mother Should Know
6. I Am the Walrus

Side two:

1. Hello, Goodbye
2. Strawberry Fields Forever
3. Penny Lane
4. Baby, You're a Rich Man
5. All You Need Is Love

Chapman notes: "The Beatles were no longer the same Beatles to whose music I had rocked back and forth on the couch in the den." Like many others who had first encountered the Fab Four as pop stars, Chapman was now encountering grown men with an artistic power never before wielded by popular musicians. Without the late sixties Beatles and their capacity to mesmerize most of the stories in the book you are now reading could not have existed. In particular the most convoluted and self-generating stories, like the tale about the death of Paul McCartney, could not exist. In regard to his ability to find personal meanings in the music and project his own fantasies on The Beatles' work Chapman was almost normal in his behaviour at the time. The Beatles' power to rule this fevered period of change in music is shown in their chart dominance in 1967 and 1968. *Sgt Pepper* topped the U.S. charts for the whole summer of 1967, clocking up 15 weeks at #1 and hovering around the charts to the very end of the year, at which point *Magical Mystery Tour* sat on top of the albums lists for the opening two months of 1968. By the end of that year *The Beatles* (aka *The White Album*) was on top of the album chart. The band placed two singles in the top five sellers of both 1967 and 1968 in the U.S. and both of the songs placed this way in 1968 – "Lady Madonna" and "Hey Jude" – were not on any album. As Mark Chapman grew away from his parents and towards his own fantasy world and hanging out with similarly disaffected kids his own age The Beatles were at the height of their powers. The band offered a seemingly inexhaustible supply of creativity and depth. They spoke – near as made no difference – to the whole world but the United States in particular had a love affair with the band that saw them hit peaks of commercial success, critical praise and fan worship few bands could ever hope to match.

Accounts of Mark Chapman's involvement with all of this vary massively, but it is inescapable that through his early teens The Beatles loomed massively in the lives of most

Americans of his age. Those who didn't personally own the albums were likely to hear them, and be aware that others cherished them. Many of those making other choices – like following the emerging acid rock or folk rock movements – would be involved in conversations comparing their favoured music to that of The Beatles. As a final tribute to the Fab Four it should be noted that another band hogged all but one week between January and June 1967 atop the the U.S. album charts. This band – The Monkees – were dubbed by some "The Pre-Fab Four" on the basis that the foursome, created for the purposes of manning a television show and selling albums, had clearly been created in the image of the fun mop-top period of The Beatles, with more than a nod to the zany comedy of The Beatles' *Help* album and movie. The first four Monkees albums all topped the American charts in 1967, and came close to matching that feat in the UK. So, as Mark Chapman gravitated towards others like himself, The Beatles' past style was informing America's biggest pop sensation since the British invasion that occurred when Mark Chapman was nine. At the same time the new sounds and styles of a range of rock musicians more likely to appeal to his crowd were being inspired and matched by the band he had always loved.

By Chapman's own admission rock music and drugs formed a soundtrack to a period of low academic achievement, missed opportunities and heavy drug use. Along the way he acted out much of his anger towards his parents, albeit in the passive manner of developing intense interests at a great distance from his father's military discipline and proneness to anger. When this lifestyle eventually left him feeling empty and unfulfilled Chapman made a seemingly dramatic shift towards God. "I felt like nobody. Like nothing," he states in *Let Me Take You Down...*, "At some point I lifted my hands and I said, 'Jesus, come to me.'" The decision was to define the next, and most significant, period of his life. Chapman may have swapped one crowd for another and moved over from seeing one set of powers as omnipotent only to find a hierarchical religious organisation waiting for him. But – as those he encountered have repeatedly testified – this life gave him periods of the greatest fulfilment he would ever know. It also allowed him to discover and employ personal talents. More than anything else, Mark Chapman appeared to find both an identity and a sense of being valued during the years he worked for God. He also found a set of values that corresponded with things he personally felt to be important.

Mark was soon working for the YMCA, an organisation with worldwide connections capable of offering him a career path and a range of responsibilities. His inability to sustain an academic career to the level of a college degree would ultimately deny him the opportunities he knew to be available. But in the short and medium term Chapman found a perfect match between his talents and some of the aims of the organisation. Before long those around him were highly impressed with what they saw, and were working with Mark to ensure his talents found the perfect project. From his first post as a YMCA summer camp counsellor Mark made friends and showed a real aptitude for working with children. He won an award for his work with children and was made up to assistant director within the camp. A measure of Mark's impact is obvious in this extract from an article in *People* magazine from 1987; "Cindy Simpson met Mark Chapman during the period of his greatest religious fervour, when she was 7 years old. He was 17 and a senior counsellor at the YMCA camp in Decatur. Like all the kids, she called him 'Nemo,' after the mysterious captain in Jules Verne's *Twenty Thousand*

Leagues Under the Sea. He led the singing in the morning on his guitar, he led the field trips, and his campers all remember him as the counsellor they would have been with all the time if they could."

Before long, the YMCA would be able to offer Mark the chance to travel abroad. A robust strand of the conspiracy theory argument regarding Chapman being a programmed assassin rests on the use of the YMCA by the CIA, specifically the way the agency can embed American operatives in foreign lands under the cover of a large organisation like the YMCA. The constant movement of people in and out of the YMCA's buildings across the globe, and – in particular – the focus on single men moving around in this way, means it is easy for any individual to book in and book out without arousing great suspicion. That much we can regard as proven in much the same way that we can regard the cover of jobs as journalists and diplomats as a means of allowing intelligence operatives to travel without arousing much suspicion.

Mark Chapman's strong and successful involvement with the YMCA presents something of a dilemma for the conspiracy argument, however, because it is so well documented that he had genuine talent in this area and that his plans, for a while, clearly revolved around making a career with them. Everything he has subsequently claimed about his aims, and disappointments, also hold up in a robust argument. When his Presbyterian faith led him to the work Mark was still finding his way. His high school grades failed to qualify him for university, but the YMCA work provided the perfect alternative. Even Fenton Bresler notes Mark Chapman "was undoubtedly quite marvellous with children." Chapman's talents included the ability to find imaginative angles on the activities that brought the kids minds into play, and allowed the kids and him to exchange ideas as they took part in treasure hunts and sports. By 1974, aged 19, Mark was assistant director at South De Kalb YMCA's summer camp, he was also enrolled at De Kalb Junior College on a two year programme to raise his high school grades to degree entry level. Tony Adams, a YMCA colleague, described Mark Chapman displaying "real leadership qualities" and showing real care for the kids in his charge. To Mark the sense of purpose in the work showed clearly that Jesus Christ had come into his life, wiping away what he now saw as the waste of his drug use years.

Even when a lack of application undermined his chances of passing his junior college course Mark stayed with the YMCA and the limited opportunities it could now offer. A college degree was essential for the level of management responsibility enjoyed by those – like Tony Adams – whom he saw as mentors. But, even without this option, the YMCA offered him the chance to travel. The Y's ICCP/Abroad programme took the camp counsellor skills Mark had used in the U.S. and made them the centre of a well thought out cultural exchange programme, moving people between countries to facilitate international understanding. Along with the obligations to further the YMCA's aims this represented an inexpensive way to see the world to those – like Mark – lacking significant funds or the opportunities offered by the higher end of education. Mark originally applied to travel to Russia but was turned down because of his inexperience and lack any knowledge of the Russian language. His application to go to The Lebanon was successful. From as long ago as the 1960s there was evidence, produced in magazine articles, that the CIA used students to gather information as they travelled, and that

Russia was one country spied on in this manner. Some conspiracy theorists, notably Mae Brussell, have argued that the CIA had contacts and a camp in The Lebanon at this time allowing them to train assassins well away from the USA. Brussell's show *Dialogue: Conspiracy* (which was later renamed *World Watchers International*) ran until her death in 1988, and dealt in a wide range of theories and ideas. Superficially Brussell's claims are a strong support for the belief Chapman was recruited by the CIA but even Fenton Bresler – who was convinced Mark Chapman was a trained assassin – is circumspect to the point of admitting Brussell was an "avant-garde radio commentator."

The truth from the point of the present chapter is that Mark Chapman did travel to The Lebanon in 1975, remaining there a few weeks before the worsening security situation obliged him to leave. The short trip to a place so far removed from his experiences to that point in life strikes conspiracy theorists as strong evidence that he was doing more than working in the YMCA. To others it represents a combination of a deliberate move out of his comfort zone from a young man desperate to make a significant mark in life. It is not disputed that Mark's brief time in Beirut changed his perceptions about some aspects of life and that he returned with a cassette recording he had made of the sounds of ongoing battles near the YMCA. He had heard gunfire, screams and explosions, recorded some of the noises and later played the tape to friends and acquaintances with very little prompting on their part to do so. He became known for doing so. Some have read this as a sinister move, though it should be noted at the time that Mark had dropped out of college and faced unemployment on his return from Beirut. With some of his peers achieving more in life, Mark's tape did, at least, offer some evidence that he had done things they couldn't match. The YMCA continued to offer demanding opportunities and to recognise Mark's particular talent for working with youngsters. He excelled at his next job, working with Vietnamese refugee children at Fort Chaffee, Arkansas. Mark worked with children displaced to America after the war in Vietnam, the bulk of his responsibilities involved arranging activities for up to five thousand people, his "staff" amounted to 15 Vietnamese volunteers and one American volunteer. His success in the role was such that David Moore, Director at Fort Chaffee, wrote a glowing letter of introduction, in effect a reference for Mark. It was that letter (arguably the single most significant piece of evidence that he had achieved something notable in his life) that formed part of the display Mark Chapman left in his hotel room as he set off to kill John Lennon.

Fort Chaffee would eventually process 29,000 refugees in an operation that demanded a lot from its staff as they dealt with a vast and unpredictable tide of people and problems. Mark's enthusiasm, and the faith that sustained it impressed those around him. By the end of 1975 he had also hit a steady and friendly patch with his on/off girlfriend – Jessica Blankinsop – and the pair were planning to enrol together at Covenant College, an institute in Tennessee offering a strict Presbyterian education. Mark would make another attempt to earn the college degree he needed to establish his future with the YMCA.

The ambition, and his plan to marry Jessica, were never realized. A number of different explanations surround these events. From a conspiracy point of view the involvement of a man Fenton Bresler grants the alias of Gene Scott and others have since named as Dana Reeves, is crucial. Reeves was a former high school friend, a few years older than Mark and a macho character who clearly had influence on Chapman. One of Mark's co-workers at Fort Chaffee described an instant change in Chapman's behaviour after Dana Reeves arrived to see him; "Mark cleaned his nails…put on clean clothes…And there was [Dana's] gun…" Prior to this incident Mark was known to be non-violent to the point his pacifism and sensitivity marked him apart from others. The sight of Mark openly playing with a firearm, engaging in rough manly play with his friend and freezing as Dana looked right at him struck the co-worker interviewed by Craig Unger as highly unusual, and very memorable.

In some accounts of the relationship between Reeves and Chapman there is clearly a hint of a gay relationship, though none of the main conspiracy theorists develops the argument to the point of making much about it. The glimpse Chapman offered his Fort Chaffee colleagues of a different character in 1975 is crucial to what followed. Jessica Blankinsop, quoted by *People* magazine and a few others close to Mark saw a battle within him; "The armor of fundamentalist faith was beginning to fail him, depriving him of its security but leaving him in its world of moral blacks and whites. The war Jessica witnessed was one between the Good Mark and the Bad Mark, both fictitious but vivid to him at the time, and both palpably engaged in battle for control of their vulnerable host."

At his moral and focussed best Mark was as good as he had ever been in dealing with refugees, avoiding temptation, staying close to his Presbyterian beliefs and aiming for the targets he and Jessica had agreed. But there were other times when he drank, hung out with other guys, played his guitar and – in a move that shattered his understanding with Jessica – lost his virginity to one of the camp refugees. A remorseful Mark poured out his guilt and confusion to Jessica in letters. As 1975 ended he and Jessica were together as they had planned, but Mark's source of self-esteem was quickly running out and the confusion within him was starting to fragment his mind. *People* noted: "When his work at Fort Chaffee ended in December, Mark enrolled with Jessica at Covenant College, a conservative Presbyterian school in Lookout Mountain, Tenn. There Jessica saw at close range the war raging inside him. He cried after their petting sessions, dreamed of making love to a prostitute in front of her and dreaded the morbid daydreams that came to him in class—the feeling that life was all about dying, that the history of man was the history of war. In the grip of a major depression, he entertained his first thoughts of suicide."

The religious sustenance offered at Covenant College didn't help and soon Mark fell behind again as a programme of study offered itself. His relationship with Jessica was the next casualty and any chance Mark had left of continuing to work at Fort Chaffee ended after he had an argument there. By early 1976, Mark – quite possibly because Dana suggested it – opted to work as a security guard. It was a massive change. The work, and the meagre prospects it offered marked such a sharp contrast from the future he had mapped out a few months before. The drift towards a job, however menial, that contained a threat of violence and confrontation was also at odds with everything Mark had done for work or leisure beforehand.

Ironically both Lennon and Mark Chapman saw massive life changes in the years from 1975 and 1980. For Chapman the stops and starts that had marked his time up to the success at Fort

Chaffee and the final attempt to study his way to a degree simply became more marked. According to June Blankinsop the woman who, in different circumstances, would have been his mother in law Mark's grades at Covenant College "were not all that bad." The real problem was his application, motivation and direction. Mark and Jessica had sought counselling before their relationship fell apart. Mark made rapid job and life changes in the aftermath of his dropping out of college after one semester but it was still a massive surprise to everyone he knew when he opted to leave Atlanta and head for Hawaii. The pattern of selling his possessions and making a big change would follow Mark until he shot John Lennon. Along the way he would unload record collections, an act that could go some way to explaining why an apparent Beatles obsessive might have no Beatle albums of his own when he shot one of the band. In *Who Killed John Lennon?* two extremes that might explain Chapman's move into the Pacific are starkly laid out. According to journalist Jim Gaines who wrote articles on Chapman for *People* magazine the move was originally intended as a suicide mission. At a great distance from those he knew best Chapman would simply spend his money on living well and then end his life when he was broke. David Moore of the YMCA believed the move was an attempt at a new start, and the attraction was the "Asian quality of serenity and calmness" more readily available in Hawaii than anywhere else in the United States. The truth may well lie somewhere between both polar opposites. Mark would never again enjoy the sense of achievement and satisfaction he had touched in Arkansas and his successful achievements from here on would often revolve around a hopeful scheme and his ability to convince others of its potential. Mark enjoyed what good life he could afford in Hawaii until the money ran out, found himself once again involved in the YMCA and came under the care of a psychiatric social worker who quickly saw how much trouble he was in. Mark made a suicide attempt in which he linked a hosepipe to the exhaust of his rental car, started the engine and passed into sleep with no expectations of waking up. The following morning he found a Japanese fisherman tapping on the car window. A short investigation showed Mark that the hosepipe he had taken from a vacuum cleaner had melted on the exhaust pipe. Had Mark's planning come good at this moment John Lennon might still be alive.

Mark was helped by local mental health services though never – as was misreported later – admitted as a full blown "mental patient." Indeed, his recovery was so quick that he made a rapid transition from being helped to helping the Castle Memorial Hospital for over two years, first through employment as a maintenance worker and later, via promotion, to the customer relations department. In the second area Mark worked on printed material and discovered almost immediately a particular talent for graphic art. He remained involved with a small Presbyterian Church and formed new relationships with women which gradually helped him recover from his split with Jessica. He had relationships with a nurse at the hospital and a member of the catering staff. Fenton Bresler and others have also uncovered a strange situation, not addressed in Mark's own account of this time, in which he seems to have lived at 112 Puwa Place with a woman and three young children, who may have been sisters of the woman. One strand of investigation has dismissed this as a co-incidence, believing the confusion to have come from the presence of a second Mark Chapman in the area. Mark, however, cited the 112 Puwa Place address on his driving licence. Whatever the case, all the inhabitants did a disappearing act leaving rent unpaid, the electricity disconnected and enough mess to warrant a $2000 clean-up bill. Given Mark's own use of the address on his driving licence the evidence seems overwhelming that he was living in a family situation and the workmates who saw the usual cheerful and outgoing young man who'd made such a success of his job at Fort Chaffee were unaware that he was defaulting on rent payments and surviving with no electricity at home. Mark's ability to keep his life in compartments and mask the confusions by presenting a positive image to workmates was now well established. His parents, visiting in December 1977, saw him stable to the point they felt they could stop worrying about him. But, in reality, they were all in trouble.

Mark's parents soon filed for divorce. Within a year his mother Diane, had moved to Hawaii, alone, and Mark had helped her find an apartment. Mark, for his part, did the thing that was by now becoming characteristic of his behaviour. Just as things looked settled, and before his mother arrived, he threw all the stability aside and decided to take a trip around the world. The inspiration, according to Mark at least, came partly from the Jules Verne novel *Around the World in Eighty Days.* This ranks as one of the most impenetrable events in Mark Chapman's life and – therefore – as a significant source of evidence for the conspiracy theorists. The obvious question is how did a junior employee in a hospital afford the journey? Mark told journalist Jim Gaines that he secured a loan from the hospital's credit union. That union refused to speak to investigative writers like Fenton Bresler. But it seems strange that a man who had briefly been in the care of the hospital and who had only risen to the junior ranks could secure a loan fit to finance a round the world trip. To conspiracists the obvious source of funds is an organisations like the CIA. In any case – as Fenton Bresler asks – "Why on earth did the twenty-three-year-old Mark, at last beginning to get his feet firmly on the ground… suddenly take it into his head to go off around the world?"

In order Mark visited: Seoul, Hong Kong, Singapore, Bangkok, Delhi, Israel, Geneva, London, Paris and Dublin before returning to see friends and family in Atlanta en-route to Honolulu. The access to YMCA buildings along the way helped make the trip affordable and Mark carried with him the letter of recommendation from David Moore that he would eventually leave in his hotel room, amongst the display of things for the police to find, after he shot John Lennon. The letter read:

"This is to introduce Mark Chapman, a staff member of the US International Division of the National Council of YMCAs. Mark was an effective and dedicated worker at the refugee camp in Fort Chaffee Arkansas following the mass influx of refugees after the change in governments in Indo-China in the spring of 1975. Mark was also the youth representative to the Board of Directors of the YMCA in his home town in Georgia. Mark will be visiting YMCAs in Asia and Europe and we look forward to his visit here in Geneva. I can commend him to you as a sincere and intelligent young man. Any assistance that you can give Mark during his travels will be greatly appreciated by this office."

The round-the-world trip certainly broadened Mark's mind. If the purpose was to give him an alternative to the college degree he seemed incapable of earning then he certainly fulfilled the need for a deep education. He encountered grinding poverty, different cultures and a range of ideas to challenge his assumptions. In London he watched a performance of *Jesus Christ Superstar,* not something likely to impress the more fundamentally minded of his fellow

Presbyterians. Nobody is in any doubt that Mark returned with over 1000 colour slides of the things he had seen and people he had met. Like his tape of gunfire and explosions in The Lebanon he had a trophy of his travels and achievement. Mark was also exhibiting a pattern he had shown on first moving to Hawaii and would demonstrate again when staying in New York before shooting John Lennon. When away from those he knew and in possession of some funds Mark could often be found living well, and acting like someone with significantly more money to his name and significantly more professional achievement than he actually had. The obvious interpretation of this, that Mark so desperately wanted to be the person he presented on these trips, has satisfied many. But another possibility sees Mark feeling confident because he knew the CIA, or some offshoot of the security forces, was there to pick up the financial tab and afford him this freedom. If he was genuinely involved with the CIA on these trips then the sense of self-worth others saw in him probably wasn't faked. There is also supposition, but no hard evidence, that Mark's travels also allowed him, however fleetingly, to experiment with some aspects of gay culture. The link between YMCA hostels and the gay community was well established at the time. Indeed, the trip more-or-less coincides with the monster hit by the Village People putting the whole issue in the public domain. Any gay feelings on Mark's part, and any actions driven by these feelings, like his behaviour hanging around the stage door after seeing *Jesus Christ Superstar* put him at odds with the teachings of the Presbyterian Church and the opinions of many of those he most cherished.

On returning to Hawaii Mark soon courted and married the helpful travel agent he'd bothered repeatedly as he planned his trip. He and Gloria Abe were married on 2 June 1979 and the conspiracy theorists, and those with a general penchant for spotting a pattern where others see only coincidence, would soon see significance in the fact she was a few years his senior and Japanese-American. Mark's mother was living on the islands and enjoying a single lifestyle that included boyfriends significantly younger than her. Mark had a fairly obvious anger at both parents. Towards his father he felt resentment because his mother had been cast adrift after years of being downtrodden, leaving her struggling to behave in a responsible adult way, as Mark saw it. He was also angry his father had manoeuvred their affairs to leave his mother without much financial independence. Mark ended up helping her organise accommodation in Hawaii and wasn't impressed with the lifestyle she led. He would later tell both psychologists and psychiatrists after the shooting of John Lennon that he had wanted to kill his father for the mistreatment of his mother during their 24 year marriage, and for his thoughtless discarding of her afterwards. He also resented having to act as a parent to his mother.

Between returning from his round the world trip and shooting John Lennon Mark Chapman's life was punctuated by destructive outbursts of anger that cost him in terms of work, friendships and respect. He had returned to the Castle Memorial Hospital but was soon forced into an effective demotion in his job because his dealings with the customers were becoming a problem. Mark was forced back to the print shop and "stuck, all alone, in this printing room, smelling of chemicals, going crazy, with the noise, the boredom." Binge eating junk food on work time brought some temporary relief but did nothing for his health and he acted out his need for control in devising new ways of working for himself and his colleagues although it was, literally, above his pay grade to do so. Despite the affection many colleagues had for him Mark was fired after a furious row with a nurse who complained when he failed to deliver a printing job on time. He was almost immediately rehired but the damage was done and soon after Christmas in 1979 Mark saw sense and took another job, the last job he would do before going to jail, working as a security guard at 444 Nahua Street, an apartment complex for holidaymakers. By this point Mark had had another row with neighbours over noise, which led to a confrontation and an uncomfortable apology from Mark that left him feeling strong resentment. Typically, in leaving his job and falling out with neighbours Mark was severing contacts that could provide stability. From the day he took his final job he had virtually no dealings with those at Castle Memorial Hospital who had provided stability and support after his suicide attempt and some of whom had seen the best in him and given him positive feedback for showing those qualities. His behaviour towards his new wife was also alarming some people, particularly her work colleagues who'd seen him sound the car horn and storm into her office when she didn't come out precisely on time. When Mark yelled at her boss for a second time he found the office door slammed in his face.

At the same time the local Scientologists were occupying 447 Nahua Street, quite literally looking across at Mark's apartment complex. The Scientologists were having problems with loud Beatles' music being blasted across the street and a particular caller ringing, announcing "Bang, bang you're dead" and hanging up. There is little doubt Mark had issues with the Scientologists' beliefs and the means by which they were accruing money from their converts. But, to give the arch conspiracist Fenton Bresler his due, even he admits "Come to think of it, one does not have to be a deeply committed fundamentalist Christian to object [to some of the demands Scientology allegedly places on its followers]." It is certain that others were also harassing the Scientologists on Nahua Street at the time.

A breakdown of communication and – in Mark's mind at least – trust duly followed in his job at the apartment complex. Mark felt blamed after a break in and nearly quit before his employers talked him back, but he transferred from security to maintenance work, though the relatively low $4 an hour remained the same. With responsibilities for both his mother and his marriage the previous strategy of escaping trouble by redefining what he needed and quite literally moving away wasn't a realistic option. Mark did, however, build up his ego with escapes of sorts, both into acquiring art prints (for which he had to borrow money, including some from Gloria's father) and into a new found obsession, reading *Catcher in the Rye*. As 1980 dawned Mark's behaviour became more erratic, with obsessions and schemes occupying his time. By March the art dealing was all but over, he got out having failed to make money and began "Operation Freedom from Debt" a convoluted series of plans that were drawn and redrawn as Mark tried to marshal his meagre resources to build financial security. Gloria Chapman would later describe moments when Mark stared into space, spoke out loud to people she couldn't see and used a pencil and ruler to chart out plans, which were then rejected to be replaced by other plans hatched on the back of the same strange behaviour. It got little better when he finally spoke to her about the little people who had occupied his consciousness when he was younger. They were now, he informed Gloria, back. Mark's plans were submitted to committee meetings of his little people, hence the conversations and redrawing. Neither Mark nor Gloria had massive salaries and the day to day costs of everything from accommodation to running a car were draining them before additional curve balls, like Mark losing one job and having to take one with less prospects, were added to the worries. Prudent management eventually did pay off and the couple's finances were under control later in the year, at which point Mark decided to quit work and, in his own words much later, "be like Lennon was, kind of like a househusband."

Conspiratorially much would later be made of Mark signing out of work on his final day as "John Lennon" and then striking the words through, as if to obliterate Lennon. In jail for the murder he would later explain: "When I quit, I already knew that I was going to go and kill John Lennon." Mark had explained to Joe Bustamonte, his supervisor at the apartment complex, that he was taking a trip, possibly to London. The issue with his final signature at work is troublesome to the conspiracy theory because in retrospect it looks like such a clear signpost to trouble. Mark usually signed out as "Chap." Mark left the holiday apartment complex on Thursday 23 October 1980. On Monday 27 October Mark legally bought a gun over the counter at J&S Enterprises in midtown Honolulu. The five shot Charter Arms Undercover .38 Special revolver wasn't a particularly special choice, Mark had selected a best-selling model from a fairly standard dealership. Mark had been seen, but not formally sectioned, at the Castle Hospital. Because he was never sectioned he had no record of commitment to a mental institution. If he had, he would have been barred from owning a gun. Mark's time was already being filled by reading. He had started visiting the local library, enjoying the way information was ordered on the shelves and the escape into reading that was available for free. The need to process and understand information was strong; Mark had even visited a local court and watched a rape trial, taking particular interest in the way the judge ensured that a female juror – who was clearly uncomfortable with being selected – served on the jury. There was method in the madness of grasping at things in search of meaning in his life, but Mark was also drinking alcohol from first thing in the morning and his rages continued.

One source of rage was the contents of the book *John Lennon: One Day at a Time* by Anthony Fawcett. The 1976 book was written by a Beatles' insider who enjoyed access to Lennon. In 1976 open-ended biographies in which the writer describes the subject but lacks conclusions were something of a rarity amongst works on pop and rock. By far the most common works at the time were scissors and paste recaps of successful careers. Only the major artists, like Lennon and Dylan, warranted more in terms of a book. *One Day at a Time* ranked amongst a select few biographies, like Toby Thompson's *Positively Main Street* where the dynamic between writer and subject was as much the point of the work as any facts recounted. Toby Thompson went to Bob Dylan's home town, Hibbing in Minnesota and set off in search of the Robert Zimmerman who became Dylan. Fawcett's journey is similar as he writes mainly in the present tense and observes Lennon from the break-up of The Beatles to the mid-seventies. The resulting portrait of the man and his art captures Lennon as his activism collides with the need to rein in such behaviour to stay in the U.S. The book is also honest about the artistic attempts and relative failures of some of his seventies work, indeed it shares its subtitle with a track on the often maligned *Mind Games* album, and the book also explores the dilemma of a man with a sense of social justice and a large personal fortune.

In the twenty first century such complex literary portraits have become defining tomes in helping to understand major figures in popular music and fans are more comfortable with their idols as flawed artists, for whom the journey is sometimes as important as the places reached. The rarity of such biographies in the mid-seventies made them harder to understand. Mark Chapman found reading *One Day at a Time* around the time he was reading *Catcher in the Rye* to be an explosive mixture. The contradictions he saw in Lennon were proof the man was a complete phoney. The same level of phoney Holden Caulfield rails against in the classic novel. To a fan raised in the simpler media age of the sixties, when audiences frequently took messages at face value and didn't look behind the superficialities *One Day at a Time* presented clear contradictions between a hero and his image.

By the end of October John Lennon was back in the public domain, his first new single in five years was climbing the charts and he was talking about his plans for the future. Mark Chapman was in meltdown, armed and beginning to be dangerous. The one thing protecting Lennon from the man who – by his own admission – was already intent on killing him was Chapman's disorganisation. For a while Mark appeared genuinely confused about whether Lennon lived in London. Once he had set himself the task of reaching New York to find his target Chapman again made a basic mistake. He checked he could carry his newly acquired gun to New York but hadn't bargained on the local laws forbidding anyone without a New York City gun permit buying ammunition over the counter. Mark reached New York but flew on to Atlanta in early November. Mark's subsequent discussions about this suggests he visited Dana Reeves, did some shooting with his old friend and then asked for enough shells to fill his .38 because – as he told Dana – he was worried about being attacked on the streets of New York and was carrying a considerable amount of cash. From Chapman's account Dana initially offered standard ammunition and Mark rejected this in favour of five hollow points, designed to crumple on impact and spin through soft tissue, tearing bigger holes and tending to remain lodged in a body rather than pass through. In military circles such bullets are nicknamed "devastator" rounds for good reason.

In New York and Atlanta Mark was up to his usual fantasy antics, taking out girls he met, spending money, staying at New York's Waldorf Hotel and visiting the theatre. An English nanny he met in New York didn't seem impressed when he told her "something" was going to happen soon and she'd know about him then, and a former Atlanta girlfriend – Lynn Watson – stood him up after he and Dana had arranged a meeting and Mark had bought her an expensive teddy bear and roses. Mark's attempts to present himself as someone of importance and achievement were convincing fewer people, probably because as he got older and relied on the shame showy shtick he was less credible to those his own age. But Mark had protection, of a sort, in *The Catcher in the Rye* where his hero went through the same rejections, but knew deep down he held the moral high ground because of his honesty and his ability to detect phonies.

To conspiracy theorists, however, the trip to Atlanta and the target practice in the woods with Dana were the dress rehearsal for the final event, now roughly one month away. It is probably too much, even for the most ardent conspiracy theorists to believe the neatly timed *Esquire* article Chapman managed to read on the plane back to New York was planted specifically to bring Mark into action. However, the article did make clear that John Lennon, the one-time activist for social justice, was returning to work because he wanted to. It was also clear in the article that Lennon's wealth and comfort were assured regardless of the sales of *Double Fantasy*. Chapman headed for the Dakota building when he was back in the Big Apple and was told the doorman didn't know where Lennon was or when he would be back.

Mark was still packing a considerable amount of money, gifted to him by his wife, and could stay longer, or travel on. But he began to feel disoriented and headed into a meltdown. He was deeply depressed, hanging about aimlessly by the entrance to the Dakota and also beset with thoughts of *Catcher in the Rye* and by the movie *Ordinary People* in which Timothy Hutton played a post-traumatically stressed young man, recovering from a suicide attempt and coming to terms with the death of his brother in a boating accident. Mark's ability to identify with fictional and troubled adolescents meant the character in the hit movie instantly struck him as a window into his own personality.

Fortunately for John Lennon Mark rang home from the YMCA where he was staying. He told Gloria her love had saved him, and began – for the first time – to tell her he had planned to kill John Lennon. Gloria told him she loved him and asked him to come home. The following day they embraced in their apartment, but Gloria was horrified when Mark opened his case and insisted she hold the .38 and pull the trigger on the unloaded weapon.

From the point of any conspiracy theory Chapman's presence at the Dakota, his conversations with the door staff and the frank admission to Gloria of what he had planned are all problematic. A brainwashed assassin surely wouldn't leak incriminating information and flag up his presence so clearly. However, if Chapman's attraction to those programming him was this very vulnerability then it sets up a scenario in which his programmers have to manage a man prone to random acts. It also sets up a scenario in which his troubled history easily explains his eventual crime, making look like the act of a madman.

Mark sought psychiatric help from local mental health services at the Makiki Clinic and was referred instead to the Catholic Social Services (CSS) locally, an appointment was scheduled for 26 November. Significantly Mark avoided calling the Waikiki Mental Health Clinic where he was known to Anne Jones who had successfully worked with him three years earlier. A conspiratorial view of this sees the act as one of avoiding a person who could have diverted him from killing John Lennon. A more pragmatic way of looking at it might suggest Mark was filled with shame to find himself back in the same meltdown situation Anne Jones had helped him escape in the past and simply wanted a new start with new helpers. Mark sounded coherent on the phone to the CSS and the appointment made was for almost a week after the initial call. Mark didn't show up, and the organisation rang him three times over the next nine days, getting no reply. By the final phone call Mark was well on his way to kill John Lennon. The sequence of events that led to Mark Chapman's troubles being missed was subsequently investigated by the press and the court trying him for murder. Amongst the experts called to work with Mark and later testify to the court was Dr Dorothy Lewis of New York University. In her opinion "the killing might have been aborted" if Mark had received help and support. Fenton Bresler's detailed analysis of all the facts cites Professor Lewis' use of the words "command hallucinations" in the report she gave to defence attorney Jonathan Marks. To Bresler this might be a tantalising glimpse into a conspiracy because it suggests someone else might have been controlling the commands. The professor refused to deal directly with Bresler when he approached her about helping with his book.

Bresler also successfully shows gaps in the events leading up to the shooting of John Lennon. Particularly in the details of how and when Mark Chapman travelled to New York so soon after returning from the city. There is no doubt Mark arrived at New York's La Guardia Airport on United Airlines Flight 904, coming in from Chicago, on 6 December. It is also clear he bought a ticket from Hawaii to Chicago, not a through ticket to New York. The evidence of when he left Honolulu is less clear, and Bresler remained convinced that Mark spent three days in Chicago and it was there, not in Hawaii, that he made up his mind, or had his mind made up, to kill John Lennon. The discrepancies and lack of evidence in this area didn't trouble the police in New York anywhere near as much as they have troubled those seeing a conspiracy in the aftermath of Lennon's death.

The police and courts didn't feel the need to look too closely into the minor details of dates and travel because they had eyewitness testimony placing Chapman at the scene and identifying him as the killer. Chapman remained in view between the killing and his arrest and – in any case – he pleaded guilty. Indeed, once he'd pulled the trigger he even said, out loud, he had killed John Lennon. There was little doubt to those up close to the events that they had the right man, and he had acted alone. One key piece of conspiracy "evidence" fails to fit the physical evidence and Fenton Bresler's discussion of the days unaccounted for between Honolulu and New York implicates some unknown person(s). It is beyond doubt that Mark Chapman's original ticket out of Honolulu was numbered 24-65607-252 and his planned flight was outbound to Chicago on 2 December with a scheduled return ticket from Chicago on 18 December. The flight tickets found in his New York hotel room after the killing clearly specify a departure date of 5 December, but the number is identical to the one sold for 2 December. It remains a mystery. To Fenton Bresler it was clear proof that the flight evidence in Mark's "display" to be found by the police had been "doctored." The baggage information, also left out in the hotel room, corresponds with the allegedly doctored ticket. There was no evidence of the used part of the ticket to show Mark had flown on 5 December. To Bresler, and the conspiracists who have followed his lead, this is a clear suggestion that Mark Chapman may have been unable to show the ticket for the original part of the flight, because it would have made it clear he travelled three days earlier, and spent the intervening time in Chicago before buying a new ticket to fly on to La Guardia.

What Mark Chapman may have done with the spare time in Chicago is central to the conspiracy theory. It is possible, though unproven, that one of his grandmothers lived in Chicago at the time and he went to see her. The conspiracy argument suggests he met a handler from the CIA and was finally deployed into action to kill John Lennon. Once again, the hard evidence doesn't easily present itself. Fenton Bresler confronted Lieutenant Arthur O' Connor with the discrepancies about the travel from Honolulu to New York and got an intriguing reply: "If there is a conspiracy it would never have been investigated and no conspiracy was investigated to my knowledge, and it would have come to my attention if it had." The reason for this was the satisfaction the NYPD had in bringing the case to a conclusion so quickly. So far as the basic investigation had gone the case went quickly from initial report to the arrest of the prime suspect, gathering solid evidence to bring charges and a guilty plea. The loose ends mainly revolved around the suspect's sanity and motivation, all of which were soon a matter for the courts. With the arrest of Mark Chapman and the gathering of evidence from witnesses and the crime scene the NYPD had done their job and signed off on the main investigation very quickly.

In retrospect there is a cinematic quality to the killing of John Lennon and a poignancy about some of Lennon's final public words and actions. John and Yoko were working hard in the early days of December 1980. *Double Fantasy* was newly released. The mixed reviews didn't appear to have dented John's joy at being back at work. He was in charge to the extent he had chosen how to work, and had complete creative freedom. *Double Fantasy* may have been middle of road by comparison to the emerging styles of the time but it represented a manageable step back for Lennon. The final music on which he would ever work was Yoko's song "Walking on Thin Ice," a choppy dance track with simple rhymes but a message hinting at deeper truths. Yoko's lead vocal has a soft echo and much of the dramatic interest on the track comes from the way it pits the pop melody and catchy rhythm against random sounds which erupt in the passages between Yoko's vocal. At worst, "Walking on Thin Ice" shoehorns the less commercial tropes of Yoko's performing style into a hit formula and adds enough window dressing to appear more down with the early eighties kids than it is. At best it shows the Lennons embracing the post punk and dance scene sounds then at the cutting edge and meeting them on their own terms; a spoken word passage near the end certainly reaches that level of creativity.

I knew a girl who tried to walk across the lake,
Course it was winter when all this was ice.
That's a hell of a thing to do, you know.
They say the lake is as big as the ocean.
I wonder if she knew about it?

It is hard to pin "Walking on Thin Ice" down to any specific meaning, though the song clearly drives at the same overarching messages in *Double Fantasy* in which it reflects on life lessons learned through mistakes and suffering, and offers up this experience to the listener. The nameless girl crossing the frozen lake could be seen as a metaphor for the inexperience of youth in general, and – in that context – "Walking on Thin Ice" does have the quality of the Lennons recognising their ability to relate to younger people, and guide them through their own experience. But, frankly, it is a massive stretch to go from that reading of the final music John Lennon ever worked on and decide that the CIA were so concerned about his ability to come back and re-ignite social unrest that the man required immediate elimination. In any case, John may have been excited by the punchy new track and the couple's ability to get down with the kids but neither of the Lennons were blind to the fact they were now fortysomethings focussed on raising a five year old child. By the admission of those closest to John his final days were energetic, excited and happy ones because he was loving his work, and his life. "Walking on Thin Ice" caused him to get up early one morning and listen again to the track because he was in love with the music, and fired up by new possibilities and – crucially – he was motivated to complete the track because he saw it as their best chance to get a hit for Yoko. "Walking on Thin Ice" is her composition, with her lead vocal, and his contributions all over it. It was eventually a minor hit, but by that time John Lennon was dead, and the meanings listeners took from the track were informed by those events. How it would have been received as a single from a fully completed follow up to *Double Fantasy* will never be known.

The final work of the Lennons certainly suggests the couple would have enjoyed a recording future in which they took more artistic chances and pushed out of the majorly comfortable style of *Double Fantasy*. John's production contributions that shaped the song also suggest he was right in guiding Yoko closer to the emerging pop/dance styles, because it was in that territory, years after his death, that she enjoyed her greatest solo success. But none of this really places John, in his final days, back in the activist/avant-garde/ menace to society territory that was always the focus of the FBI snooping.

The best summation of how he felt and what he thought at this time comes from John Lennon himself, he was still talking more freely and openly than he had in years. On the day he died he gave his final interview to Dave Sholin, a radio producer from San Francisco who was charged with putting together special programmes for distribution throughout the RKO network. John spoke in detail about the new album, the way his life revolved around his son and the fact he would only work with Yoko, on their terms because: "I want to be with my best friend. My best friend's me wife. If I couldn't have worked with her, I wouldn't have bothered." On several occasions in the lengthy interview he was clear on his priorities and where he stood musically and artistically.

The former outspoken activist was especially clear about how much he didn't know:

> "...if I knew the secrets of what is right and wrong... I wish we all knew the secrets. Nobody really knows, that's the point. Nobody knows what's best for children. They're like guinea pigs that each generation experiments on. I know if you go too far to the liberal side they'll probably grow up bein' disciplinarians. If you give 'em too much discipline, they'll end up the opposite. I'm tryin' to just have no real heavy discipline about behavior, only 'don't be impolite; don't hurt other people."

He was also fairly objective on what *Double Fantasy* meant as an artistic statement and where it fitted in to the climate in late 1980:

> "it's an album that's not gonna do too well. But, in the end, you know, maybe like two years later or something, people will say, 'ah, that was good.' Because I knew that the theme was good, I knew the dialogue was important, etcetera. And each song was alright, you know? So I had a feeling that even if it takes a long time, people would know about it. But I didn't think it was gonna be that instant, you know?"

And, he was clear on how far out of touch he was with the bands emerging at the time, he had to be "dragged" to an important discovery:

"And I was finally dragged to a disco by an assistant of mine...downstairs they were playin' Rock Lobster by the B-52s, and I said, 'That's Yoko!'...I thought it was so like Yoko, so her, I thought 'This person's studied her.' I said, 'Get the axe out, call the wife, gee have you heard this?'"

Lennon's comments in the final interview were similar to those made in other discussions promoting *Double Fantasy*. So, if the CIA or any other security agency had decided that 8 December was the day to finally kill Lennon their intelligence gathering doubtless showed they were about to end the life of a man keen to ensure his son watched *Sesame Street* and avoided the endless parade of gormless commercials aimed at kids who watched American television. A man who was playing catch up as far as the new and more dangerous end of music making was concerned and – above all – a man who had mellowed and become more accepting of the world than he had been a decade earlier.

On the morning of 8th December Lennon's killer did the kind of things he usually did when he was spending money he'd loaned and staying far from home; he fed his obsessions. Walking around near the Dakota and clutching a newly bought copy of *Double Fantasy* he diverted to buy another copy of *The Catcher in the Rye*. Along with the items displayed in the hotel room he had just left this would help others to piece together some elements of the Chapman and his rationale in killing John Lennon. When the Dakota doorman told him Lennon hadn't been sighted on the day Mark got talking to two young female Lennon fans and soon invited them for lunch. He regaled them with the usual chat about himself and his achievements and the pair appeared duly impressed about his travels and the things he had seen. When the trio returned to the Dakota one of those already standing outside was Paul Goresh, who supplemented his earnings as a store detective with a side-line as a celebrity photographer. The Dakota, which housed several rich and famous people, had already given him some useful shots on 8 December. He had snapped Lauren Bacall, Paul Simon and Mia Farrow before he got a shot of John Lennon signing Mark Chapman's copy of *Double Fantasy*. Goresh couldn't possibly know that the one shot of that autograph being etched on the album would earn around $10,000 inside the next 24 hours.

Chapman had a loaded firearm in his pocket as Lennon signed his album. He was close enough to shoot fatally, but he did nothing as Lennon climbed into the same limo as Dave Sholin and the radio crew to whom Lennon had just given an interview. From the point of the conspiracy theory the argument about Chapman's lack of action revolves around the crowd outside the building and the chance that someone would intervene to save Lennon's life. A more prosaic thought suggests Mark Chapman, in the throes of a mental meltdown, was simply acting out a combination of his usual alter-ego behaviour far from home and daring himself to do something truly catastrophic. This second interpretation is supported, albeit indirectly, by a curious incident that occurred in front of the subway station at 72nd Street on 7 December. Singer songwriter James Taylor knew John Lennon and lived in the building next door to the Dakota. He was at home the following day and heard the gunshots that killed Lennon. Taylor was accosted outside the subway station: "The guy had sort of pinned me to the wall and was glistening with maniacal sweat and talking some freak speak about what he was going to do and his stuff with how John was interested, and he was going to get in touch with John Lennon. And it was surreal to actually have contact with the guy 24 hours before he shot John." In other words, James Taylor met a madman who was making little sense but clearly had some obsession with Lennon and was spouting this "freak speak" within sight of the front door to the block in which Lennon lived.

Mark Chapman waited over five hours for the Lennons to return from the Record Plant, talking to Jose Perdomo, the doorman who had arrived for the night shift and stating he was waiting to get Yoko's autograph on the *Double Fantasy* album sleeve. Soon the waiting crowd was down to two, Mark and Paul Goresh. When the celebrity photographer left Mark alone at 8-30 Mark said to him; "I'd wait if I were you. You never know if you'll see him again." An obviously ominous remark but one that taxes those obsessing over Lennon's death. It could be read as a programmed assassin intoning his own mantra, but it is so laden with threat that it could have caused alarm, and prompted someone to take protective action.

The Lennons arrived home around 10-50, Yoko led the way into the Dakota, John clutching tapes of "Walking on Thin Ice" was a few feet behind when Mark called out "Mr Lennon." Mark crouched into a combat stance and as Lennon turned towards him Mark emptied the five chambers of the .38 at point-blank range. Four shots entered Lennon's body, hitting him in the back and left shoulder. From less than twenty feet the impact of the hollow points was instant and devastating, the fragments shattering into Lennon's blood vessels and vital organs. John managed to stagger up the steps where he fell, bringing up blood and gurgling.

In the shock and panic that followed one eye-witness – Sean Strub – who has gone on to become a writer and activist, noted Mark had "almost a smirk" as he remained in the area watching the mayhem he had just brought about. Despite a subway station entrance just across the road Mark remained and read from his copy of *Catcher in the Rye.* With Lennon still prone and rasping on the floor Jose Perdomo screamed "Leave! Get out of here." That outburst would eventually become a central plank of another branch of conspiracy theory. Perdomo and Chapman remained outside whilst those around Lennon tried to do something and suffered through the seconds until the emergency services arrived.

Mark Chapman would eventually discuss these moments in chillingly detached detail claiming to have heard a voice in his head repeating the phrase "do it" after which: "I pulled the gun out of my pocket, I handed it over to my left hand, I don't remember aiming, I must have done, but I don't remember drawing the bead or whatever you call it. And I just pulled the trigger steady five times."

The first patrolmen on the scene were Steve Spiro and Peter Cullen. Spiro pointed his weapon at Mark Chapman, who immediately begged the police not to hurt him. Spiro used Chapman's body to shield his own, suspecting further danger until Jose Perdomo told him Chapman was the only person involved and as Chapman was pushed up against the wall he told Spiro "I acted alone." Spiro's notes from the night point out he had not previously seen Perdomo whilst carrying out his police duties in the twentieth precinct. Spiro's initial suspicions were that he was dealing with a shooting linked to a robbery in the Dakota and once again it was Perdomo who pointed out to the officer that Chapman had shot John Lennon. Spiro immediately decided to take Chapman into custody and he was bundled into the police cruiser. The police officers picked up some of Chapman's clothing from the sidewalk and Chapman pointed out that "the red book" (*The Catcher in the Rye*) was his too, so that was retrieved and placed in the police car.

As Chapman was on his way to police custody another police cruiser, containing officers Tony Palma and Jimmy Moran was taking Lennon to the emergency room at the nearby Roosevelt Hospital. The last word Lennon uttered was a wheezy "Yes" as Jimmy Moran, still barely believing what was happening, asked if he was really John Lennon. Lennon was dead on arrival at the Roosevelt, the doctors knew it from the extent of his injuries, his vital signs and what the police officers could tell them about the circumstances in which he had been injured. But this was John Lennon they were dealing with. Despite the hopelessness of the situation, they tried. Dr Stephen Lynn who was on duty later told BBC correspondent Tom Brook:

"He had no signs of life, no blood pressure, no pulse. He was unresponsive. We opened his left chest, I did it, with a scalpel. We made an incision.

"I actually held his heart in my hand as the nurses rapidly transfused blood. I tried to massage the heart as we put blood into his body. We knew that there was no way that we could restore circulation, there was no way that we could repair the massive injury to all of the blood vessels in the body."

In the aftermath of the shooting the world mourned Lennon and within 24 hours the status Paul McCartney would later sum up as "a martyr. A JFK" was established. If this was an ordered killing to diminish Lennon's impact on society then those behind the plans must have shuddered at the scale of the media coverage and outpouring of love for the former Beatle. In particular they must have shuddered at the way his opinions on love and peace took an unreproachable nobility as the media focussed on the senselessness of the killing and the love between Lennon's audience and their hero. The irony that a man of peace had been so brutally slaughtered evoked comparisons with political deaths and the word "assassination" was widely used, not because anyone appeared to believe a conspiracy had ordered the death but because Lennon's status as a spokesman and activist placed him comfortably beyond the ranks of those who were simply entertainers. Any criticism of *Double Fantasy* and the recent single seemed pointless as the pair soared to the top of the charts on both sides of the Atlantic and the songs of love and looking to the future took on a poignant irony. Lennon's observation on the album that he could hardly wait to see young Sean come of age seemed particularly tragic as the world poured out sympathies to Lennon's wife and son. In a bitter kind of irony that the often cynical Lennon might just have found grimly funny the world suddenly appeared to embrace and love Yoko. In the circumstances the comparisons with JFK, Ghandi and Martin Luther King didn't appear to be out of place. Apart from anything else, it was one of those events for which everyone would remember where they were and what they were doing when they found out about it.

If this was a pre-meditated hit to silence a dangerous activist, it been achieved at a massive cost. The beliefs for which Lennon had most publicly stood were suddenly the subject of front page articles and leading items on news broadcasts, and none of these beliefs chimed well with those of the incoming Reagan regime in the USA. On the evidence of the news coverage and near-deification of Lennon it looked like he may have been wrong in declaring "the dream is over" at the end of the song "God."

The concern in the twentieth precinct was more down to earth. What the hell did Mark Chapman think he was doing and what, exactly, were they dealing with? In front of them they had a calm, rational and strangely unemotional young man. He clearly felt concern, but only for his own personal safety and the impact the press interest was likely to have on his wife. He knew exactly who he had shot but couldn't explain the act beyond stating "I had to." In 1988 former police lieutenant Arthur O'Connor fed the conspiracy theory when he told Fenton Bresler: "It's possible Mark could have been used by somebody…I studied him intensely. He looked as if he could have been programmed – and I know what use you are going to make of that word!" The police also considered Chapman may have been under the influence of drugs, but didn't test him. In terms of the investigation they had lots to go on. The suspect was in custody, the main witnesses known, they were already certain they were dealing with a murder and the evidence all pointed to one man acting alone. Pretty soon they had a statement, which read:

> "I never wanted to hurt anybody my friends will tell you that. I have two parts in me the big part is very kind the children I worked with will tell you that. I have a small part in me that cannot understand the big world and what goes on in it. I did not want to kill anybody and I really don't know why I did it. I fought against the small part for a long time. But for a few seconds the small part won. I asked Got to help me but we are responsible for our own actions. I have nothing against John Lennon or anything he has done in the way of music or personal beliefs. I came to New York about five weeks ago from Hawaii and the big part of me did not want to shoot John. I went back to Hawaii and tried to get rid of my small part but I couldn't.

> "I then returned to New York on Friday December 5, 1980 I checked into the YMCA on 62nd Street I stayed one night. Then I went to the Sheraton Center on 7th Ave. Then this morning I went to the book store and boughtThe Catcher in the Rye. I'm sure the large part of me is Holden Caulfield who is the main person in the book. The small part of me must be the Devil. I went to the building called the Dakota.

> "I stayed there until [Lennon] came out and asked him to sign my album. At that point the big part won and I wanted to go back to my hotel, but I couldn't. I waited until he came back. He came in a car. Yoko passed first and I said hello, I didn't want to hurt her. Then John came, looked at me and passed me. I took the gun from my coat pocket and fired at him. I can't believe I could do that. I just stood there clutching the book. I didn't want to run away. I don't know what happened to the gun, I just remember Jose [Perdomo, the doorman] kicking it away. Jose was crying and telling me to please leave. I felt so sorry for Jose. Then the police came and told me to put my hands on the wall and cuffed me."

Having cuffed Chapman and taken him into custody the twentieth precinct were faced with more trouble that was usual in the case of a shooting. Their prime suspect was admitting to his actions so that made things easier. But along with the routine police work attending even the most serious crimes there was the added complication that this crime was instant news, and those caught up in the proceedings became instant targets for press attention and public opinion. One of the first casualties was Herbert Adlerberg, a fifty year old attorney with two children who took the case because his name was on the homicide list that day. Herbert soon removed himself when threats started coming his way (he had two children and didn't want to run any risks) but he freely admitted later that in the first meeting with Mark Chapman he had struggled to understand the motive for the killing and considered Chapman to be "a nut." Indeed, he was so convinced of this fact he believed there was a good chance of acquittal on the basis of Chapman's mental state. Because Adlerberg was involved in the first hearing he was party to a bizarre incident. The prosecution informed the court that Mark had a criminal record dating back eight years and an arrest in 1980 for armed robbery. Very soon it emerged that another Mark Chapman was responsible for these crimes and Adlerberg's one to one interview time with the man he considered "a nut" had only been 25 minutes, so he didn't know enough about Mark to object to the misinformation put in front of the court. Looking back later what he found particularly strange was that Chapman stood perfectly still and didn't react to the wrong information being presented about him.

Mark Chapman soon found himself in Bellvue Hospital where everything was done to keep him calm and he met two court appointed psychiatrists; the only psychiatrists he would meet who didn't have a vested interest in proving him sane or insane. Dr Marvin Stone and Dr Naomi Goldstein took immediate charge of Mark. Dr Dorothy Lewis – who would later become an expert witness for the defence – was placed in the hospital at the time of Mark's admission. Her role there involved research into violent young adults, so Mark's reasons for admission were relevant to her work. In her first dealings with Mark she too could be regarded as impartial to the court case because her principal interest was in understanding violent crime and, in particular, violent young criminals. Dr Lewis wasn't on duty as a doctor to deal with mental health issues but, as discussed earlier, she was the witness who would eventually discuss his "command hallucinations." The significant point about this belief is that it suggests some sense of an outside agency motivating Mark. So, regardless of the fact some of his ideas were clearly in the realm of psychotic thinking, Dr Lewis was raising the possibility that Mark had some ability to reason his way through the main mass of delusions, as he had managed to do when he returned from New York a few weeks earlier and told Gloria her love had saved him. The problem was the commands he felt he could not resist.

By the time the trial had started the first rumours of a conspiracy to "assassinate" John Lennon had appeared. The fact that the press had discussed his killing as an assassination, and presented his significance as a world figure in their reports was some fuel to these rumours. These stories had no impact on the trial. The testimony of a range of mental health professionals was considered. Predictably those for the prosecution identified psychiatric problems, including narcissistic personality disorder and borderline issues, but considered Mark Chapman sane and fit to plead. The diagnosis of full-blown paranoid schizophrenia came from the greater number of experts employed by the defence. Dorothy Lewis, who had encountered Mark first within her role of researching violent young adults also considered him to have a "seizure disorder" which could appear "indistinguishable from the psychosis of schizophrenia." Her diagnosis put some mental health perspective on those moments when Mark's recollections became hopelessly distant and vague. New York had long abolished the death penalty so, realistically, the issue was whether Mark would spend a massive part of his future, possibly the rest of his life, in jail or hospital. The preparations for a long trial took place, including state of the art brain scanning on Mark involving an electroencephalograph (EEG), computerized axial tomography (CAT) scan and skull X-rays. Some slight abnormalities were identified, but nothing that would locate a particular problem likely to make Mark a murderer. With a trial date set for 22 June the world's media anticipated lengthy and detailed proceedings, guaranteed to put the killing of John Lennon back amongst the world's leading stories for a few weeks. All of that changed on 8 June when Mark Chapman phoned defence attorney Jonathan Marks to inform him that he was changing his plea to guilty. The reason for the about face, apparently, was the fact Mark had received a visit from God whilst in his cell. God wanted Mark to plead guilty, and Jonathan Marks could not talk his client out of this course of action. Marks did – however – ask Justice Dennis Edwards to order a new examination of his client's mental fitness to plead but this was always likely to be dismissed. The original two court appointed psychiatrists - Dr Marvin Stone and Dr Naomi Goldstein – had considered him fit to plead and the machinery of the court was ready to roll. In any case, as the judge pointed out, if reasons emerged within the trial for another assessment of Mark Chapman's sanity it could be ordered in response to those. But, in another twist that has since fuelled notions of a conspiracy, Judge Edwards engaged Mark in an exchange designed to tease out whether he understood the issues, understood the significance of his changed plea and realised the implications of what he was doing. As *People* would subsequently note; "Chapman's answers seemed fastidiously designed to follow the penal code, as if he wished to ensure that his guilty plea would be able to withstand any challenge. When Edwards had finished, the main points of the prosecution case were quickly covered. Chapman was offered a final chance to return to a plea of not guilty, which he declined. The prosecution case was going so well their court time was largely limited to focussing on specific issues that made Chapman's actions especially murderous, like the reasons for his choice of hollow point bullets. The judge allowed Assistant D.A. Allen Sullivan to question Chapman." *People* reported the ensuing exchange:

"AS: This is your own decision?

MC: It is my decision and God's decision.

AS: When you say it is God's decision...did you hear any voices actually in your ears?

MC: Any audible voices?

AS: Any audible voices.

MC: No, sir.

AS: Before you made this decision did you indulge in any prayer?

MC: Yes, there were a number of prayers.

AS: After you prayed did you come to the realization, which you understand to come from God, that you should plead guilty?

MC: Yes, that is His directive...command.

AS: [And] you would say at this time that this plea is a result of your own free will?

MC: Yes....

The Court: Have any promises been made to compel you or to induce you to plead guilty?

MC: Not in such words, but I have been assured by God that wherever I will go He will take care of me.

The Court: A good Christian ethic. I presume we all feel that God will assist us in times of need and emergency..."

That was, effectively, the end of any insanity plea. Judge Edwards' questioning had established that Mark Chapman did not feel any threats had been made to coerce him into his plea. The assistant D.A.'s question about the audible voices had proven particularly significant in establishing Mark was sincere, not crazy. Conspiracists would come to regard the exchange as proof that Mark had been coached into the shortest and most effective legal route to jail, and well away from any penetrating and lengthy analysis in the public gaze of how he came to shoot John Lennon. From the conspiracy angle, this represents a neat ending, because most of the evidence about what Chapman thought he was doing and why he did it was not tested in cross examination.

Mark had just over two months to wait between his trial on 22 June 1981 and 24 August when sentencing was due. During this period he withdrew to the point he refused to see his wife, who had travelled all the way to Attica. A second EEG on 31 July produced very similar results to the first but, without warning and just over a week before sentence was due, Mark Chapman went berserk, wrecked a television set and radio and began screaming that his crimes would see him punished in Hell. Thrown into his cell he ripped off his clothes, ripped up his Bible, stuffed the Bible pages into the cell toilet and began splashing water at the guards who came for him. After half a dozen guards had subdued him the next step was a ride to Bellvue Hospital. Doctors there heard him speaking in two distinct and different voices, neither like his own speaking voice. They were made to understand that these voices belonged to Lila and Dobar, two personal demons sent by Satan to torment Mark.

Mark had recovered enough to carry a copy of *The Catcher in the Rye* with him as he turned up to be sentenced. It was clear from the outset that no further pleas with regard to Chapman's insanity would be entertained but Jonathan Marks was able to call Dr Daniel Schwartz and Dr

Dorothy Lewis to put further context forward with regard to Chapman's mental state. Dr Schwartz' testimony included; "I believe [Mark Chapman] became perilously close to losing his own identity." As evidence for this Schwartz cited the instance of Mark signing out on his final day at work in the apartment complex as "John Lennon." When it came time for Mark to testify he read the section from *The Catcher in the Rye* in which Holden Caulfield explains his fantasy of actually catching the endangered children in the tall grass.

Justice Edwards' summing up took some of this into account but emphasized that Mark was sane in the eyes of the court and had committed an intentional crime. He sentenced Mark Chapman to a minimum term of 20 years, and a maximum term of life imprisonment.

Mark began his sentence, spending years in solitary confinement for his own protection as various theories about why he shot John Lennon grew and diversified. Along the way television documentaries, books, newspaper and magazine articles and websites poured over the details of what he had done and the conspiracy theories gradually coalesced around a set of beliefs.

Mark Chapman wasn't given to commenting on them, though he remained approachable and willing to talk when journalists like *People*'s Jim Gaines were allowed access to him. In 1987 Jim Gaines wrote a lengthy and detailed account of Mark and his crime, including detail of what had transpired since the sentencing. Gaines met Chapman in November 1983, his article included the following:

"The person I confronted now was entirely different from the one I had known before. The Mark Chapman I first met was highly excitable, subject to sudden mood shifts, with a manic brightness in his eyes and voice. This new Mark Chapman looked broken; his face was without color, his look was downcast, pleading. His nails were bitten to the quick and he shook as if with a chilling fever. For three six-hour days… he shook, rocking back and forth vigorously enough to pull his chair's front legs off the floor. Not long before, he had begun once again to proclaim the faith of a born-again Christian. 'God has brought me so low,' he said, 'I'm almost like a cripple, an invalid.'"

This version of Mark rationalized that he had committed his crime to become famous, stating that the shooting could have cancelled his past and given him an identity. "It's the greatest cop-out in life to allow yourself to become insane," Chapman claimed, going on to state that he had over-played some aspects of his mental illness to allow others to pity him. Gaines was given access to Chapman's "spiritual journal" in which he charted the way God directed his life. However, Chapman also felt Satan coming close and influencing him and at times the effect of the evil was overwhelming, and hard to tell apart from that of The Lord. Along the way Chapman reported the influence of demons and how one visit from a minister had eventually led to him being delivered from the effect of a group of six demons infesting him.

Chapman filled the first decade of his incarceration with studious projects including reading major works of scholarship in the order in which they were written and attempting to map the sum total of human knowledge. He and Gloria jointly wrote and published a fundamentalist

Christian newsletter for prisoners called New Block.

Despite the focus on long term projects Mark has remained in the grip of the obsessions that erupted in his life before the shooting of John Lennon. Extremes of behaviour have marked much of his time in prison. Jim Gaines reported periods of vegetarianism and fasting (including one of 26 days which obliged the state to get a court order permitting force feeding). Along with outbursts of paranoia Mark has remained capable of rejecting his Christian God and turning to other religions including Zen Buddhism and Judaism. Such periods typically end when he returns to God and re-establishes his belief in the nurturing God, more in line with New Testament teachings. His devotion to *The Catcher in the Rye* goes through similar periods of intense engagement and rejection. Chapman's parole hearings, for which he has been eligible since 2000, have tended to follow similar patterns. His eighth hearing in 2014 saw him refused release because of the danger he would commit another crime, or become the victim of a murderous attack himself. The same notions of Chapman having depths and secrets constantly emerge in the hearings. 59 year old Mark told his parole board in 2014 that he was no longer interested in fame, but still maintained his grim celebrity profile stating "there has been many times where I could have [achieved great fame through responding to a media request] and very recently, too. I won't mention names, but you would be surprised." His infamy has ensured a steady stream of people make contact and keep Mark engaged in discussions of his crime, his life and a great many related topics. Much of the conspiracy research that seeks to place Mark Chapman in the midst of a carefully planned professional hit relies on the ease of access people have always had to him. The travels around the world would have allowed for rendezvous those close to his homes in Atlanta and Honolulu would never have suspected and Fenton Bresler was the first, but by no means the last, writer to marvel at how easy it was in 1980 to contact a man awaiting trial in New York. Mark is known to have had telephone contact with a number of people including a church minister and his wife, but no complete record of those in touch with Mark by phone was kept, something that forms part of any argument for those claiming his sudden guilty plea was forced on him, along with the responses in court that ensured he was never tried on the basis of being innocent by reason of insanity.

Perhaps because the crime for which he remains internationally famous is the focus of the vast majority of communications he receives in jail Mark now talks openly (including at his 2014 parole hearing) of this as a well-planned crime. His religious faith, though consistently tested in jail, keeps re-emerging and a central point of his argument to parole boards is that Christ has helped him appreciate the mistakes made, and see a path toward a useful and productive life if he is ever released.

Jim Gaines' comment from his 1987 People article highlights the nagging problem that besets both conspiracy theorists and those whole believe Mark Chapman was an extremely disturbed individual who acted alone: "it seems to me that murder needs a deeper reason, a cause in some relation to the gravity of the act. The image of the exposed, shell-less conch—an organism stripped of the protective layer critical for its species' survival—suggests such a reason." Because, beyond the facts outlined so far there remains a question. Does the combination of the disturbed Chapman and the unprotected but culturally potent John Lennon give us an explanation for why Mark shot the musician? Conceivably it does, but mystery still surrounds the motivations behind the act and Mark's inconsistency, along with some nagging gaps in the story continue to feed the conspiracy theories. If the "deeper reason" comes from Mark's mind alone, then the problem is that few of us can begin to feel his disturbance, let alone fully understand it. If the deeper reason revolves around a complex plot, then we are only looking at the most random fragments of hard evidence, and connecting them with the best arguments possible.

A Simple and Non-conspiratorial Summary:

The arguments about his crime continue to feed conspiracy theories, though to many others the whole story makes sense. In the simple version of these convoluted events Chapman is cast as a hopeless narcissist, unloved by his father – who avoided him in jail after the crime – and caught in the domestic tension between both his parents. Unable to form meaningful relationships Mark's fragile psyche developed ever more complex alternatives including his world of little people to whom he was powerful and with whom he could usually reason out the logic for his personal schemes. They would approve, eventually, because he could convince them. The emotional intelligence to take this same reasoning power effectively into the world of education and careers appears conspicuously more lacking in the life Mark led up to 8 December 1980 and the frequent redefining, trips abroad where he could appear to be a different person and the stop/start schemes, like dealing art, all suggest self-obsession coupled with little real comprehension of how success has to be built. The increasing desperation to matter as he got older and the lack of a firm educational or employment base on which to build any success then appear to fuel the outbursts of anger that hampered even the most menial of Mark's jobs. In this context the convoluted scheme to find some argument that gave him moral high ground over a cultural icon, like John Lennon, coupled with the complex planning that eventually put him on the sidewalk as Lennon's limousine arrived just before 11-00pm on the night of the killing are both a perfect expression of Mark's increasing desperation and also the perfect scheme with which to become famous. The simple fact that the whole thing seems so unlikely makes the chances of being caught in preparation or prevented from shooting the accessible Lennon highly unlikely. By contrast John Hinkley (co-incidentally born in the same month as Mark) chose a well-protected target, who survived. All of the non-conspiracy arguments are supported by Mark's continued problems in jail to make sense of his life and his actions, and escape the attentions of the complicated cast of characters contained in his mind. His obsessive returns to the signifying elements of his earlier plans – like *The Catcher in the Rye* – show the same patterns of thinking and making meaning still apply to him decades after his crime. Whatever the redemptive power of his faith Mark remains a troubled individual, prone to being persuaded by the interest of others as is evidenced by the increasing pride he shows in the complex crime and his ability to plan and execute it (not something he raised when interviewed in the immediate aftermath of the shooting). His grandiose schemes to read and understand great works of scholarship are similarly expressions of a deep need he has never fulfilled to achieve some power over others and be respected in the adult world in which he failed to function comfortably or successfully before his arrest.

A More Complex Conspiratorial Summary:
Mark Chapman was programmed and is the only incarcerated member of a group of conspirators who killed John Lennon for reasons that made perfect sense to them. In this reality Chapman led a secret life away from those contacts and witnesses who have commented in the small library of books dealing directly with the killing of John Lennon. In this scenario John Lennon's death qualifies as an assassination because it was planned by a group with a political agenda and the intention was to silence a political voice and eliminate an influential leader. Some of the intention was to stop Lennon's recording career but the main aim of the plot was to stop Lennon, in all his activities. The collateral damage to the lives of others – notably his wife and his youngest son – was regrettable but necessary if the aim was to be achieved.

Chapman's usefulness to the conspirators revolved around the fact he was suggestible, making him an ideal Manchurian Candidate style assassin and the perfect fall guy when investigations probed the crime because his unstable background and inconsistent career would present him as "a nut" (as Herbert Adlerberg described him after their one meeting as attorney and client). If this conspiracy theory is fully understood then the most telling pieces of evidence are those which amount to leakage or loose ends and these random indicators are likely to have been inevitable because Chapman's instability made him a difficult assassin to manage. The discrepancy about the days spent in Chicago is one prime piece of evidence; along with the funding of Chapman's round the world trip and his various stays in YMCA buildings along the way. If we are to fully embrace the conspiracy theory then it is a given that in all of these cases there are individuals who met Chapman and provided him with funding and training for his final role. It is also a given that the time spent in Chicago as Mark travelled from Hawaii to New York involved a meeting with someone who activated Mark as an assassin, and despatched him on the final mission to kill John Lennon.

It should be noted that whilst this re-writing of the story has alluded to those points where the conspiracy theorists think the most telling evidence can be found there are two ongoing problems with taking the conspiracy theory seriously. Firstly, the hard evidence that proves any of it is conspicuously absent. The most that can be said with any certainty is that Mark Chapman definitely turned from a peace loving Presbyterian into an angry young man who practiced shooting. There are eyewitness accounts of him having contact with people like Dana Reeves, being encouraged to shoot, and acquiring bullets. There is also hard evidence that nobody at the time thought Mark Chapman was about to become a notorious, high profile, killer. Americans, at that time and now, can acquire and pass on guns and ammunition with more ease than citizens of other countries in the western world. So most of the main line of conspiracy theory argument where Mark Chapman is concerned is a combination of things known to be true, like the existence of covert programmes like MK-ULTRA and the proof that the CIA had been involved in domestic activities and operations well beyond their basic brief. There are many who claim that the erratic activities of Mark Chapman are tell-tale signs that he was working on a covert level, but that is not proven.

The second major problem with taking on board the main conspiracy theory argument outlined thus far in the chapter is that the same facts are the core of other, and more bizarre, tellings of the same story. So, ironically, this conspiracy theory and many others are permanently at risk of being destroyed because they are being overwhelmed by lovers of conspiracy theories, many of whom have their own opinions and takes on the information presented so far in this chapter. At this point in the story it is worth warning anyone unfamiliar with conspiracy theories in general that this situation is normal. Those hell bent on believing in conspiracies often cite evidence that various groups amongst the "authorities" have infiltrated the researchers with the intention polluting the research with dis-information. Strange as this sounds there is much evidence of this happening in the UFO community, but also much debate about the significance of why it happens. So, for example, the encouragement of American citizens to look to the skies and spot flying saucers in the 1950s had a lot to do with the USAF lacking complete radar coverage on their coasts and – therefore – welcoming any report of unidentified aircraft approaching American air space. If you are unfamiliar with conspiracy theories in general all you need to know from this point onwards is that most of the major events and phenomena surrounded by conspiracy arguments – from the assassination of JFK to the existence of UFOs in secret US hangers – are so mired in conflicting arguments that finding any truth likely to convince everyone becomes a near-impossibility. One reason for this is that so many followers of conspiracy theories become focussed on their own interpretation of the facts that others with a different take on the same conspiracy can often irritate them. Truly, this way madness lies. So, having warned you, I should point out the obvious, you have a choice about reading the rest of this chapter, because we are about to dip into some of this dark conspiratorial material. If you read on you will get a sense of how bizarre one story can become. John Lennon's death isn't up there with JFK in terms of the tonnage and strangeness of the various theories, but it has its moments.

Mind Games and More:
The one totally trustable thing about complex conspiracy theories relating to people like John Lennon is their ability to stretch your critical thinking above and beyond most standard stories about your musical heroes. You might choose to apply your own common sense and logic to the facts as you understand them. However, a little investigation means you'll soon discover there is some individual ranting in cyberspace and displaying a take on everyday life that has – hitherto – escaped you. It sounds simple to suggest that you Google online variations combining John Lennon's death with conspiracy and then log off after a couple of mind-altering hours. The experience of doing that might prove far from simple and may well leave you understanding the facts in front of you but struggling to understand how anyone reached the levels of reasoning that support some of the stranger takes on this story. What follows are a couple of well-developed arguments that take the known facts of the death of John Lennon and drag their interpretations to places the original conspiracy theorists never imagined and few have since explored. Before we visit these brief overviews a reality check of sorts is available. A number of books compile various conspiracy theories, often comparing and contrasting some of the main ideas. One of these conveniently applies its own "Alert Level" rating to each theory, with the higher scores indicating a very high level of probability that what you have just read is true. In *Cover-Ups* by Jon E. Lewis a rating of ten is the highest (i.e. this really did happen), and one is the lowest. On the back of the MK-ULTRA documents eventually leaking into the public domain and the court cases successfully raised against those

who conspired to cover up deaths within the programme that particular conspiracy is awarded the full ten in *Cover-Ups*. By contrast the notion that "John Lennon was assassinated by a CIA-sponsored Manchurian Candidate" merits an Alert Level of three. This makes it less likely than the notion that Christopher Marlowe wrote the plays of William Shakespeare (Alert Level five) and marginally more likely than the notion that the photograph apparently showing a massive carving of a human face on Mars is proof that this edifice was put there for us to find someday (Alert Level two).

Mark Chapman is a "Patsy" Who Only Believes he Killed John Lennon

Salvador Astucia's twice published book *Rethinking John Lennon's Assassination: The FBI's War on Rock Stars* has excited plenty of internet comment and driven others to further research which appears to support his basic theory. As might be guessed from the title the argument in the book is complicated, mainly because it locates the basic facts of the Lennon killing within a complex web of covert operation and conspiracy. Because the original book has driven subsequent online research, much of which has been posted on blogs and other public sites, the whole argument in Astucia's work has been dragged, developed and distorted into various forms. The basic argument he presents suggests Mark Chapman was indeed recruited and used in the manner described by Fenton Bresler but he remains innocent of the crime for which he has served decades of jail time because Chapman's purpose was always to appear as if he was the killer of John Lennon. Salvador Astucia names Dakota doorman Jose Joaquin Sanjenis Perdomo as the real killer. Online arguments present the same man as "an anti-Castro Cuban exile and member of Brigade 2506 during the Bay of Pigs Invasion in 1961, a failed CIA operation to overthrow Fidel Castro." The same man was the person who asked Mark Chapman if he knew what he had just done as Lennon lay dying in the hallway of the Dakota and also screamed "Leave! Get out of here" before the police arrived.

Astucia also regards it as suspicious that with Chapman crouching to the right of John Lennon the majority of bullet wounds occurred on the left side of Lennon's body; suggesting possibly another gunman on the opposite side of the target to Mark.

Astucia's agenda goes way beyond the immediate killing and ties in a range of other premature rock star deaths – including most of the notable members of the "27 Club" – suggesting they were eliminated in a long term operation in which covert U.S. security killings were used to silence activists, critics of American values and other subversives. Some of the discussion involves suppositions based on known facts. For example, one offshoot of the Chapman/Patsy discussion considers whether music industry mogul and mob associate Morris Levy might have been motivated to locate a reliable hitman to kill Lennon because he and Lennon had clashed over copyright issues a couple of times.

Astucia's interest in the possible covert war against rock is shared by others and Alex Constantine's book *The Covert War Against Rock* (2000) provides a succinct summary of suspicious circumstances in the end of most of the high profile genuine pop and rock performers who died in the twentieth century. Lennon's death nestles alongside rapper deaths – Notorious B.I.G. and Tupac – protest singers like Phil Ochs and both Bob Marley and Peter

Tosh of the Wailers. The copiously researched chapter on John Lennon provides over thirty separate citations of evidence gathered in the compiling of the argument, showing – if nothing else – that when the likes of Astucia and Constantine start researching there is no fruitful line of enquiry left alone.

Like most of the alleged assassinations of high profile musicians, Astucia and Constantine's efforts often rely on provable elements. They focus on security forces carrying out covert operations against targets they regard as legitimate and use the evidence of covert security work focussed on eliminating individuals. They do their best with the harder to support/harder to prove notions that any popular music star was a legitimate target in this context but the hard evidence proving anyone in American security wanted – say – Bob Marley dead remains very elusive. One or two related arguments have an added dimension in that it may have been in the interests of the "deceased" person to disappear. Such an argument might be applied to the death of Tupac Shakur, who clearly knew his life might have been in danger and produced work exploring the faking of death. There is also a widely available tonnage of material online and in books suggesting the pressures of fame drove Elvis Presley to fake his death to gain peace and personal space. But no such argument easily attaches itself to John Lennon's death. So, if Mark Chapman was a patsy then we still have to assume the death was an orchestrated contract killing, most likely masterminded by some element of American security. In that context the complication of a second gunman – like Perdomo – whatever his history with the CIA still presents major issues, like why none of the few people in the vicinity, including Yoko Ono who was several feet ahead of her husband when he was shot, saw anyone other than Mark Chapman with a gun. There is also the issue of how four shots from a gun other than Chapman's landed in Lennon's body and weren't heard as they were fired. Various possibilities exist, including Perdomo dropping the actual murder weapon on the sidewalk and secreting Chapman's other gun but these depend on nobody in the vicinity seeing the event. They also stretch credibility because the killing took place in public and nobody appeared to be directing the flow of footfall traffic in the area. Granted this was a quiet late night in New York, but the shooting still took place outside a central building in one of the world's busiest major cities. Anyone – within reason – could have happened by or seen something from a window, so this could never have been a controlled and secure operation.

John Lennon and Satan were Faust Friends
The notion of a Faustian pact is well established in popular music lore. The original German legend tells the story of a scholar – Faust – who can never find satisfaction despite his consistent learning. Faust trades his soul with Satan in exchange for unlimited knowledge and ceaseless pleasures. It ends badly, of course, and the longevity of the tale and its various popular interpretations over the years owes a lot to the way people consistently relate to the dissatisfaction, temptation and ultimate failure. A well-known variant on the theme concerns the alleged deal struck between Robert Johnson – blues singer and guitarist – and the Devil at the crossroads near Dockery Plantation, Mississippi at midnight. In popular legend (but not any recorded fact) Johnson met a huge black man at the crossroads. The man tuned his guitar, played some songs and handed the instrument back. The man was, in fact, the Devil and Johnson had just struck the bargain that would allow him to record 29 songs that have gone on to become one of the most treasured catalogues of all blues artists. In total, including different

takes of the same song and fragments of studio outtake, Johnson can only be credited with 42 tracks, but the power and influence of his music turns almost all of these recordings into classics.

Johnson was dead in mysterious circumstances at the age of 27, thereby cementing another legend and becoming a member of the infamous "27 Club" of artists dead at that age. Having subsequently been joined by Jimi Hendrix, Amy Winehouse, Kurt Cobain and Jim Morrison amongst others, Johnson's cool remains assured.

There are other cultish talents linked to legends of Faustian pact, including John Lennon. Joseph Niezgoda's *The Lennon Prophecy* does its level best to make a case for Lennon trading his soul for twenty years as a living legend and purveyor of some of the best rock music the world would ever hear. Despite the ravaging reviews it has received online the book has sold a few copies. The story – as with many marginal interpretations of Beatle lore – draws much of its "evidence" from the well-known mysteries and the more enigmatic elements in The Beatles' work. Central to the whole story is Lennon's comment "I've sold my soul to the Devil." Lennon was talking to fellow Liverpool musician Tony Sheridan, the context of their conversation being the incredible success and musical achievements of The Beatles. Since Sheridan had helped the band make their first recordings, and then benefitted from some of the spin-off success afforded to anyone who could claim involvement in Mersybeat, the conversation, as reported in Ray Coleman's biographical book on Lennon, was more of the "how did it come to this?" variety than any literal confession that Lennon had invited the dark lord into his life and subsequently agreed a pact with him. However, a few others have run with the idea and looked into additional material, notably Tom Slemen who quotes Lennon's remark in the context of a local Liverpool legend locating a crossroads/pact with the Devil site at a bridge on Rose Lane, Mossley Hill, Liverpool.

The Lennon Prophecy develops the initial confession into a complex argument tracking The Beatles' involvement at the cutting edge of recording technology and placing them as the first band to use backward masking. *The Lennon Prophecy* charts Lennon's singular path from pop star to social icon and the strange symbolism that infused much of his work. As with Fenton Bresler's arguments much of *The Lennon Prophecy* combines solid factual argument with supposition. But – as Niezgoda notes – "No one is sorrier than I about what is written here. It's a horrifying topic and a difficult subject for me. I wish my interpretation was wrong."

Joseph Niezgoda's "interpretation" of Lennon's life and example covers the well- trodden details of satanic lore and those who have sold their souls to the Devil before considering John Lennon's troubled young life and the seething combination of anger, frustration and the need to be recognised that eventually led him to rock 'n' roll, The Beatles and their truly phenomenal rise from unknowns to global stardom. The sheer speed and scale the early achievement strikes Niezgoda as eerie, as does the level of hysteria attending early Beatle gigs. The fan hysteria came alongside The Beatles being presented with seriously ill young people, apparently in the hope that the proximity of the desperately afflicted to the pop sensation would cure them. Niezgoda considers this strange phenomena and also the revulsion of the individual Beatles to a side of stardom they didn't court or understand, noting that "while achievement should have brought happiness [to John Lennon] he instead appeared tormented."

The Lennon Prophecy suggests a timeline of twenty years between Lennon selling his soul and the Devil collecting the debt on 8 December 1980, so the dissatisfaction brought by stardom along the way is a confirmation of the darkness at the heart of the deal. Niezgoda sees the tension building as Lennon appears to realise the enormity of what he has done and considers that Lennon then adapted his work to include a series of cautionary and revealing clues. Niezgoda heads into familiar cult Beatle fandom territory and teases out a series of symbols and clues. The Beatles' name in the shape of an inverted heart on the cover of *Rubber Soul* may – apparently – indicate a "'false soul'" whilst the fact that Lennon is the only Beatle gazing squarely into the camera on the same cover might be grimly significant. If we assume The Beatles are gathered around a grave in the picture, hence the camera's gazing up at the group, then Lennon is staring directly at death whilst the others avoid this relationship. The death imagery on the infamous "Butcher" cover also appears to allude to Lennon's pact with Satan before the depth and complexity of the hidden messages takes off once the band are freed from the rigours of touring and able to experiment at leisure. *Revolver*'s "Tomorrow Never Knows" is singled out as a turning point as Lennon, high on marijuana, becomes transfixed by the sound of a tape accidently loaded backwards and begins to grasp the possibilities of strange sounds to communicate the reality of what he is living through. The fact that Lennon attributed this revelation to "'the gift of God-of Jah, actually, the God of marijuana'" is presented as another recognition that the standard Christian God is out of the equation.

Interestingly Niezgoda also covers the familiar ground of the Paul-is-dead legend, but draws different meanings from some of the same symbolism. The cover of *A Collection of Beatles Oldies* suggests part of the prophecy because the crooked leg of the moddish figure draped over a drum on the front cover allows Niezgoda to read the right leg, crossed over the left leg and held in a position similar to the letter J, as part of a message. Taken together this single J and the word "Oldies" in the title of the album, which starts just under the heel of the boot on the right leg, spell out "Joldies" which can be broken down to "J-O-L Dies." Since Lennon had just met Yoko at the time the collection was released Niezgoda suggests the message prophesizes Lennon's name change on his second marriage, from John Winston Lennon to John Ono Lennon, and – therefore – alludes to Lennon's impending death at the hands of a killer. The apparent funeral scene on the front cover of the Sgt Pepper album which forms such a fruitful source of clues to the death of Paul McCartney in 1966 is interpreted by Niezgoda as a deluge of information about Lennon's pact with Satan. Amongst the more comprehensively explored clues are the fact that Lennon's image on the back of the Sgt Pepper cover appears under the lyrics for George's song "Within You Without You" with its discussion of spirituality and those who make mistakes and "lose their soul." These three words are printed across John's beltline, and appear perfectly centred on him.

Niezgoda rightly rubbishes the "urban legend within urban legend" suggesting the Walrus is a Nordic image of death but does take significance from the fact Lennon is the one in the Walrus costume on the cover of the *Magical Mystery Tour* album and EP, and also makes significance from Lennon writing the lyric of "I am the Walrus" with its "I'm crying, I'm dying" reference and its surreal word play and cascade of images including the reference to them "kicking Edgar Allan Poe" ("a tormented writer who was obsessed with death, violence and tragedy"). Because so many clues on album covers suggest a breakage in The Beatles the same material so neatly slotted into the Paul-is-dead story, like the crack in the wall on the back of the *Abbey Road* cover which separates the "s" from "Beatle" can be read as support for the Lennon prophecy because it could be an indication of a break in The Beatles band. Crudely, it can indicate Lennon's inevitable death as easily as it indicates McCartney's death in a car accident and replacement by an imposter.

Because the Lennon story concerns a prophecy there is no break in the logic required to shoe-horn a song like "One After 909" into the argument, despite the fact it was one of the earliest Lennon and McCartney compositions and was revisited for the sessions that ultimately produced the *Let it Be* album. The song is generally regarded as a standard rock 'n' roll tune with a lyric built around tensions concerning seeing a lover and train times. Niezgoda points out there were only two 9th days of the month that fell on a Tuesday in 1980. One in September and one in December, the second date being the one [Tuesday] "after 9/09." Since "I am the Walrus" had already referred to a "Stupid bloody Tuesday" and – therefore – discussed Lennon's senseless and grisly killing on that day of the week, "One After 909" can be taken in tandem with that song as a prophetic locating of the date and day of Lennon's death. The obvious problem, that Lennon was killed late on Monday 8 December in New York, is alleviated if you consider local time in his birthplace, Liverpool, where it was already Tuesday 9 December when he was shot. Of course, with this fluid approach to factual support for the argument a lot of random elements, like numerology, soon become involved. But the argument sustains itself for nigh on 200 pages without too much repetition, hesitation or deviation. A few choice diversions of logic include the fact that "The Beatles" is revealed to be an anagram of "seal the bet" and – therefore – potentially a recognition of the fact that the group was the vehicle by which Lennon achieved fame and world-wide notoriety as a creative artist. So it was the means by which he sealed the deal for which he had sold his soul.

"Good night sleep tight"
The beautiful haunting and melodious ballad closing *The Beatles* (aka The White Album) has been widely mistaken for a McCartney composition. In fact it's a Lennon song, pure and simple, and it was his genius idea to allow Ringo to wrap a mournful vocal around the lilting melody, all of it accompanied by a "really cheesy" orchestral arrangement. If the Lennon chapter of this book has been a strange, surreal and sometimes scary tour of the dark side of human nature then it's appropriate to remind you that John Lennon was capable of a level of pure tenderness in his music that has often been eclipsed by those praising his edgier artistic legacy. "Good Night" is a lullaby written for Lennon's eldest son, Julian, and in that context it's the perfect companion to "Beautiful Boy" on *Double Fantasy*. The man who wrote "Power to the People" and "Cold Turkey" also wrote love songs of spellbinding intimacy. That range of artistic power has inspired so many different thoughts and appreciations of John Lennon that nobody now could justifiably claim to know everything about the man, or his work. So, before we acquaint ourselves with other myths and legends about the most successful musical group the world has ever seen, a few reality checks are in order.

Firstly, with regard to the interpretations of John Lennon seen in this chapter, it is worth reminding ourselves that these are amongst the more extreme ideas advanced and we've spent almost 35,000 words in territory often associated with the paranoid and delusional. Lennon's work and legacy also exist in less challenging territory. Songs like "Imagine" are almost secular hymns that see action in school assemblies these days. The arguments explored in this chapter may have evidence and logic, but so does the argument that Lennon was a product of the time and place in which he grew up and an inspired and highly talented musician who pushed his creative abilities above and beyond those of his peers, making a permanent mark on the history of popular music, and his era. Secondly, it is worth reminding ourselves that the ideas in this chapter are the best researched and most supported by evidence of any Beatle legends you will read in this book, and – for all that - Jon E. Lewis' well researched tome on *Cover-Ups* still gives them three out of ten likelihood of being true, a rating many would regard as highly generous. So, the probability on that rating is that the alleged assassination of John Lennon by the CIA (or whichever maverick offshoot of the U.S. security services may have considered it) is a legend. In that scenario the stories in this chapter have much more to teach us about the imaginative nature of extreme fandom, and the need for people to believe in conspiracies than they do about the way the world really works. The point of this chapter, and this book, is to explore these strange stories. So, that focus on imaginative fandom is the one that will be emphasised repeatedly as the other chapters unfold. This book isn't about concluding anything, simply presenting the evidence and letting the reader decide, or start Googling and spend the rest of his/her life trying to make sense of any of it. Frankly, I'd recommend the second option, it'll mess you up in ways you'll struggle to imagine beforehand but it will also mean life continues to surprise you!

But, whatever you make of all of the above, as the presenters of *Crimewatch* are fond of saying; cases like this are very rare, don't have nightmares.

Chapter 2

Paul McCartney Died in a Car Crash and was Replaced by an Imposter

Of all the Beatle related urban legends this story is both the best known and most celebrated. Apart from anything else the "Paul is Dead" rumour has maximum entertainment value and manages to attract many fans for whom the playfulness and surreal artistry of clue spotting and theory forming is an enjoyable game. This crowd also includes McCartney himself, who playfully reworked a few of the standard visual clues to his "death" by parodying the *Abbey Road* cover for his own *Paul is Live* (1993) album. On Paul's live album the black van is missing, he is being dragged across the zebra crossing by one of the descendants of his sheepdog Martha – the subject of "Martha My Dear" - and the number plate on the white VW Beetle reads "51 IS" at the end. Perhaps a fairer way of discussing Paul's McCartney's own view of his death legend would be to say he is capable of having some fun with it but in the end it's been more of a burden than a blessing.

Unlike the Lennon "assassination" story the tale of the death of Paul McCartney generally appears without any sinister or threatening angle. In this reality the gist of the story is that McCartney left Abbey Road recording studios after loud disagreements with his fellow Beatles, and was subsequently killed in a car accident; usually timed and dated as occurring at 5 am on the morning of 9 November 1966, after which the band resolved to continue. Since most Paul-is-dead "research" revolves around the clues on record covers and in songs there is less speculation than might be expected on the motives for the deception. The obvious reasons for such a strange course of action are to maintain the artistic vision and huge earning power of the most successful musical group in history; though it isn't hard to pursue some blogs and Paul is dead speculation online and find yourself in occult territory where darker motives are considered.

The Paul is dead rumour, and the next chapter's George is dead story both pre-date the internet, or the kind of electronic communications that record messages. Subsequently, any research done into the stories soon descends into identifying the discoveries made by "researchers." In most cases these researchers were people motivated enough to spend hours wrapped in headphones, energetically listening to sounds at the edge of a stereo mix. The same researchers were prone to pouring over lyric sheets, album covers, photographs of Beatles and any other useful source of clues. Who they were, why they bothered and what they thought of their discoveries remains largely unchronicled. To put this crudely, the Paul is dead story is largely a focussed game of Chinese whispers fuelled by a few magazine articles and some media coverage at the time. The Harrison story is more of the same but has way fewer articles or Chinese-whispering-researchers to support it.

In this context it makes sense to lay out the main gist of the story and how it started before breaking down the evidence into albums, songs and lyrics to shape the story. Frankly, there is so much of the story that what follows is a greatest hits of this greatest hit of Beatle legends. As with the killing of John Lennon, if you want to follow up any loose end or clue in the following chapter the internet is both your best friend, and most addictive enemy.

Nobody has laid provable and legitimate claim to starting the McCartney death rumour. Standard sources, like Wikipedia state accurately: "American college students published articles claiming that clues to McCartney's supposed death could be found among the lyrics and artwork of the Beatles' recordings. Clue-hunting proved infectious…" whilst one of the more detailed specialist websites devoted to the story describes the beginning of the rumour in this fashion:

> "In the fall of 1969—shortly after the release of the Beatles' Abbey Road—a rumor swept America concerning the death of Paul McCartney. While this rumor was very popular on college campuses, the widespread acceptance of this rumor reached such proportions that stories of the phenomenon were subjects of news reports and publications no less respect than the New York Times, Time Magazine, and the cover story of Life Magazine. It was the cover of Abbey Road that started it all."

From this one thing is clear. The release of *Abbey Road* (26 September 1969 – UK/ 1 October 1969 – U.S.) prompted the first thoughts that Paul was already dead, after which "college students" in America drove the first discoveries supporting this idea. A few of those advancing the theory got their names into print, but most continue to remain anonymous and it is hard at this distance in time to discern how many people took the idea seriously for even a few seconds, and how many simply enjoyed the treasure hunting amongst words, sounds and signs on the Beatles' artwork. What is certain is that an article in *Life* magazine in November 1969 put a damper on the death rumours. Paul McCartney along with wife Linda and their two daughters was pictured very much alive, scruffy but clearly quite content near his farm on the Mull of Kintyre in Scotland. He denied that he was dead, and that was good enough for most people. However the rumour had enough roots to continue growing in the shadows, a place it still twists and thrives today.

It wasn't the first semi-serious McCartney death rumour. That came on 7 January 1967 when icy conditions on the roads were behind a story that McCartney had been killed on the M1 motorway. The story grew enough momentum to oblige Beatles' publicist Derek Taylor to ring Paul's home in St John's Wood where the Beatles' bassist answered his own phone to inform Taylor that he'd been home all day. In fact, McCartney's black Mini Cooper had been involved in an incident around that time. Some years later *Gadfly* magazine related the story in discussing the Paul is dead rumour. The fact that McCartney's car was very distinctive, unique in fact, and that it was being driven by someone who bore a passing resemblance to Paul

McCartney is also relevant. It will be discussed later in this chapter.

Because the band were off the road and confined largely to studio work it was possible for such rumours to spread. If anything, their power as potent cultural icons grew in the period between their last live show at Candlestick Park in San Francisco on 29 August 1966 and the release of *Abbey Road*. With their focus on creating music that pushed the possibilities of recording technology and wasn't intended for live performance by a four piece pop group The Beatles created a series of albums that set new standards for popular music. Few acts could match their combination of creativity and commercial success and those that attempted to do so – like Brian Wilson of The Beach Boys – risked their own sanity in trying to keep pace. In bedrooms all over the world Beatle music was devoured and set about its work of changing perceptions.

No catalogue in popular music history has been more dissected or discussed so it is not the purpose of this book to add greatly to the consideration of The Beatles as artists. What matters from the point of the Paul is dead rumours is that the band, metaphorically speaking, were on fire for most of the period. So much so that every single track has subsequently been poured over and analysed to the extent that the identity of almost every musician featured is now known, each song has an online presence where its meaning(s) can be discussed and the artistic legacy of all of the work is assured. The fact that this music matters so much decades after its first release is proof enough of its value. At the time this work was incendiary to the extent that many fans would stumble upon John Lennon's Lewis Carrollesque wordplay, or the fluid sitar lines George was contributing to a few tracks and find their lives changed as they made it their business to chase these inspirations to source, and find what their heroes had found. Off the road, and free to experiment The Beatles remained a band for business and recording purposes but as they matured they were no longer one focus for hero worship. From *Revolver* to *Abbey Road* it might be more truthful to regard The Beatles as some unholy collision between skilfully managed brand awareness and a vibrant arts lab with an unbelievable ability to guess their business and creative decisions correctly.

Their public were starved of live concerts, the band's public appearances were few and far between and, increasingly, were appearances where one member was seen out at a specific event. George Harrison took a stroll around San Francisco at the height of the hippie explosion, John and Yoko were prone to public activism in support of peace and the rights of the downtrodden and Paul was keeping a relatively low profile. Though locals on The Mull of Kintyre were fairly used to seeing him with a toddler in tow as he refuelled his Land Rover or wandered down the quiet roads in the area. With the music becoming richer and more challenging and the band less ready than before to explain it in witty press conferences or play it live it was often down to the fans to make the meanings for themselves.

The first overground breaking of the Paul is dead story is generally located to 17 September 1969 and the student newspaper of Drake University in Iowa. Their article – "Is Beatle Paul McCartney Dead?" – discussed a campus rumour and was the first to discuss items that have since become the bedrock of the story. Central to this story was the claim that played backwards the track "Revolution 9" revealed a message that said "turn me on, dead man." The story generated enough interest that three and a half weeks later Derek Taylor discussed the regular flood of enquiries the band's press office received and noted that enquiries about death rumours were a regular part of his work but the Paul is dead story was exceptional for two reasons. Firstly, the scale of the enquiries was unusual and secondly some industry insiders – like prominent DJs in the USA – were amongst those contacting the office. Paul was alive and well according to Taylor.

Taylor spoke out in 11 October. It may well be the case that this uncharacteristic response to a death rumour by the Beatles' press office actually fuelled the story because the next few weeks were the height of the silliness. The day after Taylor responded to the rumours DJ Russ Gibb of WKNR-FM, Detroit took a strange late-night call, apparently from a listener called Tom. He was told that if he played some tracks off *The Beatles* (aka The White Album) backwards he would find more of the messages that were already the substance of the death rumours. Gibb followed the directions and heard what he was told he would hear.

As Gibb, along with a few other prominent people, began sharing their discoveries the Beatles' most recent back catalogue albums began to climb the charts again. The 1967 albums, *Sgt Pepper* and *Magical Mystery Tour* (released as an album in the U.S. but not the UK in 1967) came back into the Billboard top 200 albums in late 1969 and stayed there until well into the following year. These – of course – would have been the first releases without Paul had he died late in 1966 as the rumours were increasingly claiming. It made a general sense. The band's failure to undertake international tours, which had been a staple of their career from the British invasion of the USA in 1964 until the final date in San Francisco seemed out of character. Therefore, locating Paul's death to sometime soon after that final live date was logical. One element unrecorded in the increased sales is how many albums were being destroyed as anyone with an interest put their hands on the vinyl and forced it to play backwards. This was years ahead of scratching and these early turntablists were in search of sounds that revealed hitherto hidden messages. They set off in this search informed by the directions that had started with the campus newspaper story, and grown via the WKNR-FM broadcast and a few similar events. The meanings they found spurred others to join the same search.

The press and radio, especially in the USA were fuelling the hysteria. The first separate publication on the topic was probably a 22-page booklet printed in September 1969. Credited to J. Lancelot Turner and printed by Stone Garden Press the publication is now Beatle collectors gold, more for its rarity value than any significant insights it provides. It appears self-published and consists of photocopied typed pages and hand drawn illustrations. It does, however, run through the main clues that first spread the rumours of McCartney's death.

On 14 October the *Michigan Daily* newspaper ran a belated review of *Abbey Road* with something of a twist; the review was effectively Paul's obituary, complete with an illustration of a severed head. In his book on the McCartney death rumour – *The Great Beatle Death Clues* - R Gary Patterson even cites a television special on whether McCartney had died, in which F. Lee Bailey questioned a series of witnesses as WKNR-FM presenter Russ Gibb presented his evidence. F. Lee Bailey is a criminal attorney who – at that time – included involvement in The Boston Strangler case on his CV. Bailey's colourful career went on to include involvement in the defence of O.J. Simpson before he was finally debarred in some states from practicing in 2014. So the television special had some credibility. The witnesses called included Beatle manager Allen Klein and Peter Asher, brother of McCartney's former fiancée Jane Asher. The special ended with F. Lee Bailey earnestly facing the camera and suggesting viewers make up their own minds. The special aired in New York on RKO on 30 November 1969, weeks after the *Life* article. Subsequent investigations into the programme reveal that the main protagonists were already tiring of the tale. One witness was journalist Fred LaBour, the man whose article in *The Michigan Daily* had taken the initial underground rumour to a higher public profile. In 2009 *The Michigan Daily* reported that LaBour had informed Bailey before the show that most of the story was made up, only for F. Lee Bailey to reply; "Well, we have an hour of television to do. You're going to have to go along with this."

McCartney himself had told *Life* magazine that those concerned about his alleged death should "worry about themselves instead of worrying about whether I'm dead or not...Can you spread it around that I'm just an ordinary person and want to live in peace?" McCartney would later reveal that he had encouraged the Beatles' publicity staff to get the denials out, realising that any publicity in this context could be good publicity.

Media coverage continues to this day and the internet boosted the search for evidence by offering everyone with a theory and the motivation to share it a platform. However, the end of November 1969 marked a falling off in any serious consideration of the story as fact by the main news media. Since this time Paul McCartney's career has been the main plank of evidence proving the whole caper to be an urban legend. If McCartney genuinely was replaced by an imposter then the chances that a lookalike, aided by plastic surgery, could go on to fake one of the most lucrative and lengthy solo careers in rock are incalculably high.

In the immediate aftermath of the first hysteria there clearly was debate and activity. Nobody has seriously suggested The Beatles or their direct employees were behind stoking the rumour, although McCartney and Derek Taylor were obviously aware of its usefulness in drawing attention to the band's recordings and artwork, and boosting sales as a result. The increased sales of older albums suggest the rumour may well have been good for business. It would be impossible now to make an accurate measurement of how many people involved in the music industry reacted to it in ways encouraging the legend to continue. What, for example, would a record shop manager do confronted with a group of kids pouring over the *Abbey Road* cover for clues? If he let them hear a snatch of "Revolution 9" and suggested "if you really listen you can hear..." he might just add a lucrative sale to his accounts that day. Similarly, how many people in the employ of Capitol Records, various radio stations or the rock press found themselves discussing the rumour in a manner that led to more publicity, and created more work for them by way of radio features, articles and the like?

There isn't much evidence that people seriously believed the story, then or since, but there is lots of evidence that it grew a body of evidence. In effect this is the lore, the substance of the urban legend. The fact it has grown, continued and produced different tellings of the tale is the thing to be celebrated. At best we are looking at the imaginative genius of fandom, at worst the unchallenged outpourings of paranoid fantasists feeding each other's frenzy as they go. But, for the most part, the death rumour has been grim fun with a serious element. The serious element largely concerns the ability of the most celebrated group in popular music history to create work of depth and intrigue, and present it as inventive, listenable and highly creative music.

If there is one close precedent for the McCartney death rumour it is probably the infamous *War of the Worlds* radio broadcast of 30 October 1938, presented by Orson Welles and Mercury Theatre on the Air. Most of the radio drama took the form of a live news broadcast following the landing of Martians in Grover's Mill, New Jersey, and their subsequent breaking out across country. On the spot announcers, clearly panicked, relayed events that suggested an all-out hostile invasion. Some listeners panicked themselves and in the aftermath of the show Welles was forced to account for his actions. He was suitably contrite, though the fuss amounted to a major public arrival for the man, and his career soon benefitted from the notoriety. Unlike the McCartney rumour *War of the Worlds* caused serious concern at a national level in the U.S. and something was done to understand how and why some of the nation had panicked.

The subsequent academic investigation, carried out at Princeton University, can lay claim to being the first serious piece of Media Studies research. Some of its conclusions bear comparison with the McCartney story. Firstly, the numbers alleged to have believed and panicked over the broadcast were hard to ascertain, but were certainly much fewer than the most lurid tellings of the story suggested. There was clear evidence in the aftermath of the broadcast that people had enjoyed discussing the panic. Years later a BBC *Timewatch* programme marked the 50th anniversary of the broadcast by finding some who remembered the panic. One man interviewed for the programme couldn't tell his story without breaking into chuckles as he described how he and his brothers – clearly aware it was a drama – had failed to point this out as their father panicked in front of them. They "let Dad go for a bit" simply because they were enjoying the wind up so much. Once again, the numbers of older rock fans enjoying the sheer wind up of initiating impressionable youngsters into the Paul is dead legend has never been accurately researched. But the Paul is dead legend spread largely by word of mouth and its sheer persistence long after any serious media interest fell away suggests people continued to discover the story and find it intriguing. An intriguing story is often one people want to believe, even if their more logical instincts tell them it can't possibly be true.

One of the more fruitful lines of enquiry regarding the *War of the Worlds* panic was the extent to which people's existing beliefs directed the way they responded to the apparent invasion from space. Those with a strong Christian faith were amongst the most likely to panic, especially those with a strong belief in that the end of the world would take the form of the conflagration depicted in the Book of Revelations. Some of these people did their own reality checks and still came to the conclusion the invasion was real. A lot of reality checks provided little reality, because people saw what they expected to see. In one case chronicled by the Princeton researchers a New York resident realised people were hurrying past in the street and then noticed the crowd had suddenly vanished. This seemed like confirmation that everyone was fleeing the area at once. In fact the crowd were hurrying to catch the start of a film in a nearby cinema, and crowds flocking to the movie theatre were common on that street. But to one resident panicking about an alien invasion all of that usual Sunday night routine was suddenly forgotten.

Some of the panic over the alien invasion occurred by accident. The Mercury Theatre on the Air had broadcast a clear declaration that their work was a drama, and repeated the message at the end of the broadcast, stating their work was the closest they could come to scaring the American public for Halloween. One problem with the announcements was that many people joined the broadcast a few minutes in because they had opted to switch over from other shows after deciding the guest stars on offer weren't worth waiting to hear. Some of these late arrivals were amongst the first to panic and some of those panicking made decisions to flee their homes long before they could hear the closing announcement. If they fled without a car radio (i.e. by heading to a railway station, running or simply not having a radio in their car) they had no way of hearing the final announcement making it clear *The War of the Worlds* was a drama.

So context and the existing beliefs of those hearing the broadcast made a major difference. So too, with the Paul is dead rumour. In the time since the rumour first broke a great deal of research has been done into fringe beliefs, especially into the beliefs people hold regarding UFOs and other paranormal phenomena. It is too much of a diversion to lump all of this research into the present chapter but a brief summary suggests people prone to experiencing an external locus of control; i.e. feeling strongly that others are in a position to control their lives, are more prone to believing conspiracy theories. So too those for whom their intelligence and education might feel incompatible with their levels of employment and those who have suffered emotional trauma in growing up, like a vicious divorce of their parents.

Whilst the above is a very trite list of reasons people might be more prone to believe urban legends and conspiracy theories there are some other elements to the argument. Firstly, some of the stories people struggle to believe at first actually turn out to be true. Bob Woodward and Carl Bernstein were initially reluctant to believe the unfolding facts coming their way were an indication of a genuine political conspiracy, but the evidence in front of them forced them to accept the truth of the Watergate scandal. The regular leaking of conspiracies into the mainstream media, and the fact some of the strangest ones prove to have elements of truth, makes it more likely that people will believe conspiracy stories in general. Secondly, the Chinese whispers nature of rumour spreading in the pre-internet age meant that many people were first told the basics of the rumour by someone they knew or trusted. In many cases this would involve an older and respected person initiating someone else into the story. As with any secret lore there was status in simply knowing the facts, and kudos to be gained by repeating them to others who didn't know. Pre-internet there was much less opportunity to find out stories like this, or hear the music that was never played on the radio, so knowing the stories, and the songs was a means of gaining status. The Beatles were more played on the radio than almost any other band at the time but it may be significant that some of the tracks central to the death rumour – like "Revolution 9," "Don't Pass Me By" or "I Am The Walrus" (banned by most UK radio stations) – are amongst the least played on radio. In the present century when almost any music is available online it is hard to imagine how hard it was to track down the harder to find sounds. The Beatles' records were, just about, everywhere but that still left many people unfamiliar with their contents. A great number of those getting to know the Paul is dead story and examining the clues did so in the company of people who already knew the territory. So the newbies were often influenced in their perceptions. To put it crudely, the introduction was similar to an experienced pot-head passing you your first joint. The experience of staying in that circle, with its shared knowledge and different way of looking at the world was also similar to joining the circle of regular smokers, indeed, those most knowledgeable about the secret messages in rock music in general were often those most acquainted with the mystical secrets of good weed.

In this context the question of how many people seriously believed Paul McCartney to be dead, or for how long this minority actually believed this, is not really the point. The sense of belonging and sharing a journey by way of a strange story is really the issue. So much the better if the story revolved around levels of reality more likely found in the works of Lewis Carroll or some half-obscure tome of eastern thought. Around the time of the Paul is dead rumour the British sociologist Paul Willis researched hippie and biker cultures. His work eventually appeared as *Profane Culture* (1978). His work relies on an approach characterised by those in the field as "thick description" as it employs nuances of speech and scene to convey meaning. In this extract Willis observes humour amongst the hippies (or "Heads"):

Head humour was characteristically articulated around bizarre and distorted expressions of unspoken but fundamental attitudes. This account of Les was greeted with great hilarity.

Les: I had a fantastic experience [at] Bath [Pop Festival]...this friend of mine went to score...and he came back with the shit...it was...really bad shit...I took about five drags...I went to sleep and I woke up...and I was tripping...it suddenly went dark...I looked up... there was this great big cunt...massive...beautiful...it was just looking at me...then it suddenly went blue sky again...I looked up...there was this chick walking through the crowd, and she stood over me for about thirty seconds...I'll never forget that. [Laughter.]

The humorous point of such stories was to bind groups together through sharing an experience they could find amusing, whilst at the same time knowing that "straight" society couldn't hope to share the values or the perceptions that made this story such a laugh. Such stories were shared in the knowledge that they would be passed on within the community. So Les' experience was doubtless recounted when he wasn't there, at which point others hearing the story would be prompted to share their best mind-fucks on dodgy dope. For all its illegalities there was a glorious naïve innocence about this sharing culture that the internet age can't hope to replicate. So the present Paul is dead experience revolves around a totally different set of values in which those of the most extreme persuasion can find friends and supporters. In this culture it is much harder to check whether anyone supporting you is who they say they are. The most extreme ideas and acts find supporters. At its worst internet sharing means the 14 year old who stabbed a teacher, endangering his life, in Bradford in 2015 got almost 70 Facebook likes when he posted afterwards: "Teacher's getin so funny so I stick the blade straight in his tummy." On the positive side the online presence of the Paul is dead story means every single fact and scrap of evidence is so easily available that anyone can gather as much material as s/he can stand and make up their own minds.

The fact that Paul is dead has survived the transition from urban legend to stalwart story of internet conspiracy theorists suggests it always had some strength. It also speaks volumes about the power of The Beatles as one of the most enduring artistic forces of all time. By contrast, the George is dead story that forms the following chapter was there and gone as a high profile rumour in weeks and never found significant support; but the main evidence for that tale is one person, who identified herself immediately and based most of her argument on photographs and her own experience.

Paul is Dead's Top Ten
This story continues to expand more rapidly than most people could cope with so the greatest hits forming the bulk what follows are intended to help you focus on the main foundations of the ongoing story. There's near enough unlimited amounts of all of this online, should you feel the need to search it.

The man masquerading as Paul McCartney is really called Billy Shears

There's more than most people imagine on this. For starters, Billy Shears has billyshears.com and his own book is promoted on the site with some awesome promises:

> "Read it as an amazing "Paul is Dead" fantasy...including verifiable facts about William Shepherd taking over The Beatles and the McCartney estate. In the end, it tells you which parts were fiction...

> "...you will also learn the hard physical evidence. Here are a few examples: DNA Chapter 4 reveals how it was proven in court, in Germany, that the current Paul does not have the same DNA as the earlier Paul. Chapter 34 identifies the professor in Florida who first published the fact that the new and old Paul have different voiceprints, proving again they cannot be the same person since each voiceprint is unique (like each fingerprint)."

Shears also has his own Facebook page under the name of William Shears Campbell which you can like. It tells you:

> Billy Shears, also known as William Campbell, (born 15 November 1943) is most commonly known for replacing Paul McCartney after his death in 1966. He remains to be the recent Paul McCartney and is said to be more talented, refined, and down to earth than the first.

But then, it would be unlikely to tell you Billy was less likeable than the original Paul, right? Billy Shears' first and only appearance in the work of The Beatles is as the singer in Sgt Pepper's Lonely Hearts Club Band. In the title track opening of the album we're told "the singer's going to sing a song" and the track ends with the introduction of "the one and only Billy Shears." The major problem with this clear sign that Billy Shears is the new Beatle is that the second song on the album is "With a Little Help from my Friends" and the lead vocal is blatantly that of Ringo Starr. So, obviously, Ringo *is* Billy Shears. Though, this impediment hasn't greatly stalled the ongoing Paul is dead legend. The myth that grew up around Shears continues to support the serious and satirical takes on the death legend, summed up succinctly at ispauldead.com it runs: "William Campbell had won a Paul McCartney look-alike contest a year earlier in Scotland and was carefully trained and groomed in Paul McCartney's music style, to replace the dead Beatle." Add that claim to the lack of live Beatle action and a few ructions in McCartney's life after 9 November 1966, like his split with fiancé Jane Asher and eventual marriage to Linda Eastman, and you get a picture of the new boy settling in, whilst his band mates support the delusion and others likely to be emotionally impacted, like Paul's fiancé, all finding it too much and leaving the Beatle inner sanctum.

The above is a short version of the most common story regarding the arrival of the imposter Paul, though – as with most of the evidence in the Paul is dead legend – there are many variants, including one that identifies the imposter Paul as a Canadian police guard who had worked with the band when they toured that country and who had struck them as an uncanny ringer for McCartney (so much so that Lennon, told of McCartney's death at a 6-30am meeting with Brian Epstein on 9 November 1966, suggested finding him and using him as the replacement).

Paul Died in a Car Crash in the Early Hours of 9 November 1966
The date and time of the crash have become a shaping element of the legend. They matter because dating Paul's death to a specific point in time and establishing this as a sudden and accidental death makes for a better legend. The specifics of the date and time create a watershed between Beatle works involving the Fab Four and works dripping with hidden clues from the three survivors and Billy Shears. The later works, predictably, can be understood better if we assume they leak information about the true nature of what is going on. In the real world it is certain that Paul McCartney did not crash his car in London in the early hours of 9 November 1966. That much is clear because decades of rabid Beatle scholarship and obsessive fandom have promoted a forensic approach to gathering trivia. Every verifiable scrap of information relating to the thoughts and actions of the band has been gathered and used in some variant of publishing or broadcasting because the market for such minutiae shows no signs of slowing down (and, yes, I know it's ironic to be making that statement in a book about The Beatles). There are two books using the title *The Beatles Day by Day*, one of which chronicles the daily activities so far as is possible of the band from 1962 to 1989. In addition a number of websites chronicle these details. One of the saner sites – The Beatles Bible (beatlesbible.com) – puts it simply; "In fact, the crash never happened. Between 6 and 19 November 1966, McCartney and his girlfriend Jane Asher were on holiday, travelling through France and Kenya."

The origin of the date and time of the crash starts with the belief that the *Sgt Pepper's...* album is a revealing testament to the change in The Beatles line up. Specifically, it revolves around the cover. If you take a small mirror and line it up so it bisects the words "LONELY HEARTS" on the drum on the album cover an enigmatic message appears. It shows the phrase "I ONE IX HE ◊ DIE." From this point onwards you can interpret "I ONE" as two ones, in other words the number "11." IX is the Roman numeral for "9." So the mirror appears to reveal the message "11 9 HE DIE." American dating puts the month to the left of the day of the month, meaning Paul McCartney died on 9 November.

On the strength of this revelation a number of vivid descriptions have been developed, rich in detail and description. In researching the present book the account below became a particular favourite read. It currently lies on the AltHistory Wiki (althistory.wikia.com/wiki/ Paul_Really_Is_Dead)

Paul was under the influence of LSD. This, combined with Carolyn's [a hitchhiker he had picked up who was amazed to find herself with McCartney] excitement at meeting Paul, distracted him from the road. At 4:38 AM, he went through an intersection, not noticing the light was red. Someone going through the intersection from the left slammed into the car, not having time to stop or dodge. The collision sent Paul—and Carolyn—veering head-on into a telephone pole. Carolyn's face went into the windshield, killing her within minutes. Paul's mouth and nose hit the steering wheel, knocking out all of his teeth and crushing his nose and right eyeball socket. He also crushed his fingers—and his entire right hand—against the dashboard. Finally, he broke both his right knee and thigh. (Thigh fractures are potentially fatal as the muscles can move the pieces of the bone around, causing severe internal bleeding). The driver who had hit them pulled over to help them, but upon recognizing Paul he was so overcome with shock and guilt that he drove away, seconds before the car caught fire.

Because of his injuries, Paul was unable to get out of the car, so he started screaming, "Get me out! Get me out!". Several people came over, but there was nothing they could do since the car was on fire. Paul himself caught fire at 4:42 AM. An ambulance, fire engine, and two police cars arrived at 4:47 AM. The blaze was extinguished within a couple of minutes, but by that time, Paul had died. His hair, clothing, and most of his skin had been burned away. Much of Carolyn's body had been burned all the way to the skeleton, so she could only be identified by her dental records. Both were pronounced dead at 4:56 AM.

The Cover-Up
At 6:30 AM, Brian Epstein called the three surviving Beatles and asked them to come into the studio immediately. Once they arrived, George Martin and Brian Epstein told them what had happened. After several minutes of just thinking about their friend, Ringo asked what this would mean for the band. They all agreed that Paul's death would hurt the band and considered disbanding both out of respect for Paul and because they feared their fans would not accept them if they brought in a new member to replace him. Epstein reminded the group that splitting at that stage would be too much of a legal headache given the amount of agreements and contracts which the band were tied into while John believed that the group were at their creative peak and wanted them to carry on. Then John suggested covering it up

Granted, the Alternate History Wiki openly invites contributors to share "Any and all original alternate histories" so the site is a free for all. But the account above is typical of both the best and worst aspects of the date and time of Paul McCartney's death. The tale is cinematic in its imagery and strong in Beatle lore, presenting the band as a powerful unit, aware of their influence. The unwitting contribution of the star-struck hitchhiker to Paul's agonised death is also a backhanded reference to the distance between adoring fans and their idols, suggestive of both the attraction between each and the inherent dangers when they do meet. It also references Beatle lyrics, Paul didn't notice the changed traffic light, i.e. "he didn't notice that the light had changed". Paul's hair was burned away, referencing Ringo's line from "Don't Pass Me By" stating; "you were in a car crash and you lost your hair."

The account is also typical of many elements of the Paul is dead and George is dead stories in the way it contains a certain logic but also offers up evidence that stretches credibility to breaking point. The specifics of the injuries sustained and the exact time Paul caught fire make gripping reading. But if they were true they suggest witnesses with the ability to ascertain all of this. They also suggest a ridiculously detailed forensic analysis for the bodies of two people clearly killed as the result of an inferno following a car accident. Possible, but unlikely. Since the other driver fled and the emergency services didn't arrive until 4.47 the whole tale would be dependent on witnesses, who aren't named or even numbered, despite the attention to detail elsewhere in the account. Above all, the detail puts the teller of the tale in a very strong position of possessing a level of knowledge bound to attract others to the story. Something that also occurs in the George is dead legend from the mid-seventies where Claudia Gates – who broke the story – was in personal touch with the deceased George. Finally, despite all the credibility issues, there is some basis in truth for the story. In this case, it is tenuous. But there were two road accidents involving Paul McCartney in the sixties. On Boxing Day 1965 McCartney crashed his moped, breaking a tooth and sustaining scarring to his upper lip. Avid Beatle fans know exactly where to find evidence, for example in stills from the video for "Rain." McCartney grew a moustache partly to hide the evidence of the injury whilst his lip healed.

The "Paul is dead" rumour dating from January 1967, and already mentioned in this chapter, also relates to a road accident with McCartney's involvement. Although, he was nowhere near when the accident occurred. A full account of the events has been published in a few places, one of the more illuminating accounts comes from *Gadfly* magazine's May/June 2000 edition, which still appears online. This points out that the 7 January accident involved Paul's distinctive Mini Cooper, but when it crashed the car was being driven by Mohammed Chtaibi. Chtaibi (then better known as Mohammed Hadjij) worked for gallery owner Robert Hugh Fraser, officially to support work with artists, but – according to a few accounts available online - his duties often amounted to the kind of activities that totally blur the boundary between PA and good mate (cooking, carrying dope etc.) On 7 January 1967 Fraser and Chtaibi visited Paul McCartney to party the night away. *Gadfly*'s vivid account sets both the scene and the context:

Fraser and Chtaibi's taxi pulls up to the gate at 7 Cavendish Avenue, McCartney's London home located in the swank St. John's Wood area, late in the afternoon. Twenty or so fans, mostly girls, were already camped outside hoping to get a glimpse of the elusive Beatle. When the slight, dark-haired Chtaibi gets out of the cab the girls all scream, thinking at first glance that he's McCartney, but McCartney is already shuttered inside the three-story detached house, playing rock 'n' roll records. Fraser goes to the gate and presses the intercom button several times. It's many full minutes before McCartney (thinking it's the girls playing pranks again) answers with a laconic "Yeah?" After a brief exchange, the gate swings open just enough for Fraser and Chtaibi to squeeze through, and then clicks closed again.

Once safely ensconced inside the house, the trio retires to McCartney's cluttered back-room lounge to relax. After a few minutes of chat, McCartney exits, but quickly returns with a large book, which he places on a table. Chtaibi watches as McCartney opens up the book. He's surprised to learn it's actually hollowed out in the middle, making the book a secret box, and the box is filled with all manner of hard and soft drugs, from hashish to cocaine, heroin and acid. This is the stash, the heart of the party. McCartney takes out a bag of hash and assigns Mohammed the task of rolling the "Benson & Hashish B-52 Bombers," joints made from a mixture of dope and tobacco, while he and Fraser chat. A few Bombers later, the intercom buzzes again. Within moments, Mick Jagger, Keith Richards, Brian Jones and mutual hipster friend Christopher Gibbs (the nephew of a former British Governor of Rhodesia) are standing in the middle of the room. Now the party starts to get serious, and the Bombers are augmented by some of the harder drugs.

After a few hours of fun, and with darkness falling, the group decides to "make a weekender out of it." Plans are made to drive to Redlands, Richards' secluded thatched-roofed country mansion in West Wittering, Sussex…

These party plans were ultimately the source of the rumour of McCartney's death in a car crash and the reason the hard evidence of McCartney's injuries never emerged. The tale goes on to describe Chtaibi driving Paul McCartney's distinctive Mini and trying to keep sight of the taillights of another car, containing the various Stones and a Beatle. Because Chtaibi was pushing his driving skills and the car to their limits there was clear danger with the plan from the start. Along with driving he was also worrying about carrying the book stuffed with drugs and coping with his own intoxicated state. The tale goes on to describe a situation in which Chtaibi, not realising he has left a length of seat belt trailing outside the Mini, is stunned when the car pulls to the right as it is being overtaken. He corrects to the left as the passing car clears the trailing belt and McCartney's Mini shoots straight into a lamppost, car and driver (Chtaibi) both taking a serious pounding in the process. With enough presence of mind and physical strength to cope with the situation Chtaibi succeeds in locating and ditching the drug stash before the police arrive, and also discharges himself from hospital when it becomes apparent his life isn't in danger. There is a coda to the story involving Chtaibi's bemusement that his employer and pop star friends don't call from their weekend to find out what happened to him or the drugs. His next contact with McCartney involves a fairly unsympathetic tongue lashing from the Beatle bassist over the wrecked car and a refusal of help to get medical treatment to help with lingering injuries from the accident.

The story matters here because it does establish that Paul McCartney's prized Mini was involved in an accident in January 1967 and also establishes that the driver, though Moroccan, bore such a resemblance to McCartney that genuine Beatle fans were momentarily confused as they watched him earlier emerging from a taxi outside McCartney's home.

There are interviews with all of The Beatles in which they dismiss the rumours regarding hidden insider messages in songs or artwork. There are a few exceptions to this like the McCartney/ Harrison backing vocal of "tit-tit-tit" on "Girl." But in the aftermath of the accident involving McCartney's Mini it is also notable that the doll on the cover of *Sgt Pepper's Lonely Hearts Club Band* is wearing a top emblazoned with the words "Welcome The Rolling Stones" and she nurses a toy car on her knee.

So, whilst Paul McCartney did not die in a car accident in the early hours of 9 November 1966 there is a link between real events and this rumour. The true story also supports the gist of the rumour and provides some tenuous support for the belief that hidden insider messages appear in Beatles' work.

The Sgt Pepper Album is Dripping Clues and Symbolic References to Paul's Death
Here we go into the circular logic and inescapable strangeness of secret Beatle missives. This way, truly, madness lies, but a sparing study of the main points is probably survivable. There's way more "evidence" than the material listed here, but some celebrated Sgt Pepper clues include:

The Beatles are no longer The Beatles, the opening track and cover art make it obvious this is Sgt Pepper's Lonely Hearts Club Band. And, if anyone is in any doubt, the lyrics of the title track specify the band is performing and Billy Shears is about to sing. The uniformed line up on the cover are stood next to The Beatles, so clearly they are separate from them. Their colourful clothing contrasts with the Merserybeat era Beatle suits. The entire crowd are gathered around a site that looks like a fresh dug grave and this is the grave of The Beatles because the name Beatles is spelled out in flowers in the plot. The crowd gathered behind are – therefore – mourners. Whilst no obvious priest is conducting a service there is the hand of writer Stephen Crane hovering over McCartney's head in a gesture that might either be blessing a dead Beatle or anointing the new blessed one (i.e. Billy Shears). Curiously Crane died aged 28, the age McCartney might have lived to had he not had his fatal accident. Also the age referred to on the VW Beetle number plate on the *Abbey Road* cover. More significantly Crane wrote a well-known story called "The Open Boat" in which four men are confined to a lifeboat. Three eventually survive but in an ironic twist the fourth man, who dies, is the one who struggles hardest to keep the group together. His efforts must be remembered and so it is down to the survivors to tell the story. The small crowd includes a significant number of those who died tragic early deaths, collectively their fates might reveal something of Paul's death. In 1967 Marilyn Monroe's death was more widely accepted as suicide at the end of a period of reckless activity than it is today. Two tragic young heroes – James Dean and Jayne Mansfield – died in road accidents. Dean's driving was fast and dangerous and, perhaps significantly, Mansfield was decapitated (a widely rumoured fate for the dead McCartney). Edgar Allan Poe reached the age of 40 but his death – like that of Paul McCartney - is shrouded in myth and legend and lacks documentation. On the inside cover of the album the four Beatles stare back at the viewer but only Paul wears black trim on his epaulettes (possibly signifying death) and only he has the initials OPD (which could mean officially pronounced dead – a UK equivalent of the American DOA). Paul's back is to the viewer on the back cover, though the other three Beatles look directly at us and part of the line "Wednesday morning at five o' clock as the day begins" touches Paul's left arm, linking the line to him and

– possibly – linking with the message on the drum to locate a Wednesday (9 Nov 1966) with the specific time of Paul's fatal accident. The importance of the line is further emphasized by George pointing a finger at the text on the back cover.

A number of lyrics on the album can be taken to provide enigmatic clues. Paul "blew his mind out in a car" having failed to notice changing lights. The new Beatle (Billy Shears) is getting by with a little help from his friends and may sing "out of tune." In the desperate attempt to replace the dead Beatle with an untried imposter things are "getting better all the time." Other offshoots of the urban legend begin to link named characters in songs, like Rita – the meter maid – with characters in the Paul McCartney death drama. There is discussion in some places that Rita was the hitchhiker he picked up and who was with him in the accident, not Carolyn as quoted earlier. At which point it is probably sufficient to point out that the wealth of contradictions in the different versions of the story, along with a strong basic narrative and underlying themes, are indicative of urban legends. But you will easily find intense discussions of the ways in which the complex masterpiece reveals a wealth of detail regarding the early death of Paul McCartney.

As a final point, the sheer scale of success enjoyed by *Sgt Pepper's Lonely Hearts Club Band* as a major work of art has been a strong factor in the enduring Paul is dead legend. It is generally regarded as a good sign when a band can produce an original album that outsells any greatest hits collection and *Sgt Pepper's...* currently sits well inside the top 20 biggest selling albums of all time, still marginally ahead of *1* which contains Beatles chartoppers from around the world. The certified sales of the album are lower than many others around it, but this owes a good deal to the fact that sales in the sixties were manually recorded, so the claimed sales figure of well beyond 30 million copies may well have some claim to be reasonably accurate. Critically an album so widely known has – predictably – drawn every kind of comment. The worst and most telling commentators are those, like Lester Bangs, who have taken issue with the artiness of the whole album, seeing it as a stepping off point into hopeless self-indulgence and excess, and therefore a dangerous work to those who love rock 'n' roll with balls and attitude. By contrast the album tops chart after chart of the best records ever made. In 1978 Paul Gambaccini polled a small army of the most respected rock critics he could persuade to identify the best albums ever made and *Sgt Pepper's...* won, with *Blonde on Blonde, Highway 61 Revisted, Astral Weeks* and The Beatles' *Rubber Soul* making up the top five. 25 years later a special edition of *Rolling Stone* was devoted to the 500 greatest albums of all time and *Sgt Pepper's...* topped that list, which included 10 Beatles studio albums and put the band's best work right at the top. The top five in that poll are:

Beatles – *Sgt Pepper's Lonely Hearts Club Band*
Beach Boys – *Pet Sounds*
Beatles – *Revolver*
Bob Dylan – *Highway 61 Revisited*
Beatles – *Rubber Soul*

No poll of the best of anything can truly claim to be definitive and there are other lists that see things very differently. But *Sgt Pepper's...* commercial and critical success goes on and on. In the *Rolling Stone* list it's notable that The Beatles grab the majority of the top five before a single black artist, heavy metal band, or progressive rock band make an appearance. Other *Rolling Stone* favourites – like Bruce Springsteen – are duly rewarded with high places on the list and glowing write ups, but The Beatles and their most celebrated works appear to exist in a class above everyone else. So audiences keep finding them and devouring them. Day by day some of these people are initiated into the myths and legends around *Sgt Pepper's*... and, as Kurt Vonneget would say; so it goes.

The Magical Mystery Tour Album is Dripping Clues and Symbolic References to Paul's Death

To be more precise, the album (released in America and most of the world) and the EP released in Britain containing the songs from side one of the album are oozing clues and symbols. According to legend the black Walrus on the cover is Paul and the black costume, against the colourful costumes of the other Beatles is symbolic of death, as is the figure of the Walrus itself (though only in Scandinavia). In reality John is in the Walrus costume and the role of the Walrus in symbolising death belongs more in this Beatle legend than reality, but you'll still find people and websites claiming the Paul is dead angle on these points as the truth. There is also a belief about placing the "Beatles" spelled out in yellow stars on the front cover in front of a mirror and getting a phone number leading to the M&D Company of Funeral Directors. Phone numbers in the UK have changed mightily since 1967 so don't try this at home. However, the M&D C name appears in a scene from the television film and a still from this scene, showing the name on a sign, is in the booklet inside the album and EP. Many of the outdoor scenes for *Magical Mystery Tour* were filmed in and around West Malling in Kent. In 1967 this was still a working airfield and well-remembered locally for its part in the Battle of Britain. In that year the US Air Force ceased regular operations on the base but it was placed on a "care and maintenance" standing. In the early seventies the accommodation blocks were put into service to house Asians expelled by Ugandan leader Idi Amin. Today the same site is Kings Hill, a modern business park. But in 1967 the local bus company was Maidstone and District (M&D) and they had a major share of local travel, including coach trips. So they could claim to be "the best way to go." Incidentally, *The Lennon Prophecy* book makes some mileage from the fact Lennon is depicted next to the sign and the initials MDC might prophesy his death at the hands of Mark David Chapman.

The stills from the 24 page booklet with *Magical Mystery Tour* appear to have been an almost inexhaustible source of evidence to the Paul is dead story. A few of the more blatant clues include one photograph of Paul dressed in military uniform behind a desk name sign that says "I was." Significantly the sign points away from Paul so his face and the message are full on to the viewer. A cartoon drawing of Paul which appears in the "Fool on the Hill" sequence in the book elongates the final "l" in "Hill" with a wavy line that runs across the top of Paul's head, effectively splitting it and appearing to refer to the fatal head injury of some legends. Although, of course, the story presented above suggests serious head injuries followed by death in a burning car. In one shot, and sequence from the film, the band perform with Paul standing shoeless. His shoes are on the ground next to Ringo's bass drum. The shoes appear bloodstained. There is clearly colouring on the shoes apart from their usual leather appearance. Some have suggested this is a printing error caused by the colour of ink needed for the bright orange bass drum. The drum says; "Love The Beatles" which could be an incitement for fans to love the band without condition, or could be a parting message of affection to the dead Paul (who is signified by his shoes). In one of the more notable and loved sequences of the film The Beatles dress in white evening dress to perform "Your Mother Should Know." As can be seen watching the film online or perusing any good quality still, Paul is alone in sporting a black carnation, all the others sport red ones.

It is widely reported that the *Magical Mystery Tour* television film was a complete critical failure. This is not so and a few Beatle expert authors, including Alan Clayson and Spencer Leigh in their book debunking Beatle myths – *The Walrus was Ringo* – have successfully pointed out that the critical reaction has always been mixed. Never-the-less to a band used to a mixture of respect, love and awed admiration the most scathing reviews were an unpleasant surprise. Most Beatle histories see the problems stemming partly from the death of Brian Epstein and the band flailing in the wake of losing the focussed management he provided. Another interpretation of the same situation suggests simply the band in *Magical Mystery Tour* are only three quarters of the band that made *Revolver* and the apparent creative mistakes are understandable if one quarter of the group is being blooded into his new role, and the most reliable doer in the old line-up has died suddenly.

Having said this, the best songs on the *Magical Mystery Tour* album are amongst the best pop songs ever written and these include masterpieces like Paul's "Penny Lane." The fantasy word play on Lennon's "I am the Walrus" has provided more fuel to the Paul is dead story than any other song on *Magical Mystery Tour*. Some of this revolves around the alleged symbolic place of the Walrus in representing death but the mystical lyric with its changing viewpoints and enigmatic symbolism goes way beyond one simple image substituting as the announcement of a death. The fact that Lennon sings "I am the Walrus" and the title of the song includes the subtitle "'No You're Not said Little Nicola'" suggests some dispute over who is really dead. The "stupid bloody Tuesday" line in the song is part of the Lennon prophecy story but has also been interpreted as Lennon reflecting on an argument that led to Paul McCartney storming from the recording studio on a Tuesday night before his fatal car accident in the early hours of the following day. Lennon's refrain of "I'm crying" and "I'm dying" might also be understood as going through a range of grieving emotions over his unwitting part in the death of the friend who stormed off after a row. One of the more involved discussions of "I am the Walrus" occurs in Forrest Dailey's book *The Fifth Magician*. The book admits in its own publicity it is "difficult to categorize" because "It is somewhere between fact and fiction. Truthful facts and events have been put together to form what is considered an untrue urban legend." Dailey's focus is on being as fluid and creative as possible in looking into meanings, but "I am the Walrus" lends itself to such an exploration. This interpretation sees each vivid vignette as a different item in the story of Paul's death. So the line about sitting on a cornflake as the van is coming translates into McCartney in a wrecked car as an ambulance heads for the scene, the following reference to a girl letting her knickers down is taken to refer to a besotted female hitchhiker with Paul and the sexual tension in the air before the gruesome yellow matter custard dripping from a dead dog's eye depicts horrific crash injuries.

Another strong element of *Magical Mystery Tour*'s (album) contribution to the rumour is in the apparent messages heard despite what appears on lyric sheets. The second and final fade in "Strawberry Fields Forever" is widely reported to feature John Lennon saying "I buried Paul" whilst some people hear the hidden message "Paul died, Paul is very bloody!" in George's "Blue Jay Way." In "Blue Jay Way" the hidden message is there in the echoing extremities of the vocal track, which also feature some production effects. It is very hard to hear in the original version of the song but some clips exist online in which the specific sounds have been filtered out, including a YouTube clip that offers the additional words on screen whilst playing the sounds edited out of the song.

The "White Album" is Dripping Clues and Symbolic References to Paul's Death
The sprawling and occasionally self-referential double set released late in 1968 has many supporters and critics. At the time of its release, and subsequently on internet forums, Beatle fans have enjoyed a great deal of fun and debate in attempts to cull the four sides of vinyl into a running order for one single album. Officially titled *The Beatles* but widely known as both "double white" and "The White Album," the collection features some of the fiercest rock the band ever recorded, hosts some of the simplest and gentlest songs in their catalogue and famously ends with "Revolution 9" followed by "Good Night." These closing tracks pit two of John Lennon's most contradictory works side by side. "Revolution 9" is easily the most avant-garde work released during the Beatles' career, a piece of sound art compiled of found and invented loops. "Good Night" is a syrupy lullaby, sung with a beautiful hint of melancholy by Ringo. The band appear on the double set in their full complement and sometimes as solo performers and with occasional help; like George Harrison engaging Eric Clapton as lead guitarist on "While My Guitar Gently Weeps." The double album – other than the impenetrable "Revolution 9" – appears to be a simpler set than its two lavishly produced predecessors but the various lyrical twists and production asides soon dispel this deceit. America in particular loves *The Beatles*. The album has achieved sales in excess of ten million copies in that country alone, it spent years in the top ten American sellers of all time and is now approaching 20x platinum rating for the U.S.

Despite the white cover with solo shots of each Beatle the packaging is still a rich source of McCartney death rumour material. The original albums included a large folded sheet with montage photographs of the various Beatles. One image in the collection shows McCartney lying back in the bath with his head mainly submerged. His face and torso are sticking out of the water, effectively decapitating him. Another shot on the fold out shows Paul with slicked back hair and glasses, looking very unlike the mop topped Beatle. An obvious interpretation of the look-alike picture is that we are looking at William Campbell Shears, or whoever else replaced the deceased Paul, and the picture is included so the slight differences in their appearances will be less apparent as a result of Beatle fans becoming familiar with Shears' likeness. On the original insert poster this photo is towards a far corner, making it less likely to get spotted unless the person looking at the insert is a dedicated fan and likely to pour over every detail. The photo appears online in various places, like checktheevidence.com, in which it is animated with other photos of Paul, past and present and/or placed alongside for comparison. Another photo of Paul on the insert shows him in a blurry black and white image, clapping and appearing to dance. A closer look reveals what appear to be a pair of skeletal hands reaching towards him from behind. The obvious interpretations include death stalking him, or the dead Paul reaching from beyond the grave to signify his replacement (in the picture) isn't the real Paul McCartney.

The sessions for the album ran from May to October 1968 and marked a point in the band's career when creative and personal tensions reached new heights. The constant presence of Yoko Ono when John Lennon was in the studio marked a breaking of an unwritten rule that the band were a self-contained unit, as did the appearance (albeit uncredited) of Eric Clapton. In fact Clapton's original guitar work was fed through post-production effects to make it sound more like a Beatles' guitar track. The first Beatle to leave the group was Ringo, who got so fed up with the behaviour and bickering he announced he was off and promptly took a holiday. A number of written histories of the band report he returned to the studio to find his drums decked in flowers from the others, at which point the band resolved to knuckle down and continue working. The tensions go some way to explaining the way the main band pictures on the inside gatefold of the record are individual portraits rather than one photograph of all four. The close up of Paul clearly shows a thickening on the left side of his top lip, consistent with an accident or – allegedly – plastic surgery (to make Billy Shears look more like the dead Beatle he was replacing).

The Beatles making their 1968 album were a mature and self-aware group and also becoming used to rumours about themselves circulating. The song "Glass Onion" tackles these head on. The refrain of "looking through a glass onion" is enigmatic. The most obvious interpretation sees this as John Lennon making a sarcastic comment about the way others saw the band, specifically the fact that their vision was distorted and they were missing the real picture. In that case the line "now here's another clue for you all, the Walrus was Paul" is a barb aimed directly at those intent on finding hidden meanings, and it's funnier because John knows it was him (John) inside the Walrus suit. It is also a hostage to the death rumour theory because Lennon refers to Paul/Walrus in the past tense. The calls to Russ Gibb's radio show led to another meaning for the song. There were claims a "glass onion" was an old and peculiarly British slang relating to the appearance of the handles on a coffin. Victorian era caskets, apparently, having ornate glass handles resembling the layers of an onion. If that is true then Paul is looking out from the casket and looking through the glass onions at us all.

Because it makes so little sense in a literal way "Revolution 9" is a rich source of rumour evidence, the most famous piece of which is the apparent appearance of the phrase "turn me on, dead man" if the track is played backwards. Because reel to reel tape recorders were becoming more common in homes in the late sixties a number of people experimented with their own recordings and backward sounds became an abiding interest for some. The ability to analyse speech heard backwards led to a small number of experts developing the theories about the way messages generated in backward recordings might be the subconscious intention of the speaker. If we take this theory seriously then it doesn't matter if John Lennon denied he ever intended the backward message to appear. Experts like Vancouver-based speech analyst Jon Kelly have gradually identified and shared a number of enigmatic messages, some of which appear ironically funny or starkly revealing. Disgraced cyclist Lance Armstrong once stated: "Well, if it can't be any clearer than 'I've never taken drugs,' then incidents like that could never have happened. How clear is that?" Played backwards the message – as heard by some – appears to reveal: "The pill. Some secret."

Intentional or not, some the alleged messages in "Revolution 9" include: "Who buried Paul?" "Paul no more," and "there were two – there is none now" (supposedly a reference to the fact McCartney and a female hitchhiker both perished in the fatal accident). "I'm so Tired" also appears to reveal the message "Paul is dead man, miss him, miss him." This message appears – running backwards – at the end of the song. "I'm so Tired" is an exploration of exhaustion caused by mental torment, though Lennon never specifies what is causing such a problem. The obvious conclusion to some being that the song is an outpouring of his guilt and lingering suffering over the death of the man who wrote so many songs with him. The various sounds in "Revolution 9" can be considered to reveal the noises of a crash, followed by a babble of voices, maybe from by-standers, a siren, screams, fire and shattering glass. In fact, much of the detail in the various accounts of the car accident, like the vivid tale printed earlier in this chapter, rely on the sequence of events supposedly revealed by the sound clues in this track.

The double album also contains the first Ringo-penned song to get an official release on a Beatles' album. "Don't Pass Me By" tells a tale of anguish as the singer waits for a visit from someone he cares about. Versions of the death rumour frequently quote the lines: "I'm sorry that I doubted you I was so unfair/ You were in a car crash and you lost your hair." Not a combination of self-reprimanding emotion and specific image you'll find in many songs. The song ends without the singer and the person to whom he addresses the song actually meeting, suggesting – perhaps – Ringo mulling over the argument that drove Paul from the studio and preceded his fatal crash.

John and Ringo are both revealing their incurable pain at their loss but another clue seems to suggest the whole band want to turn back the clock. This may be the most obvious hidden clue simply because a fragment of a song appears on the album but remains uncredited on the running order (as is "Her Majesty" on *Abbey Road*) and also fails to appear on the insert for the album, which prints the other lyrics. The lyrics for the fragment run:

Can you take me back where I came from?
Can you take me back?
Can you take me back where I came from?
Brother can you take me back?
Can you take me back?
Mm can you take me where I came from?
Can you take me back?

The little fragment is so non-specific that it could be interpreted in a number of ways but an obvious angle with regard to the death rumour sees this as the band inserting a forlorn plea to their dead colleague expressing a wish to rewind time and reunite the old line-up. The fragment is also an expression of one particular skill Paul possessed. McCartney in particular could work up a small piece of a song to the point that an effective melody, vocal inflection or distinctive lick might emerge. Many of these were recorded and would eventually become complete songs. The second side of *Abbey Road* shows some of the best of these works compiled into one lengthy track.

The Abbey Road Album is Dripping Clues and Symbolic References to Paul's Death
This album was the new release when the death rumour first broke and of all the tell-tale clues to the untimely death of Paul McCartney it is likely that the front cover of *Abbey Road* is the best known of all. The four Beatles are spread out walking left to right as the viewer looks across the zebra crossing near the recording studio they had known and loved for most of their career with EMI. Each is dressed distinctively and no two appear to have dressed for the same occasion. Although one interpretation suggests the only occasion likely to unite their dressing is a funeral. In front John in his white suit may be dressed as a preacher, next in line Ringo is immaculate in a tailored suit and polished shoes and looks like an undertaker, Paul also sports a suit but looks generally dishevelled and casual, and has bare feet, leading rumour-mongers to see him dressed as a corpse might be, George, in double denim is taken to be the gravedigger. Paul is out of step with his bandmates, all of whom lead their stride with their left foot, Paul leads with his right. The VW Beetle placed to the left of the shot has a number plate clearly visible between the heads of Paul and George and ending in the digits 281F, suggesting Paul would have been 28 if he had made his next birthday. *Abbey Road* was released when McCartney was 27, he turned 28 on 18 June 1970. The black police van to the right of the shot is a reference to the police who were called to the fatal accident in November 1966. In some versions of the story it also confirms that the police attending the fatal accident were paid off to keep the secret and symbolises the ongoing link between the band and those police. The registration plate on the van is so new that it can't possibly have been on the road to attend an accident in November 1966. A series of other inferences have been made from the cover, which counts as one of the most iconic images from the rich collection of imagery generated by the band. A minor row brought the cover back to prominence in the twenty first century when – in 2003 – poster companies in the USA airbrushed out the cigarette in Paul McCartney's right hand. This was done without the consent of Paul or the copyright holders for the image: Apple Records. The cigarette is also part of the death rumour because a slang term for cigarettes is coffin nails.

On the back of the album cover the Beatles' name appears in the same type as the genuine London street sign below it. Both show evidence of being cracked as the wall behind them is cracked. Clearly the real sign is cracked with age but the Beatles' name is placed there for the purposes of creating a photograph for the album cover, so the crack is more likely to be deliberate because this is a new sign. Therefore, the death rumour suggests, the crack symbolizes the fracture in the line-up of the band. R Gary Patterson goes further than some in his discussion of the sign and draws parallels between the sign and shapeshifting supernatural characters. Typically in folklore these creatures can assume the shapes of real beings but often betray themselves through slight imperfections or mistakes when exposed to close examination. The suggestion is that the sign symbolises the compromised Beatles who might give themselves away in this manner. There is an obvious extension of logic from this argument to the fact the band never again toured after 1966, and, therefore, failed to subject themselves to the most telling exposure of all. The eight dots to the left of the sign can easily be read as a number three, with fairly obvious implications to the number of surviving Beatles. To further complicate this particular issue Joel Glazier, investigating the death rumour, visited the exact spot on the wall which features on the album cover in 1970 and found 13 dots. A discovery which suggests the band and those involved in producing the cover did some deliberate cropping, which must have taken place for a good reason.

The songs on *Abbey Road* also suggest some death rumour meanings. The opening "Come Together" includes a reference to "old flat top" which – with Lennon's noted grim sense of humour – could be heard as a reference to a decapitated person. The song builds a bizarre nonsense series of images apparently about one person who has "walrus gumboot" and shoots "Coca Cola." If we hear the chorus line of "Come together...over me" as an incitement to gather round a grave, and therefore be "over" the person, there is a fairly obvious link between the whole song and Paul's death. "Sun King" which forms part of the medley on side two shares its name with Louis XIV, France's "Sun King." The "Sun King" is linked strongly to Alexander Dumas' story "The Man In The Iron Mask" in which a twin replaces a monarch, having first had his identity as a twin hidden by an iron mask. "Sun King" also offers a strange and impenetrable section towards the end in which Spanish, scouse and nonsense phrases make a beautiful harmonic incantation. In reality this probably means nothing specific, but that very quality allows almost any interpretation, up to and including it being a death rite being performed over McCartney. "Sun King" is a Lennon song so could have been written after Paul's death to make the link between Dumas' story and Billy Shears, before the strange rite requiring the enigmatic lyric is performed to ensure the improbable scheme will work.

Andru Reeve's book *Turn Me On, Dead Man: The Beatles and the "Paul Is Dead" Hoax*, goes a lot further than most in finding some points of interest in the *Abbey Road* medley, noting "You Never Give Me Your Money" offers up a death reference with the line "All good children go to Heaven," "Golden Slumbers" can be heard as a direct reference to death because death is "the Big Sleep—death," and final track on the medley is "The End." Reeve also points out "Carry That Weight" is exactly what a pallbearer is expected to do. Co-incidentally that task and song are linked in a scene from the infamous Bee Gees/Peter Frampton musical movie *Sgt. Pepper's Lonely Hearts Club Band*, though nobody has seriously advanced a theory linking Frampton and the Gibb brothers as initiates into the dark secret of The Beatles.

The Let It Be Album is – Just About - Dripping Clues and Symbolic References to Paul's Death

Let It Be was recorded before *Abbey Road* but lay around unloved and generally considered incomplete. Its release drew an apt metaphor of a "cardboard tombstone" from *Rolling Stone* magazine. At its best *Let It Be* offers the likes of the title track, "The Long and Winding Road," "Get Back" and "Across the Universe" to rival the best moments in The Beatles' late period, but at its worst it sounds like the miserable and unproductive sessions that make up the lowest points in the movie of the same name. As with the double album in 1968 *Let It Be* places the four Beatles on the cover in separate close up shots. Only McCartney is pictured against a blood red background, the others are all against white backgrounds. McCartney's face is obscured by a large microphone, conveniently covering up the site of the damage to his top lip that is evident in the close up on the White Album cover. This could be seen as significant because the filming of *Let It Be* occurred mostly in early 1969, earlier than the *Abbey Road* sessions and slightly closer in time to the alleged date of Paul's death.

The songs on the album include Paul's "Let It Be," an emotional meditation on death and despair that still finds hope that there is an answer to everything. Significantly the song builds a bridge between life and death because "mother Mary" is generally taken as a reference to his own deceased mother, whom he lost as a teenager. There is some support for elements of the death rumour if the song is considered as a general meditation on the way those who have lost someone close can still feel their influence and presence; suggestive perhaps of the dead Paul supporting his colleagues from beyond the grave. There could also be significance in the fact that the plea to accept things in the title track references the state of The Beatles in their final days and appears on the same album as "One After 909," one of the first Lennon/McCartney songs. "One After 909" may have been written as early as 1957, mainly by John but with input from Paul. Another song on the album "Two of Us" is claimed to be about Paul and Linda but discusses the length of memories between the couple being "longer than the road that stretches out ahead" so it might be more accurately applied to the long relationship between John and Paul. In this context the *Let It Be* album subtly hints at charting the end of the Lennon/McCartney partnership. The opening line of the album sees the two of us/them "going nowhere" after which the same pair are "not arriving" on their way home. No reason is given for the lack of closure, though if it is a love song to Linda it's obviously about the simple joys of being together and how these outshine actually achieving anything. If the song refers to a finished relationship and plans that can never be completed it takes on some significance in the death rumour. The movie filmed as tracks for the album were being recorded makes clear that the 1969 Paul is singing the songs so the death rumour variant on this situation suggests the new Paul's role is to speak for his deceased predecessor. George's "I Me Mine" is a fairly blatant comment on the deteriorating communications within the band. Though apparently simple it skilfully pits a Hindu view of the ego existing in different states represented in the titular words: "I/ me/ mine." In this reading "I Me Mine" is a deft survey of the worries George was experiencing as a Beatle and a clinical strike at the way his colleagues in the band were creating this morass of mental instability. Beatles' histories see the band breaking apart as the main creative forces of Lennon and McCartney increasingly battled. Lennon often let Yoko answer questions to him, to the obvious infuriation of the band, whilst McCartney's frustration at their lack of cohesion led him to put himself forward as a leader. An obvious view of this situation from the death rumour angle sees the band trapped by their own decision to go on with a fake Paul, unable to come clean on the pact they had made, increasingly aware that the old chemistry had gone and disabled by the death of the manager who had steered the career of the band to the late summer of 1967. All of the above is – potentially – being channelled through the subtle messages in "I me Mine."

The Break-up of The Beatles Led to a few Solo Records – Just About - Dripping Clues and Symbolic References to Paul's Death
Let It Be was a posthumous release. The various Beatles were already at work on solo projects before the band brought a formal halt to their career. There are a few direct references to the Paul is dead story in songs by solo Beatles. "How do you Sleep," John's celebrated sideswipe at Paul on the *Imagine* album includes the line "those freaks was right when they said you was

dead," and the vinyl album makes another blatant dig at Paul by including a free photograph of John Lennon grasping a pig. The picture is a fairly obvious pastiche of McCartney's photograph with a ram on the cover of his then recently released *Ram* album. Ringo's solo hit "Back off Boogaloo" is also believed by many to be a sideswipe at Paul and Paul's snide comments directed towards his former bandmates. Ringo asks the subject of the song to "get yourself together now and give me something tasty" which can be seen as a missive to McCartney to start knocking out the quality of music that made his Beatle output so distinctive. Of course, if this is aimed at Billy Shears it's a fairly desperate plea for him to step up and avoid blowing his cover. At the point of "Back off Boogaloo"'s release McCartney's work with Wings was going through a critical and commercial dip. 1972 opened for McCartney with "Give Ireland Back to the Irish" being slammed as an ill-thought through and trite protest song. A BBC ban on broadcast for the record did it few favours and it stalled at #16 in the UK and #21 in the U.S. Paul and Wings responded by going to the other extreme and covering "Mary Had a Little Lamb" which fared better in the UK but only just scratched the top 30 in America. Ringo's "Back off Boogaloo" sounded more relevant and in touch and was released between both Wings' singles. Opening with a military rap on the drums the song soon morphs into a catchy rocker with clear influence from the emerging glam rock style of the time. Starr is credited as sole composer of the song but the extent to which his friend Marc Bolan might have "influenced" him has been the subject of some debate because with "Back off Boogaloo" Ringo was clearly walking the walk as well, offering up an improbably simple corker of a riff that sounded straight out of the top drawer of T.Rexstacy (the name the British press gave to the mania surrounding Marc Bolan). His song hit the top ten on both sides of the Atlantic and almost made the very top spot with its #2 position in the UK (as close as Ringo has ever come to topping that chart). George Harrison appears on both "How do you Sleep" and "Back Off Boogaloo" and produced the latter of the two. Ringo, interviewed by *Melody Maker* in 1971, spoke about the quality of Paul's output: "He disappoints me on his albums. I don't think there's one [good] tune on the last one ... It's like he's not admitting that he can write a great tune." That sentiment, and the widespread belief that "Boogaloo" was a code name used by Starr for McCartney have perpetuated the place of Ringo's tune in the Paul is dead story. Ringo covered "Back off Boogaloo" for his 1981 album *Stop and Smell the Roses*, incorporating sampled snatches of other songs including The Beatles' "Help" and "Lady Madonna." A move that further fuelled the idea that he sees it as a composition about his relationship to his former bandmates.

A few other solo tracks by former Beatles are directed at McCartney or otherwise contribute to the death rumour. Perhaps the most notable is George's song "Wah-Wah" which features on both *All Things Must Pass* and *The Concert for Bangla Desh*. The "wah-wah" in question is a combination of frustration and anger directed at Harrison's bickering bandmates. One of Harrison's biographers – Graeme Thompson – describes it as "A song of creative frustration and ultimate emancipation." The song dates from early 1969, when Harrison's frustration boiled over to the point he walked out on the sessions that would eventually become *Let It Be* so, from the point of the death rumour, "Wah-Wah" exists in the same place as Harrison's "I Me Mine" and it is possible to read the frustration and anger as being down to finding himself trapped, with the other Beatles, including Billy Shears, in a conspiracy of silence.

Finally it is worth noting that on the fringes of the Paul is dead presence online there are those who have found hidden messages in Paul's solo work. One of the clearest appears on Paul's 1997 album *Flaming Pie*. As with much solo Beatle work the album alludes to the performer's Beatle past. In this case the title "Flaming Pie" comes from an inventive reply from John Lennon. Asked "How did the band [The Beatles] get its name?" Lennon said: "I had a vision that a man came unto us on a flaming pie, and he said, 'You are Beatles with an 'A,' and so we were." McCartney's album release was actually delayed by Beatle business because EMI were busy rolling out the three volumes of The Beatles' *Anthology*, and – by his own admission – Paul had been influenced by having to go over the old material and consider how his old band had worked and how much they had achieved. On the eventual release of *Flaming Pie* a few people spotted an apparent backward mask in the song "The World Tonight." Towards the middle of the song Paul sings "I can see the world tonight" but employs an echo that is absent elsewhere in the track. Heard backwards it sounds like an advert for the causes he and Linda held dear because the phrase "Save animal's fur, Linda Eastman" can just about be heard. It is something of a stretch to see this backward mask – if indeed it was ever intended as such - as a means by which Billy Shears, comfortably established in his solo career, chose to allude to the clever tricks played by his former band. However, this particular backward mask is mentioned on the Paul is dead page of The Internet Beatles Album (a busy and regularly updated shrine to the band and serves as an example of the way die-hard fans continue to unearth and share nuggets of information).

The various former Beatles have made so many references to their former band in the solo works released since the break-up that it would be tiresome and pointless to list them in the context of the present, Paul is dead, argument. Some online discussions have sought to find Paul is dead evidence in works not mentioned in this short section. The marginality of some arguments and the desperation by which some of the evidence is forced into the Paul is dead narrative probably damages the central core of the story by polluting it with weak evidence. But, it *is* out there and – of course - should you decide to investigate for yourself, you may feel differently.

There were people outside the band involved in the Paul is dead cover up.
The most obvious candidate for outside inclusion in the massive deception is actress Jane Asher. According to some versions of the Paul is dead story this is proven because it is Jane Asher striding past the road sign on the back of the *Abbey Road* album cover. Her presence in the blue dress walking quickly past a "Beatles" sign with a crack running through it confirms that the band are fractured with the loss of her former fiancé and she is confirming the covert messages by turning up on the album cover. In fact the identity of the woman in the blue dress isn't known to this day. Another version of who she is and what she symbolises appears on the news and gossip site Bio. (www.biography.com). Bio.'s consideration of evidence for Paul's death on the *Abbey Road* jacket says: "On the night of Paul's supposed car accident, he was believed to have been driving with a fan named Rita. Theorists say the girl in the dress featured on the back cover was meant to be her, fleeing from the car crash." So, she may have been a hired model, and have been briefed on what the symbolism of her appearance meant. Or the photographer may have been aware of why that particular blurred movement was important."

Speaking of photographers; Paul's first wife Linda Eastman was a rock music photographer who first met, and possibly slept with, Paul during his long relationship with Jane Asher. Howard Sounes' salacious book *Fab: An Intimate Life of Paul McCartney* charts the start of their relationship and spares few details in presenting Paul as a womaniser who frequently cheated on Jane during their relationship, but still got engaged to her well after the date he was supposed to have died. Linda Eastman – as she then was – comes out of the book in much the same way as Paul, someone who quite literally embraced the free love ethos of the late sixties to the point that she had been sexually active with a few household names before Paul McCartney. It also presents her as ambitious and fixated on snagging the cuddly Beatle as a husband. For Sounes one thing that drew her and Paul together was his recognition of her maternal qualities, because whilst she was photographing rock stars and becoming close with some of her subjects she was also raising her daughter Heather, the product of an unplanned pregnancy and a highly unsuccessful first marriage.

Jane Asher and Paul finally split when Jane near-enough caught him in their bed with another woman and couldn't be talked round. Paul led her into the garden to reason with her but the other woman appeared at an upstairs window and Jane was finally finished. It was Linda at Paul's side, with Heather and baby Stella, on the *Life* magazine cover which fronted Paul's bemused interview in response to the death rumours. So Linda was on hand when it all broke. If the story was true, how could she have lasted so long as Mrs McCartney, giving birth to three of his children, without being aware of the truth. Her relationship with him was so long and so close that the couple spent little time apart, even when he was working. A closer and longer working relationship than he had enjoyed with any fellow Beatle. McCartney's marriage to Heather Mills might euphemistically be described as different to that with Linda. Mills' post marriage tirades against her ex-husband have been curtailed by what people widely understand to be a clause in the divorce agreement obliging her to silence. She has, however, pushed what freedom she has to the limit by making suggestions. Talking to Access Hollywood's Billy Bush Mills said she told McCartney; "You know why I've left you. Protect me, and I will say nothing." Her suggestion being that something so bad happened in their marriage that the public would struggle to understand it, and they wouldn't want to know the truth because it would be hard for them to handle. The "plasticmacca" blog discussed this in September 2009 and linked it to a BBC interview in which Mills said: "I have a box of evidence that's going to a certain person, should anything happen to me, so if you top me off it's still going to that person, and the truth will come out." The blog's implications about Mills finding out the secret discussed in this chapter are obvious. Mills' history with those who have been close to her is sometimes explosive and several people have raised issues about her relationship with the truth, so it is worth comparing the interview and her claims about holding secrets from the marriage with the views of someone else working with her at the time. In a *Daily Mail* article headed "'Heather Mills is a bitch who tricked me into spreading lies about Paul McCartney,' claims her ex-Hollywood PR" Michele Elyzabeth is quoted lambasting Mills with lines like "That witch tricked me into spreading lies about Paul. She's a bitch." Given that confidentiality and good working relationships are vital to Ms Elyabeth's business it is clear that Mills really annoyed her to the point she stepped out of her role and unloaded her anger in public. It takes serious provocation to drive a seasoned PR professional – acquainted with the best and the worst of media personalities – to say "Heather is a calculating pathological liar and the biggest bitch on the planet. She not only misled me, she misled the entire world." Then again, a really cynical view would suggest that a perfect place to hide a secret as big as the fact you are Billy Shears, and have been living a lie since the mid-sixties, might be in plain sight, by imparting it to someone capable of provoking a reaction like the one from Michelle Elyabeth. Conspiracy theorists consistently see evidence of disinformation in the material they gather, and there is evidence that some areas – like UFO reports – are indeed the focus of erroneous material planted with the intention of provoking investigators to share it and obscure the real truth. The art of disinformation is often to feed credible and true details into a web of spurious leads, allowing the potentially dangerous truth to be discredited to the point nobody would believe it. Heather Mills has yet to comment specifically on the Paul is dead rumour.

This Paul is Dead Shit is Serious – Because it's Part of a Larger Conspiracy.
If you read the entire chapter on John Lennon you'll realise already that Beatle legends spin their own offshoots and land themselves in some very strange and little frequented corners of thought. Unsurprisingly there is a marginal but highly vivid corner of Paul is dead belief that ties his elimination in with other legends of assassination and intrigue. The plasticmacca blog, and a few other internet backwaters are your friend in navigating this particular story. Plasticmacca has taken the trouble to collate the greatest hits listed in this chapter with some tirades and links to online messages, introducing the collection with a summary of how Paul's "death" links to the wider picture:

As shocking as it may seem, the real Paul McCartney is dead. He was imposter-replaced in 1966 by a double. This "conspiracy theory," called PID (Paul is Dead) for short, involves some of the following tangential issues:

- public figures (including doubles) used as puppets to manipulate the masses;
- elimination of opposition to this elite by horizontalization (the likely assassination of James Paul McCartney with impunity);
- deception of the public by a cartel of media groups controlled by a governing Luciferian elite (Illuminati);
- social control through Psychological Operations (PsyOps); and
- Info War in cyberspace using disinformation, debunking and counter Intelligence techniques to discredit ideas and individuals who oppose their plans.

If plastic Macca proves one thing it is that the McCartney death rumour has a future because it has energy and a number of angles that are likely to link it to other ongoing tales. How much time Paul McCartney spends surfing or reading his way through any of this is not recorded but in his more introspective moments it is possible he thinks back to those first days of the rumour in 1969 and his bemused response to *Life* magazine and hankers after those more innocent times.

Chapter 3

George Harrison: Died in 1974 and was
Replaced by an Imposter

A
h, the great overlooked dead Beatle conspiracy rears its head again. This one appeared to come out of nowhere, a location to which it has returned, given the lack of significant internet material currently available. But, there is a printed record of the whole caper, so that's where we'll begin.

In the edition dated 7 February 1976 the UK music paper *Sounds* devoted half of page 8 to a disturbing and somewhat surreal claim. George Harrison was dead and replaced by an imposter. In fact, the claim didn't begin life as a rumour, or a general collecting of random pieces of evidence. The story emerged, fully formed, from a very specific source; Claudia Gates. Gates included her full address when corresponding with a range of publications. *Sounds* saw fit to print her address in case George "who is alive and well, wishes to get in touch with the young lady."

Gates was at the time resident at 255 Marsh Road, Pittsford, New York 14534. She claimed George had died "two years ago this February (i.e. February 1974) from a crazy scheme to cure cancer." This was no ordinary misguided death or medical negligence case because Harrison had endured "more physical pain than any man since Jesus, enough to turn himself into a white light." The George Harrison taking the position of the deceased original was – according to Gates – an "imposter" who "through black witchcraft, has usurped not only his [George Harrison's] being and his mannerisms, but his musical ability as well (or tried to, shall we say)."

The musical ability argument is central to the whole notion of the imposter replacing the original George and we'll deal with the details of that in due course. However, it would be doing a disservice to Gates to ignore another strand of her argument and evidence. Despite being physically dead, she claimed, George could still communicate with her; "Harrison and I can still communicate – he has lost much of his memory and such, but is living as the only physical spirit in existence." The black magic power wielded by the imposter was, apparently, key to the imposter's ability to fool long standing friends and associates of Harrison – including Eric Clapton, Ringo Starr and Ravi Shankar – but the imposter's understandable wish to avoid being tested beyond his limits was key to Harrison's reluctance to be part of any Beatle reunion (considered a serious possibility in 1976).

Aside from the musical evidence, Gates cited some other clues to exposing the deceit. "Harrison has always talked and side smiled out of the right side of his mouth. Why suddenly should he do this to the left?" At which point Gates invited anyone to study appropriate film and photographs to prove the point. Similarly, "George had long wavy hair" and even the moist English conditions encountered in the misty English garden scene (actually shot at George's home in Henley on Thames) for the front cover of *All Things Must Pass* (1971) "he never had curls." There are clear and pronounced curls in his long hair as George reclines on a park bench on the back cover shot of the *Dark Horse* album (1974). Though Gates claim, "knowing George's personality…it is obvious he wouldn't curl his hair" would be tested to destruction within a few years when the man could be seen sporting a curly perm in line with late seventies footballer fashion trends, as demonstrated by other public figures like Kevin Keegan.

Gates also cited Harrison's failure to answer mail as proof that the period of the imposter's arrival was a troubled one. Her concerns about the failing quality of his music were strongly expressed. So too her belief that "what he was put through was totally gruesome; I'm (i.e. Gates) not about to let the truth go unnoticed if someone will only listen." Nobody, it seems, did listen to her, or chase up the story, beyond *Sounds* enjoying some subsequent fun at her expense by posting details of sightings of George, alive and well, in their gossip columns in the weeks after they ran Gates' letter.

Considerations of Harrison's music aside, Gates' bizarre claims are open ended and screaming conspiracy theory from the outset. Those conspiring against the saintly George include a black magician imposter and sleazy shamanic conman. Only Gates can communicate with Harrison, who exists as the only physical spirit on the planet. How he and a virtual identikit imposter manage to co-exist amongst those closest to George isn't fully addressed. Indeed, apart from fleeting communications with Claudia Gates it isn't by any means clear what the physical spirit George does all day, assuming that the imposter is the one inhabiting his Friar Park mansion, sleeping with Olivia Arias (then Harrison's girlfriend and subsequently his wife and mother to his son, Dhani). The imposter, after all, has the career, the contacts and the ability to phone up the various musicians central to Harrison's musical endeavours. At the time of Gates' claim Harrison was assembling the songs that would be recorded from May to September of 1976 and released on the album *Thirty Three and 1/3* (1976), an important move in his career as it was the first Harrison solo long player released on his own Dark Horse record label.

Claudia Gates' claims about the changes in Harrison's music do address some specific points. In particular she wonders aloud "why has Harrison's music changed so much?" She cites his new propensity for using musicians like Tom Scott (leader of the L.A. Express band who backed Harrison on his North American tour of 1974) "instead of people like Jim Horn and Badfinger." She goes on to slam the music issued under Harrison's name since the apparent arrival of the imposter as containing "tinny one line garbagers," totally uncharacteristic of the "perfectionist who created the 'All Things Must Pass' album and 'Living in the Material World.'"

At the time of writing to *Sounds* Claudia Gates could only have been referring negatively to the albums *Dark Horse* and *Extra Texture (Read all About it)* (1975) and their attendant singles. Both of the albums following *Living in the Material World* showed a heavy involvement of L.A. musicians and a sound more influenced by American AOR and soul than the acoustically based albums preceding them. At the time Harrison was spending a great deal of time in the USA, having based his recording company there, at first in a deal with A&M records and – when he parted company with that label and returned his personal advance to seal the partition – Warner Brothers. Harrison's friend and former Beatles' publicist Derek Taylor had a position at Warner Brothers and was central to the deal that took Harrison there. We'll examine the Harrison albums central to her claims soon enough but, having itemised those claims in detail we need to make a few important points about Beatle urban legends.

Firstly, the George was replaced by an imposter story was published, discussed by some, became a brief running joke – as witnessed when *Sounds* saw fit to remind people George continued to live – and was known amongst music fans at the time. Indeed, when I started working on the present book I checked in with a few die-hard Beatle fans known to me who either remembered the tale or had heard it more recently. It never climbed to the heights of a genuine conspiracy, there is no evidence anyone other than the original author of the letter ever took it seriously and it remains elusive to the point of near-invisibility online and in printed sources. I'll personally vouch for the difficulty of finding hard evidence that anyone took this seriously because I have written up the story once before, for a short-lived British magazine called *Dodge* in the early nineties. That adventure brought me close to meeting George Harrison himself, but more of that later.

I'm not for one second trying to convince you that Claudia Gates' claims have any substance beyond their life in her own fevered imagination. But, oddly, when I set about writing up the story in the nineties, and went looking for evidence in the same places the "Paul is dead" brigade had found it; basically lyrics, album covers and chronological curiosities, I found that evidence plastered all over George Harrison's work. What matters now about this strange tale is that its very failure to take off in the manner of the theories about John and Paul can teach us a lot about the way people are motivated to believe things, and how the lives of music fans and musicians in the pre-internet age were almost perfectly matched to create the strange symbiosis that brought about that letter to *Sounds* in 1976.

So, this is the Beatle legend that got away; because its tortured beginnings strangled its life chances from the outset. It is a salutary lesson in how legends can be concocted from little more than misreading the intentions of the artist, and needing to believe badly in something. In researching the story decades ago and asking what if this were true, some odd patterns began to emerge.

If the real George had died an agonising death in early 1974 that places his illness and demise squarely between two albums. The last recording by the real George would have been *Living in the Material World* and the first by the imposter the *Dark Horse* album. So, the real Beatle signed off with an album drawing attention to the fact he was alive in the physical -"material" – realm. The imposter opened his account with an album title suggesting he wasn't what he seemed. Indeed, this chronology makes the first release by the imposter the single "Dark Horse" (title track of the album) punted into the American market on 18 November 1974, three weeks ahead of the album's US release. In the UK the first single was "Ding Dong" released on 6 December and the parent album wasn't released until 20 December. The album and single were promoted with a seven week trek around north America, taking in dates in the USA and Canada on the Dark Horse Tour. The tour – on which George shared billing with Ravi Shankar – opened in Vancouver on 2 November and took in some iconic and significant venues. San Francisco (scene of the final date on the final Beatles' tour) was visited on 6-7 November and some major venues were booked to capacity, necessitating additional shows. These venues included some of the biggest and most prestigious on the live circuit; the entourage performed three times in two days at both the Oakland Coliseum and Madison Square Gardens. George was the first Beatle to undertake a major tour in this territory, so he was clearly keen to be seen and deliver the message. The set list drew from recent Harrison solo records as much as it relied on his Beatles' material and some old songs had reworked lyrics (a move that went down badly with some fans and most critics). Harrison played:

"Hari's on Tour (Express)"
"The Lord Loves the One (That Loves the Lord)"
"Who Can See It"
"Something"
"While My Guitar Gently Weeps"
"Sue Me, Sue You Blues"
"For You Blue"
"Give Me Love (Give Me Peace on Earth)"
 "In My Life"
"Māya Love"
"What Is Life"
"My Sweet Lord"
And, of course: "Dark Horse"

The rest of a lengthy set list was comprised of material performed by Ravi Shankar and a formidable ensemble of Indian musicians he had gathered for the tour, along with solo spots for both Tom Scott and keyboardist Billy Preston (who got to perform his recent US hits). The Dark Horse branding was central with the album providing three numbers on the set list - "Hari's on Tour (Express)," "Māya Love" and "Dark Horse." The new material was a regular feature of press conferences and radio play associated with the tour. Officially called the North American Tour, the seven week series of dates was often given the unofficial title of the "Dark Horse Tour." "Dark Horse" (song) climbed to #15 in the US, a notable under-achievement in comparison to Harrison's previous single "Give me Love (Give me Peace on Earth)" which had topped the list. Lyrically, the song is fairly clear in presenting a message that the singer is not who he seems:

You thought that you knew where I was and when
Baby looks I keep foolin' you again
You thought that you'd got me all staked out

Baby looks like I've been breaking out

I'm a dark horse running on a dark race course...

The consistent message throughout is that the singer has held powers from early in his life and that the "baby" who under-estimated him has made a costly mistake. The chorus references "cool jerk" and "blue moon," making fairly obvious references to early rock 'n' roll records, but also dragging in the power and meaning of those releases to the story unfolding in "Dark Horse." So the singer keeps reminding us he is a "dark horse" and "running on a dark race course."

In other words, "George Harrison" is not who he appears to be and his path isn't what we assume either. Standard interpretations of the song link it to Harrison's break up with Patti Boyd and/or his break up with his former bandmates. Simon Leng in *The Music of George Harrison: While my Guitar Gently Weeps* noting the song: "exposes the confusion in the heart of a superstar." In this reading Harrison acknowledges he has a double, though this is his "'media self'" and the lyric is a reaction to the mixed reviews given to Harrison's previous album and a statement that Harrison is capable of responding and managing his own life and art, albeit by creating a new persona and concealing the real person.

Whatever its meaning the song went on to lead a charmed life in Harrison's recording and performing work, it appears on the *Live in Japan* (1992) double album and on *The Best of George Harrison* (1976), compiled by George. Harrison only undertook two major tours, the North American venture in 1974 and a tour of Japan in 1991. Of his solo work only "What is Life," "Give me Love (Give Me Peace on Earth)" and "My Sweet Lord" joined "Dark Horse" in being performed on both tours. Of those tracks only "Dark Horse" had failed to dent the US top ten. "What is Life" was a considerable world-wide hit, though never released in the UK as a single by Harrison. So, if Harrison wasn't exactly flogging a dead "Dark Horse" he was, at least, showing a strong faith in a tune others didn't regard as highly as he seemed to.

Harrison's views on "Dark Horse" were explained in his autobiography *I Me Mine* (1980) as: "the old story. 'Mr Penguin's poking Mrs. Johnson from the Co-op'" Harrison claimed to be "a bit thick really" by not realising the phrase "dark horse" could refer to an unlikely winner.

The other single from the *Dark Horse* album hasn't fared anywhere near as well with regard to compilation and live performance. "Ding Dong, Ding Dong" is one of the most repetitive and simplistic songs ever recorded by George Harrison (regardless of whether George is one person, or two). It has its defenders, though many of these have emerged subsequent to the release of a song widely derided on first issue. At the time the single's failure to dent the top 35 in either the UK or US was deemed a sign of George's declining fortunes and the crumbs of comfort offered by the song's better showing in places like Holland weren't likely to change opinions. "Ding Dong, Ding Dong" only appears on the compilations it can't avoid, like box sets compiled of original albums. It's also conspicuously ignored in the brief discussions of the *Dark Horse* album offered in books like Joshua M. Greene's *Here Comes the Sun* (2006), Geoffrey Giulano's *Dark Horse* (1989) and Mark Shapiro's *All Things Must Pass* (2002).

Assuming for one second that the George who recorded *Dark Horse* isn't the same man who recorded previous albums, the apparently simplistic and inane lyrics of "Ding Dong, Ding Dong" are positively electrifying, and the refrain is repeated to drive home the message:

Ring out the old ring in the new
Ring out the false ring in the true
Ding dong

That, along with the observation that yesterday today was tomorrow, with the subsequent twist that tomorrow the situation will be different again is – near enough – the whole story in the song. UK promotion of the single included ads featuring the lyrics, so someone was clearly keen that the message was grasped. "Ding Dong, Ding Dong" was so much regarded as the low point of a patchy album that one review, in *Sounds* (who also saw fit to publish Claudia Gates' letter) headlined their review of the album "Ding Bloody Dong." The song's big wall of sound production swamps Harrison's reedy and failing voice. "Ding Dong, Ding Dong" is - apparently - a blatant attempt at a novelty hit, neatly midway between Paul McCartney's catchy "Wonderful Christmastime" and Lennon's more meaningful "Happy Xmas (War is Over)." The one place the song makes perfect sense is in the promo video clip filmed (as were a few of George's videos) at Friar Park. With George donning a chronological series of Beatle costumes, swapping guitars to fit different periods of his recording life and fronting a strange and surreal cast of backing singers "Ding Dong, Ding Dong" is a kiss off to his past and a statement of his independence. With few outlets to show such a video and the poor chart performance of the record further restricting the exposure of the film, the promo remained little known at the time. It is available in the usual online homes of video clips today.

George's own explanation from *I Me Mine* also links the song strongly to his home, commenting that he noticed the lines of the song inscribed in stone at the house and reworked a few of these inscriptions into "Ding Dong, Ding Dong." In fact, the lines originated in Alfred, Lord Tennyson's poem "Ring Out Wild Bells." In context, they read:

Ring out, wild bells, and let him die.
Ring out the old, ring in the new,
Ring, happy bells, across the snow:
The year is going, let him go;
Ring out the false, ring in the true.
Ring out the grief that saps the mind,
For those that here we see no more,
Ring out the feud of rich and poor,
Ring in redress to all mankind.

But, clearly, Sir Frank Crisp, previous owner of Friar Park, only saw fit to inscribe a small portion of the long work. If Claudia Gates' dig at Harrison's "tinny one line garbagers" is directed at any one recording then "Ding Dong, Ding Dong" is one of the strongest contenders, along with "You," the lead single from *Extra Texture (Read All About It)*.

Elsewhere the *Dark Horse* album offers some other tantalizing clues that the singer/songwriter behind the work is playing with our perceptions of him, and leading us on a journey. Though, oddly in the light of Claudia Gates' clear obsession with the black magic employed by the imposter Harrison the message is a positive and spiritual one, in line with the devotions driven at on *Living in the Material World*. *Dark Horse*, on the original vinyl, lines up:

Side one:
1."Hari's on Tour (Express)" – 4:43
2."Simply Shady" – 4:38
3."So Sad" – 5:00
4."Bye Bye, Love" – 4:08
5."Māya Love" – 4:24

Side two:
6."Ding Dong, Ding Dong" – 3:40
7."Dark Horse" – 3:54
8."Far East Man" (Harrison, Ron Wood) – 5:52
9."It Is 'He' (Jai Sri Krishna)" – 4:50

"Bye Bye, Love" (credited to Felice Bryant, Boudleaux Bryant, Harrison) is a reworking of the classic Everly Brothers' hit, with additional lyrics by George and written to make the song a specific kiss-off to the departing Patti Boyd, and "Far East Man" is a co-composition with Ron Wood. The Harrison/Wood song had appeared in a different version on Wood's first solo collection, *I've Got My Own Album To Do* released in September 1974. Wood's version featured George on slide guitar and backing vocals.

Dark Horse is something of a musical journey, opening with an instrumental overture "Hari's on Tour (Express)" which revved up the North American tour crowds and serves the same function on the opening of the original vinyl side one. "Simply Shady," "So Sad" and "Bye Bye, Love" are outpourings of Harrison's soul, missives to things lost and frustrating situations. Simon Leng perceptively links "Simply Shady" to the rootless but willing Neil Young songs that mark the same period for him and appear on *Time Fades Away* (1973) and *On The Beach* (1974). Indeed, Young's albums of the period are similar to the bulk of side one of *Dark Horse* in their simplistic production and unrepentantly ragged vocal lines. "Simply Shady" comes in for short shrift from a few commentators on Harrison's work. The detailed *George Harrison Encyclopedia* by Bill Harry (2003) dismisses it in three lines, including: "George penned the number in India and was inspired by his split with Patti." "Simply Shady" with its tale of indulgence leads to the mordant "So Sad" and the personified and resigned re-working of the Everly Brothers. The three tracks chronicle a downward spiral, though the jokey reference to "our lady" departing with "old Clapper" in Harrison's modified "Bye Bye, Love" does, at least, suggest some ability to cope. One of Harrison's biographers – Alan Clayson – presents a portrait of 1974 George Harrison greatly changed from the deep, shy but approachable Beatle; "Old at 31, a crashing bore and wearing his virtuous observance of his beliefs like [a] sandwich board, he was nicknamed 'his lectureship' behind his back. Visitors to Friar Park tended not to swear in his presence." To a small extent it was as if the old George had been replaced. The two singles open side two of the original vinyl and are followed by "Far East Man." In the welter of critical mauling that attended the *Dark Horse* album and the supporting tour "Far East Man" has largely been overlooked. A sly and beguiling gem that almost totally avoids major chords, "Far East Man" appears as a statement of devotion to an unspecified mentor. It could be addressed to a deity or a friend, but Harrison places himself in a world that "wages war" before asserting his faith; "I won't let him down/ Got to do what I can…" The middle eight of the song slows the tempo and brings in a sense of spiritual doubt; "Wondering…if I'm wrong" though the solution appears in the next line; "Even then my heart seems/ To be the one in charge…" Notably Harrison's lyrics differ slightly from those Ronnie Wood recorded for the song, predictably the piece is more obviously spiritual in his hands, down to the languid and expressive saxophone. It is widely accepted that though Harrison and Wood share composition credits, the lyrics are – basically – George's work. It's a personal opinion but I've argued to many people over the years that this number is the saving grace of *Dark Horse*. Never performed live, not used as a B-Side and seldom played on radio (though my *Strange Fruit* show has gone there a few times) "Far East Man" works in ways the rest of the album is often slammed for not working. Firstly, for all its devout sentiments it keeps the message real. It opens with a truly idiosyncratic spoken word introduction aimed – apparently – at Frank Sinatra and imploring him to cover the song (as he covered "Something"). All of which is surely intended as an ironic gag with George knowing full well Frank wouldn't touch this song with its palpable whiff of religious devotion within an eastern tradition. Secondly, "Far East Man" has the same deft lyricism George displayed on tracks like "Give Me Love (Give Me Peace on Earth)" and "That Is All" and combines a hefty sentiment with a disarming simplicity. With its stumbling lyric and shift from the early "I can't let him down" to the later "We can't…," the song appears to be channelled as much as written, and has the intimate quality of a close conversation with a sense of gentle persuasion. By Harrison's own admission he worked on the lyrics driving down the M4 to record with Ronnie Wood and had to remember them rather than write them down. There is also some dispute about the title, everyone agrees it came from a T-shirt picked up when The Faces had toured the far east, but whether Ronnie Wood or his wife Chrissie wore the shirt spotted by George varies depending on which source you read. *Dark Horse* closes with a simple spiritual work, delivered in an uptempo chant and reliant on the same basics as a traditional Hindu bhajan (Hindu devotional song). Taken as a whole *Dark Horse* delivers the negative thoughts and self-doubts early (basically in the three songs that form the middle of the first vinyl side), chants in search of solace and finds self-meaning (the two singles), resolves to grasp the positive ("Far East Man") and affirms its faith in the closing explosion of "It Is 'He' (Jai Sri Krishna)" which blasts a Spectoresque wall of sound into its Hindu form, and collides western and eastern instrumentation, including George playing a Bengali khomok (stringed drum). The art of sequencing an album is generally lost on twenty first century audiences, but if George Harrison was marshalling a depleted creative armoury on *Dark Horse* he still did it to near-perfection to deliver the message, of ultimate hope after suffering, he wanted. Perhaps he did it so skilfully that his true intentions were lost, even to his most rabid fans, like Claudia Gates.

Claudia Gates' general argument about changes might have found some favour with people who had known George a while, and – crucially for this investigation – with the millions of fans who felt they knew him because his music had an emotional impact on them. He was changed from before, and that much was clear from the simple comparison of *Dark Horse* with the preceding album, *Living in the Material World*. Superficially, at least, *Living in the Material World* offers up the same kind of clues in support of Gates' claims as does *Dark Horse*. There are lyrical references that make a specific sense if we consider the singer to be facing his own imminent death. The album cover is as rich in clues as *Sgt Pepper* in the legend of Paul's death. In fact, the cover of *Living in the Material World* is positively screaming a message about George's impending death. We'll consider the visual clues later. Lyrically and musically, *Living in the Material World* has a lot to contribute to Gates' claims and the – apparent – death of its creator.

The album was eagerly awaited. Mainly recorded in London between January and April 1973, and largely written and demoed before the recording started, *Living in the Material World* is a fairly obvious extension of the musical themes and production that made *All Things Must Pass* a massive success. Advance orders alone assured the album of high chart placings and it duly landed the #1 spot in the USA and in a few other countries. In the UK it reached #3. The single "Give Me Love (Give Me Peace on Earth)" also topped the US charts and fared well in most territories, earning massive airplay on its way to top ten positions around the world. More than any other Harrison single, even "My Sweet Lord," "Give Me Love..." puts spirituality centre stage. If "My Sweet Lord" is a message of seeking and devotion "Give Me Love..." is a stronger statement because it is delivered from inside the faith, by someone who knows the realities of what he wants. It also contains some lines that make little, literal, sense unless the tenets of Harrison's Hindu belief are taken into account. "Give me life, keep me free from birth" isn't a conundrum if you consider it to be a plea to avoid reincarnation in physical form once the present life is over. Similarly, Harrison's own presentation of the song in *I Me Mine* makes clear that one line has been frequently misprinted in the various ripping and pasting of lyrics that now abound online. It's "OM...My Lord" and "this song is a prayer and personal statement between me, the Lord, and whoever likes it." Considering Harrison's spiritual journey the inclusion of the sacred sound "Om" rather than the often used English expression "Oh" is a typically skilful blending of eastern spirituality and western popular music. Joshua M. Greene extols the achievements of "Give Me Love..." noting: "Some of the songs [on *Living in the Material World*] distilled spiritual concepts into phrases so elegant they resembled Vedic *sutras*; short codes that contain volumes of meaning." At which point Greene discusses the "Oh/Ommm" line.

If this really was the work of a man strong in his faith and sure of his imminent physical death then "Give Me Love..." is the strongest statement possible of Harrison's readiness to be freed from the limits of the flesh. In the context of it opening an album drawing attention to the fact we all live in the material world it is also a marker for the journey that follows. Like *Dark Horse* Harrison sequenced *Living in the Material World* to deliver a message, and make the most of the varied musical moods. It lines up:

Side one:

1."Give Me Love (Give Me Peace on Earth)" – 3:36
2."Sue Me, Sue You Blues" – 4:48
3."The Light That Has Lighted the World" – 3:31
4."Don't Let Me Wait Too Long" – 2:57
5."Who Can See It" – 3:52
6."Living in the Material World" – 5:31

Side two

7."The Lord Loves the One (That Loves the Lord)" – 4:34
8."Be Here Now" – 4:09
9."Try Some, Buy Some" – 4:08
10."The Day the World Gets 'Round" – 2:53
11."That Is All" – 3:43

From the point of Claudia Gates' claim the most significant song other than "Give Me Love…" is "That Is All." Significant both because of its lyric and because the last song on the final album released by the "genuine" George is called "That Is All." Recorded late in 1972 "That Is All" pulls the same master stroke as "Far East Man" in sounding both conversational and assured and expertly avoiding the question of whether Harrison is speaking personally to one person or to a deity. The last line of the lyric intones the title, so if this really was the final moment on the final official album by Harrison, he hid the signing off in plain sight. "That Is All" asserts Harrison's need "to give my love" because "our love could save the day." Crucially it also finds the strongest love in places traditional love songs frequently avoid; "Silence often says much more…" This reflection on silence comes in a middle eight that creates a pause in the narrative; more or less the same narrative device employed in the middle eight of "Far East Man." If we make the imaginative leap of seeing a devout Hindu facing physical death the song is the perfect bookend to an album started by "Give Me Love…" because it reasserts the need to be free from birth and the mundane concerns of human existence. The love that could save the day in "That Is All" is a silent acceptance, more a meeting of souls than a compatible existence or a sexual relationship. Or, to be more precise, in Harrison's reading of the gentle melody and flowing sound that is how the song appears. Andy Williams' sublime and orchestrated cover of the song on his *Solitaire* album finds the romantic love lurking in the piece and re-invents it much in the manner of Frank Sinatra making "Something" his own. Another crude interpretation of "That Is All" drops it right into Claudia Gates' theory because the silence saying more could simply be the absence from physical life of a person. Someone reincarnated in a higher realm is silent amongst human beings.

"That Is All" reconciles the themes developed throughout *Living In The Material World*. The album rotates tales of everyday worry – "Sue Me, Sue You Blues" is an angry blast about Harrison's place in the legal battles then being fought over various aspects of Beatle business

– with spiritual missives. George's love/hate relationship with his past as a Beatle is tracked over most of his recording career. In 1987 "When We Was Fab," took a positive view of the whole period, but still hinted that Harrison was comfortable with the thought those days were firmly in the past. Its supporting video repeated a few of the visual tricks that made the video for "Ding Dong, Ding Dong" such a riot. Coming to terms with that past, and the expectations placed on Harrison is a more convoluted and opaque theme that haunts *Living In The Material World*, colliding repeatedly with Harrison's need for spiritual peace. The album's title track which concludes the first side presents the conflict starkly. Harrison is "Living in the material world" he can't say why he is here but hopes to learn on the journey, he likens his body to a car suitable for journeys, namechecks his friends, finds time to make a joking referral to Beatle legend: "Though we started out quite poor/ We got 'Ritchie' on a tour" and ends on a full blown spiritual meditation "I pray/ That I won't get lost/ Or go astray." Ironically the full blast of the band maintains through the soulful searching finale of the lyric. Elsewhere the same history is explored in another frequently overlooked gem "Be Here Now." It should be noted that learned opinions on "Be Here Now" vary greatly, Harrison biographer Alan Clayson seeing that: "the stodgy arrangement" of the song masks "a lyric born of a funny story." Specifically, as Harrison himself noted, the song tracks the same story arc explored in the story "Journey: The Transformation: Dr Richard Alpert, PhD. into Baba Ram Dass." The story forms the first section of the book *Be Here Now*, a text following the spiritual journey of a PhD Psychologist into a spiritual teacher. Ram Dass returned to the west to teach others to follow the same path. By Harrison's own admission "the melody came fast" and it might be fairer to see "Be Here Now" as the same intuitive channelling as "Far East Man" and a song in which the spiritual and mundane co-exist comfortably. In this context, the slow, mantra like expression of the simple lyric can be seen as a very western expression of the Hindu focus on the moment. A number of those expressing an opinion on the song see it very much in this manner, with the line "it's not, like it was – before" being both an affirmation of the meditative living in the moment and a statement that the Beatle past is over for Harrison. The simple elegance of the words and music present Harrison proving the truth of his sentiment in the most meaningful way possible, by sounding like he has moved on both in his message and in creating a song that sits comfortably amongst the intimate gems forming the core of *Living In The Material World.* "Be Here Now" would probably have made the cut for The Beatles' "double white" album, or anything thereafter but would have sat less comfortably in the company it would have kept there.

Living In The Material World explores themes and finally reconciles itself in the closing two songs with "The Day The World Gets Round" expressing a belief that spiritual awaking can save humanity, despite the small proportion of the human race who "bow" before their Lord. Despite its sluggish pace this penultimate song on *Living In The Material World* bears some resemblance to Cat Stevens' hit single from *Catch Bull At Four* "Can't Keep It In." Stevens is animated about the love he has to share with the world, Harrison is more sedate and thoughtful, but both see a deep, connected, spiritual love as the means of saving the world, and believe sharing their example to be a means of achieving this. "The Day The World Gets Round" is also the perfect lead in to "That Is All" because the closing song reaffirms all the statements made, marking the whole work of *Living In The Material World* as a coherent statement of Harrison's position in his journey through life. Taken in detail it is an ambitious work, though frequently derided, disliked and misunderstood. Some reviews at the time expressed disappointment and the belief that the whole album fell far short of the standards expected of a major artist. Of all the negative comments it may be Bob Woofinden in *The Beatles Apart* who nailed the problem most astutely; claiming Harrison's "pedestal" was "an exposed, rather than a comfortable, place to be".

The cover art for *Living in the Material World* is a bizarre collision of subtleties and an outright assault of symbolism making its spiritual point. "His lectureship" may be in full flow here. A striking image of a hand on the front appears to hover in some semi-real state. In reality this is one of Harrison's hands taken in a Kirlian photograph (i.e. a form of photography sensitive to electrical energy around a body). On the front he holds a Hindu medallion. The same kind of shot on the back shows Harrison's hand holding coins. The battle of the spiritual vs mercenary covered in the songs is – therefore – represented on the front and back of the record, making a perfect wrapping for the contents. The gatefold inside devotes one panel to credits and words and another to a photograph of some of the album's main musicians arrayed in a clear parody of Leonardo da Vinci's Last Supper painting. Ringo Starr, Jim Horn, Klaus Voorman, George Harrison, Nicky Hopkins, Jim Keltner and Gary Wright are front on to the viewer. On the original vinyl edition only Harrison is in colour and only Harrison is standing and looking the viewer full in the eyes. Like Jesus in the famous painting he appears aware of a fate lost to the others (like the death Claudia Gates suggests followed the album). It is commonly – and wrongly – believed the shot was taken at Harrison's home but – as Bruce Spizer has noted in chronicling the solo Beatles – the home in the background is the sumptuous residence of entertainment lawyer Abe Somers and Hollywood glamour photographer Ken Marcus took the shot. Placed strategically in the background a nurse walks with a pram, a Mercedes limousine stands waiting with a black coated driver, an empty wheelchair stands at the edge of the manicured lawn and an empty black Ferrari stands on the drive.

One interpretation of the shot sees it as a clear meditation on spiritual values against those of material comfort. The tonnage of food on the table and other earthly delights appear in black and white and only the enlightened Harrison is in colour and offering himself to us. In that reading the complex shot has a lot to say but could be simplified as a message of the futility of trusting in earthly wealth. In another reading the shot appears to have much to say about Gates' claim that Harrison was facing death. In this reality the picture may literally be taken as a last supper, having wrapped up his final work. The birth and death symbolism in the pram and wheelchair are obvious and the awaiting limo is conspicuously large because it is the kind of car that takes mourners to a funeral. Beyond which I would recommend strongly you seek it out, and do what any dedicated Beatle myth seeker would do, and interpret the minor clues for yourself. There may be significance in anything from the collection of fruit, bread and wine on the table to the light being stronger between the diners and the vehicles than it is in the foreground. I would simply make one further observation. Even in his most pious period of spiritual devotion George Harrison liked a joke and *Living In The Material World* offers one good one on the back cover where readers are informed of the existence of the Jim Keltner Fan Club and told they should send a "stamped undressed elephant" to a Los Angeles address to join up. Ringo's *Ringo* album in the same year offered a similar gag and it appears fairly clear both Beatles were having a dig at the recently formed fan club for Paul McCartney's band Wings. It also appears clear that in the midst of a portentous album cover, the like of which he would never attempt with the same complexity again, George Harrison was still capable of having a laugh. So, a third reading of the cover might suggest it is there to make Harrison's point but also to bite back at anyone so intent on studying his album artwork down to the finest detail. You needed to be a dedicated fan to spot the line about the Keltner fan club. No site online I could find whilst researching this chapter recorded how many letters, or undressed elephants, arrived in response to the message on the cover.

Claudia Gates' argument about the quality of George Harrison's music after the imposter began releasing albums was made in early 1976, so to be fair to her claims we have to consider at least one more work in detail. *Extra Texture (Read All About It)* released on 22 September 1975 in the U.S. and 3 October 1975 in the UK is Harrison's sixth studio album and the last long-playing outing on his Apple contract. By the time Harrison released the album his Dark Horse label was already established and his links to Warner Brothers were strengthening. So *Extra Texture...* was a parting shot to Apple and EMI, putting it in limbo to some extent. It was customary with any solo Beatle, and also within the contract, that appropriate promotion should be done for the album. But EMI and Capitol in America were dealing with an artist who had already signed his next contract, who had produced an album and tour gathering poor reviews and who was already ensconced in Los Angeles, devoting office time to his new label, which belonged to Warners. In fact *Extra Texture...* did some good with regard to reversing the downturn of fortunes brought about by *Dark Horse*. The album reached #16 in the UK and #8 in the U.S. despite mixed (generally lukewarm) reviews and no live work to promote it.

In the context of Claudia Gates' claims the post 1973 albums are the work of an imposter *Extra Texture...* is something of a conundrum. It conspicuously lacks the self-conscious clues oozing from *Living In The Material World* and *Dark Horse*. So, it doesn't address the deep, spiritual, life and death themes in either the artwork or lyrics. On the other hand Gates' question; "why has Harrison's music changed so much?" And her discussion of his reliance on the cream of L.A. session talent and his propensity for "tinny one line garbagers" (i.e. crudely simplistic songs) totally uncharacteristic of the "perfectionist" of the earlier solo work all apply here. The real *Extra Texture...* issue with regard to the imposter claim is that this album is the most atypical of all George's solo releases. In the period up to 1975 there was nothing like it in the catalogue, in the period since Harrison retreated from the voyage taken on *Extra Texture...* and honed a path combining the slick AOR session sounds and his own insights and spirituality, effectively bringing in humour, warmth, some idiosyncrasy and some very skilled mates to sugar the more self-indulgent pills. If *Extra Texture...* has relatives in its own time they are the journeys into black music made by some of George's peers. It sounds very little like David Bowie's *Young Americans* set, but does mash soul and very white sensibilities in such an overt fashion as to qualify for the mid-seventies fashion briefly dubbed "blue eyed soul." Harrison didn't have blue eyes, but he certainly had soul, just a different take on soulfulness to most of those bracketed as soul artists. In the mid-seventies with Hall and Oates in their ascendency and Bowie so far into the area he snagged an appearance on *Soul Train* this music enjoyed a flavour of the month favour that lasted a few years. Somewhere between his former Beatle colleagues and that growing fashion George placed his 1975 album.

If we are to look at it now as the work of someone other than the musician who created *All Things Must Pass* then Claudia Gates' claims are best supported by some broad brushstroke arguments. *Extra Texture...* is far enough away from George's previous output that anyone studying his career tends to accept it as unusual. Crucially to Gates' claims it stands out massively in George's song-based outings because of the lack of spiritual work. The two previous albums combine personal insight and Hindu thoughts so closely they show an artistic position that makes George Harrison unique amongst major selling artists of his time. The crafted sutra like meditations of *Living In The Material World* and the journey through the sequencing of *Dark Horse* from depression, through renewal and affirmation of faith are nowhere on *Extra Texture...* The title celebrates the wider sound of the production, but lyrically the album collects and presents experiences, wallowing rather than moving. "His lectureship" might have been in full flow little more than two years previously but he's completely absent from *Extra Texture...* having been replaced by a morose, unlucky in love man, living in the moment and channelling the demons that beset him. That same creature on *Dark Horse* turned to the guidance offered by his "Far East Man" and concluded his album with. "It Is 'He' (Jai Sri Krishna)." The main hopes on *Extra Texture...* are firmly rooted on earth and loaded onto the bookends of the collection. The infatuated love song "You" and the closing "His Name Is Legs (Ladies And Gentlemen)" present Harrison looking for a new love and finding solace bantering with his friends. "His Name Is…" is a comedy song in praise of drummer "Legs" Larry Smith, one of George's Henley friends and a former member of the Bonzo Dog Doo-Dah Band. In between the solace of infatuation and partying *Extra Texture...* takes its soulful grooves and slow tempos into a series of personal vignettes, lined up more on the basis of which sounds and tempos flow best rather than presenting any coherent artistic vision. The ten tracks line up:

Side one

1."You" – 3:41
2."The Answer's at the End" – 5:32
3."This Guitar (Can't Keep from Crying)" – 4:11
4."Ooh Baby (You Know That I Love You)" – 3:59
5."World of Stone" – 4:40

Side two

6."A Bit More of You" – 0:45
7."Can't Stop Thinking About You" – 4:30
8."Tired of Midnight Blue" – 4:51
9."Grey Cloudy Lies" – 3:41
10."His Name Is Legs (Ladies and Gentlemen)" – 5:46

Claudia Gates' identification of "tinny one line garbagers" might usefully apply itself to the opening track and the single from the album, "You." She is right to point out the jaw dropping simplicity of some of George's songs on the mid-seventies albums. "You" trades on a simple hypnotic riff which combines Harrison's guitar and the horn power of a session crew and a disarming lyric with the same basic idea as "Ding Dong, Ding Dong" wherein it uses the subject of the song as the focus of very simple lines. "Ding Dong, Ding Dong" is ringing out and ringing in the passage of time, "You" literally says "I love you and you love me" after which – like "Ding Dong, Ding Dong" – it rambles very simply around that theme, repeatedly falls back on a big wall of sound to make itself catchy and listenable and vanishes before any further creative ideas are required. If you love the honest, deep thinking, George who is capable of making the gently companionable "Be Here Now" and "Give Me Love (Give Me Peace On Earth)" into accessible spiritual gems, you may well be aghast at the sheer gleeful focus on infatuation offered by "You." "One line garbagers" is something of a sideswipe, but Gates has a point. However, she has also missed a major point where this song is concerned. "You" dates back to early 1971 when Ronnie Spector, wife of Phil, recorded it for a proposed solo album to be released on the Apple label. The album never came out. Harrison offered the song to her and four years later helped himself to the backing track for his own version. The Spector production is thick and nowhere near tinny but that is a minor point in response to Gates' claims. The major point is that – whilst she and many others were unaware of it at the time – this song was written by the *All Things Must Pass* period Harrison. It is by far the simplest lyric on the album and up there with "Ding Dong, Ding Dong" as Harrison's simplest lyric ever. But if a central plank of Gates' imposter argument revolves around the change in music, it is notable that the real George and the imposter both had an uncanny ability to build a song around little more than one clear thought and a few lines tossing a simple notion about.
The opening and closing jollities aside *Extra Texture...* is an in the moment ramble through the troubling thoughts in the head of a depressed Harrison. A man prone to lingering irritability and medicating himself with cocaine. The songs sound like they have come from those down and despondent moments in which George goes in search of some meaning. The

Krishna consciousness so prevalent in his recent past doesn't appear in so much as one line of lyric. George is disarmingly honest and soulful, and also stripped back in his approach to the point of demonstrating some of the craft and tricks that under-pin his work. "This Guitar (Can't Keep From Crying)" is one craftsman like effort, written by George's own admission as a companion piece to "While My Guitar Gently Weeps." One positive of the North American tour of 1974 was the rapture with which audiences received "While My Guitar Gently Weeps" and the new song reaffirmed the idea that Harrison's playing was the way his inner feelings were expressed. George had met and rapidly fallen in love with Olivia Arias, though his changeable moods and indulgent ways still make the opening verse sound suspect. Harrison sings: "Found myself out on a limb/ But I'm happier than I've ever been/ But this guitar can't keep from crying…" from which point on the lyrics contrast the honesty of the emotion through his crying guitar with the way people fail to grasp George's meaning and the way George can't climb "Rolling Stone walls." So, the world might not get him all the time, but he's an artist and that is its own reward. The insularity is also strong on "Tired of Midnight Blue" a guileless account of Harrison finding himself involved in "naughtiness" at a Los Angeles club before a wave of depression swept him. In the most general sense this is Harrison addressing spirituality, but it stops short by offering no redemption beyond the recognition of regret and the hope that he could behave better next time.

Made me chill right to the bone
Made me wish that I'd stayed home – along with you

Time alone with Olivia may have been a better option than a night out in an LA club. The misery of the bad choice is compounded because Harrison throws in enough bluesy chords to suggest the lingering depression is still troubling him. The song is a noted standout on the album and "one of the better tracks" according to Harrison biographer Graeme Thompson. In isolation the song is probably stronger than it is sandwiched between "Can't Stop Thinking About You" and "Grey Cloudy Lies." The three songs making up the substance of side two are the artistic heart of the album but they are also mordant and slow. "Can't Stop Thinking About You" presents new love as painful, and actually concerns Maureen Starkey (Ringo's wife), not Olivia Arias. It dates from late 1973 (so pre the supposed death of the old George) and chronicles what Simon Leng calls "many nights spent nursing a bottle of brandy" as George's marriage with Patti collapsed.

"Grey Cloudy Lies" is – if anything – bleaker than the two songs preceding it. It shows Harrison's concern at being overwhelmed by the reactions to the 1974 tour and lets the listener in to how bleak the feelings were for him. Harrison had started writing the song on an upright piano in late 1973, but the lyrics specific to his feelings of depression also relate to the reactions to his tour. As Graeme Thompson notes, the song has "the weary roll of a funeral march and a lyric [speaking] of utter depression." And, it marks the end of the dirge trilogy on the album's second side. Harrison plays synthesiser and moog, effectively stripping the song of the emotive guitar licks that might have hinted at his melancholy slowly being purged, so "Grey Cloudy Lies" hangs, appropriately, like an immobile heavy sky.

The first side of the album includes the most obvious spiritual references on *Extra Texture...* although nothing on the album is blatantly in that vein. "The Answer's At The End" and "World Of Stone" both chart an introspective path, Harrison allowing the listener in to his personal thoughts. In a track by track interview with Paul Gambaccini Harrison was generally reluctant to pin songs down to specific meanings. His various biographers and the musicologists who have subsequently examined *Extra Texture...* see these two songs as a response to the critical mauling Harrison received. Once again the original compositions pre-date the *Extra Texture...* sessions and the *Dark Horse* album. A theme running through *Extra Texture...* though clearly never originally intended by Harrison is that the self-doubts and personal reflections arising from the traumatic failure of this first marriage provided a resonance when he felt rejected by his audience and derided by critics in the wake of the *Dark Horse* album and accompanying tour, at which point the fragments and demos he had in preparation formed into a focussed album. Another less romantic view of the whole process suggests this process may have been accompanied by a degree of creative inhibition in the wake of what he had suffered, and – possibly – a reluctance to invest monumental new creative effort in the signing off album for his EMI contract. Harrison already knew when *Extra Texture...* was being recorded that he had a multi-album deal with Warners to fulfil and that he would be the marquee artist on his own Dark Horse label, distributed by the U.S. giant. "The Answer's at the End" pits the lonely and misunderstood Harrison against the world, allowing us into his musings. The song started life as Harrison drew inspiration from inscriptions at his Friar Park home, and in that context it mimics the origin of "Ding Dong, Ding Dong" but offers a different perspective as Harrison presents his inner self

Now, I only want to be
With no pistol at my brain
But at times it gets so lonely
Could go insane
Could lose my aim.

The traditional sources of hope, like the whole experience making perfect sense in the context of his faith, are lacking. Harrison doesn't specifically turn away from his Hindu beliefs on *Extra Texture...* but in the context of the albums preceding it *Extra Texture...* is notably reluctant to see spiritual rewards as a consolation when troubles gather around a person. Other than romantic infatuation, notably on "You." There's a secular sense to "The Answer's at the End" with Harrison eschewing spiritual comforts and suggesting life will only reveal itself to us when it is done.

You know my faults, now let the foibles pass
'cause life is one long enigma, my friend
Live on, live on, the answer's at the end

In this context the main hope comes from mankind's willingness to achieve mutual understanding. There is also some sense of hope in the continuity from Sir Frankie Crisp's inscriptions on the idiosyncratic home, and their inspiration on its rock star owner. But the only certainties presented in "The Answer's at the End" are in Harrison's predicament, everything else is plea or a possibility. There is solace to be had, but there are no guarantees in couplets like

The speech of flowers excels the flowers of speech
But what's often in your heart, is the hardest thing to reach

Another take on hopefulness on *Extra Texture...* arrives in "World of Stone." The song made the B-Side of "You" and offered a deeper view of love. When writing about the song for *Dodge* magazine years ago and pouring over the *Extra Texture...* lyrics it also struck me that "World of Stone" had the two lines on the whole album that could be twisted perfectly into a blatant clue with regard to the Harrison/imposter story propagated by Claudia Gates.

Wise man, you won't be
To follow the like of me

In this context you could make an argument that the imposter Harrison is bemoaning his plight and realising a monumental mistake. Diligent research and Harrison's own openness in the autobiography *I Me Mine* make it clear that "World Of Stone" started life in 1973, and concerns itself more with the fact that Harrison hasn't got the answers he or his followers seek. The song isn't entirely hopeless, but it is assertive about the fact Harrison is no longer standing as any kind of spiritual guru. One thing that hurt him massively, to the point of emotional outbursts, was the negative reaction to his changing of well-known lyrics so he could perform songs with a greater spiritual message on stage. Of particular annoyance to some dedicated Beatle fans on the 1974 tour was Harrison's appropriating John's "In My Life" and changing the "I love you more" line to "love God more." Harrison also drew some derision with comments like: "I'm not up here jumping like a loony for my own sake, but to tell you that the Lord is in your hearts. Somebody's got to tell you." In the present day the comment would probably be lambasted because the "loony" reference is politically incorrect but in the live and let live times of the North American tour Harrison's evangelism for his spiritual path struck many who had found freedom to think through imbibing the imaginative genius of The Beatles as needlessly dictatorial.

"World of Stone" might have started life in the ruins of his failing marriage but the message of tolerance makes a lot of sense in the wake of *Dark Horse* and the tour.

We may disagree
We all have the right to be
In this world made of stone

And the song also has something to say about the gulf between intellectual achievement and spirituality.

The wiser you may be
The harder it can be to see

It is possible to read the "wiser you may be" thought as a specific dig at knowledgeable critics who had torn into George, but there is also a danger in over intellectualising any of the lyrics on *Extra Texture...* George's own descriptions of the writing of the songs, and his explanations to Paul Gambaccini frequently cover the same ground. These messages felt right, they focussed thoughts for him, the roots of the work were in found inspirations, like inscriptions in his house and all of these threads gradually coalesced into the album released in September 1975. Other factors driving the process included the need to get an album out quickly and – therefore – move on from *Dark Horse*.

Finally, we should note that Harrison's pythonesque humour remains present in the usual places on *Extra Texture...* Anyone scouring the whole package for secreted messages would find two very quickly. The Apple Records logo displayed on solo Beatle work is uniquely presented as an eaten away apple, clearly signifying the end of his contract. A gleefully grinning Harrison, portrayed on the inner sleeve (ironically photographed during the ill-starred 1974 tour) is captioned "OHNOTHIMAGEN" ("Oh not him again"). A clear joke at the expense of those who had fallen out of love with George. The radio and press ads for the album and single also traded on the "OHNOTHIMAGEN" gag, suggesting both that George had a level of self-awareness some doubted, and secondly that he had moved on personally from the lowest points of self-doubt.

With regard to the brief explosion of conspiracy theory in 1976 Claudia Gates is right to see George's music as exhibiting significant changes from the early seventies. If *Extra Texture...* was her reality check then it is indeed a massive move from the mysticism and spiritual focus of the lush and largely acoustic *All Things Must Pass* to the more distant and lightly electronic *Extra Texture...* The imposter theory is extreme and utterly implausible in the light of every scrap of evidence subsequently unearthed. *Extra Texture...* was, mainly, recorded in 1975 although the backing track lifted from the 1971 Apple session for Ronnie Spector does fit fairly well. However, the Harrison speaking to us from the album is a composite and confused character. The words, tempos and melodies are frequently dragged forward in time and the crack team of hand-picked musical collaborators working on the Los Angeles sessions for the album give it a sound miles away from the acoustic demos Harrison was cutting when he first worked on many of the songs in 1973. That much is literally there in front of you on *Extra Texture...* because the slanted typography of the brilliant orange sleeve puts the album title in a massive typeface, dwarfing Harrison's name on the front. The "extra texture" in question is the sound on the record and the message is that the artist has moved on.

The composite character speaking to us is part craftsman, cutting an album by applying his professional skills and work ethic to blend pre-written songs and some newer numbers. He offers a general message that he wants to sound different and move on artistically. There is clear confusion in the absence of the spiritual message that had so recently been the central purpose of much of the work Harrison regarded as his best, and also a confusion of direction from Harrison. His lyrics suggest he can live in the moment but long-term goals are vague at best. The answer may be at the end but how the end will be reached and what any of this will mean are less certain than they were on "That Is All" which closed *Living In The Material World*. So George's doubts are explored, themes emerge and they are turned over, put down and turned over again. In this reality there is a general focus and George's exceptional gift for sequencing records and grouping songs emerges intact from *Extra Texture...* This may be an art almost lost in the twenty first century but George, in particular, amongst his musical peers appears to have been a master of it. All the more so when on albums like *Dark Horse* and *Extra Texture...* he was working with doubts and difficulties and – probably – remained intensely aware that he would have liked more options than he had. In that context the focus on stepping back from spiritual pronouncements on side one of the original vinyl and the stark introspections on side two are like chapters in a short autobiographical account of his life at the time.

The art of sequencing records is all but lost in the present era when music is downloaded and passed around with a freedom that David Bowie famously compared to the availability of water. It is something worth briefly considering because George's subtle skills mean a lot less in the present time, but they may well give us some insight into Claudia Gates' relationship with him. During the period of George's greatest solo success the price of records against other entertainment was much higher than it is today. Albums of any kind represented a significant purchase. George placed a triple vinyl set at the top of the charts around the world and masterminded the release of another triple collection that performed at similar levels. Financially he asked a lot, and his fans, and record buyers in general responded. Record buyers of the period can often still recall the running order of tracks on their favourite releases. These albums were treasured, played repeatedly, smoked to, talked over, and frequently formed the backing track for sexual activity. The closest equivalents to file sharing whilst George was capable of placing albums in the top places of the charts were literally taking an armload of albums round to a friend's house and huddling in the bedroom to peruse covers and discuss what you were hearing. It was either that or run off clearly substandard audio copies on cassette tape; which allowed some sharing of sounds but reduced the experience to a lower fidelity. The platinum sales of later records by major artists can be misleading. Sales in the late eighties and nineties may have been higher before ubiquitous file sharing and the advent of sites like Napster killed the market but many of the additional sales were people re-buying on CD the albums they'd originally bought on vinyl, and a lot of the other sales were casual buying by well-paid types who simply wanted to acquire everything they could. In other words, the behaviour of consumers from the late eighties onwards meant the days of albums being poured over in every detail were diminishing.

By contrast, the highest profile days of the singer songwriter era saw devoted fans considering every lyrical nuance and reading album covers down to the fine print, where they'd find the in-jokes like the reference to the Jim Keltner Fan Club. Successful artists of that era needed elaborate album art work and the skill to sequence records so the songs would withstand repeated listening to gradually reveal more than the first layer of meaning. Steve Miller (as in the leader of The Steve Miller Band) once stated in an interview that he didn't see why a 35 minute album should take more than 35 minutes to record. He was being deliberately provocative but he went on to discuss the time he spent sequencing his albums. One almighty series of sessions produced his massive selling *Fly Like An Eagle* and *Book Of Dreams* collections. He spent ages getting the running order for the collections that fuelled the longest high-profile of his roller-coaster career and supported a series of lucrative tours. So, he had the touch when it came to making the most of the varied songs in any collection. George Harrison's less well remembered album tracks of the early seventies still enjoyed plenty of needle time in bedrooms all over the world where the familiar ebb and flow of *All Things Must Pass* and *Living In The Material World* accompanied everything from homework to debates about the meaning of life. The many hours the albums were played by individuals were probably the most important in terms of forging the devotion between Harrison and his most loyal listeners. In those moments the lush arrangement and slow incantation of "Be Here Now" or "Far East Man" might well prompt thoughts and speculation that allowed the listener to see George as a wise friend to rank alongside Joni Mitchell, Jackson Browne or Neil Young. In that relationship the skilful sequencing of a work like *Dark Horse* which presents the lowest moods before working its way through seizing the moment and reaching a spiritual solace is a potent artistic move. George unmistakably had that subtle touch just as he had the ability to craft simple lyrics with the strength of sutras and a deft touch in slide guitar that was only effortless until someone attempted to replicate lick.

The one thing George, or any other singer songwriter couldn't easily control in those times was the various unpredictable tangents the imagination of fans would take. Well over half of the meaning generated when fans listened in this way and weren't constantly bombarded by other interpretations on the internet came from the need of the fans themselves. Some artists, notably Alice Cooper, used this dynamic effectively. Cooper's best work both celebrates and satirises horror and rock, and he was careful never to deny the worst atrocities of which he was accused. Some believed him to be the Devil incarnate and that shifted albums as much as the interest of those who took his albums home and laughed out loud. The one thing Cooper kept firmly in the closet was his passion for golf; that would have been damaging to his career if it had come out too early.

Somewhere in the complex dynamic of needy fans and complex albums with a range of messages to deliver Claudia Gates and George Harrison collided to produce the story that forms the backbone of this chapter. Well, that's my contention anyway. If George (as in the real one and not the imposter) contacts you from beyond the grave, I'd recommend seeking medical help before the conversation develops too far.

Claudia Gates may have had a point about how far George had come from the man she loved, but most of the main points about Harrison and his artistic journey were missed in her argument. To be fair, she couldn't have easily foreseen George's future in which the conflicting strands of the music he made in the first half of the seventies would be comfortably reconciled. She also couldn't have foreseen the conscious stepping back from cutting edge musical artistry that made Harrison a more contented person, and allowed him to grow artistically in his own niche, often with little thought to whether he was changing fashions.

It would be tiresome to examine the George Harrison albums released after Claudia Gates' claims in the same detail as those she had to hand, but a brief overview of Harrison's life and work afterwards does allow us to pit her theory against the established views. Crudely you could look at the following story in two ways. Firstly, you could see George Harrison reconcile the warring elements in his life to the point that the differing artistic and personal pressures coalesced into a productive working life on his own terms, and a relatively happy private life largely free from the massive shifts of the first half of the seventies. Or, you could take Claudia Gates ideas and run with them to the point that every new move in Harrison's life post 1974 represents the imposter imposing a different vision on the world. In that reality you could just about argue Eric Clapton's line in "Layla" about giving his love "consolation" when her "old man" let her down is tantamount to spilling the beans that Harrison let Patti Boyd down by developing cancer and everyone from Harrison's first wife, to his best friends and the man masquerading as George since 1974 were in on an almighty secret that remains tightly protected. If – as Gates claims – Harrison suffered "more physical pain than any man since Jesus, enough to turn himself into a white light," you have to wonder what would motivate those who cared about him to keep quiet. Or, indeed, whether they could keep quiet at all after witnessing such trauma.

Post 1976 Harrison saw a brief upturn in his commercial fortunes but soon became less competitive in his musical work to the point that the gaps between albums got noticeably longer. In his typically quiet manner Harrison continued to combine spirituality and pragmatism and also continued to be something of an understated trailblazer amongst his generation of well-known musicians. The gaps between his albums were gradually mirrored by the gaps between the recorded works of a few others of his generation. In retrospect some of the artists who continued to knock out albums annually through the eighties did their critical standing some damage. For example, the decade represented a critical nadir for Harrison's good friend Bob Dylan and the reaction to Dylan albums like *Knocked Out Loaded* put them in the same category as widely derided works around a decade older, like *Dark Horse*. Harrison also led the field with regard to rock musicians diversifying successfully into business. The key to most successes in this area has been some display of genuine passion. Around the same time that Ian Anderson of Jethro Tull was acquiring land in Scotland and starting to farm salmon in that area George Harrison made the first moves to establish HandMade Films, largely because he was friends with members of the Monty Python team and cared when the funding for their *Life of Brian* movie fell through. Graeme Thompson is one biographer who has noted that the Pythons and Beatles shared a trait in displaying a zany creativity in public and a sharp focus and seriousness in private. So, George's pronouncement that he was motivated to fund *Monty Python's Life of Brian* because he wanted to see the movie was only part of the story. He understood the business well enough to see the potential and HandMade Films went on to a number of notable successes, and a few failures. In the final reckoning HandMade outlasted many independent competitors in a very tough market because it made a conspicuously good calls. During Harrison's tenure, most of which involved co-managing the operation with Dennis O'Brien, the company carved a particular path in support of individual voices amongst film directors. The hits were both critical and commercial and a few astute distribution deals were cut. Years after the event HandMade is remembered for the likes of *Monty Python's Life of Brian* (1979), *The Long Good Friday* (1980), *The Missionary* (1982), *Mona Lisa* (1986), and *Withnail and I* (1987). George's albums over the same period were generally received with some affection, but little excitement. The five years between *Gone Troppo* (1982) which failed to dent the top 100 in the U.S. and failed to chart in Britain and his renewed success with *Cloud Nine* (1987) marked a high point for his involvement with film production.

Musically George Harrison changed direction and achieved a steady focus from 1976 onwards. Around the time Claudia Gates was making her claims George was fighting hepatitis in hospital. He blamed the onset of the illness on his indulgence, especially in drinking, and vowed to clean up his act. George's relationship with Olivia Arias strengthened and when he returned to recording he made another strong decision, to work with a co-producer. The next five solo albums were less rushed and more balanced affairs. Middle-of-the-road by the standards of their time, the albums from *Thirty Three And A Third* (1976) to *Cloud Nine* (1987) mined a guitar based formula, kept the rockers restrained, enjoyed lush production and built their best songs on slowly unfolding melodies and the lyrical traits that made the best of George's work so appealing. If he won few new fans he managed moments when the loyal fan base was very happy indeed and his massive return to success at the end of this period showed there were millions more who could easily be persuaded to love George again when his work was good enough.

The devotional songs that had forced the agenda on *Living In The Material World* were still there. But they remained limited, and from "Dear One" on *Thirty Three And A Third* generally took the form of personal messages addressed to spiritual leaders, allowing the audience to gain an insight through listening, but seldom preaching directly to the listener. "Dear One" sounds like most of the other cuts on *Thirty Three And A Third* and left playing in the background could easily be mistaken for a standard man-to-woman love song. In reality it speaks to Premavatar Paramahansa Yogananda, the author of *Autobiography of a Yogi*. A healthy and focussed George got himself out there to promote the 1976 album, and showed a clear-headed awareness of what he was doing. Interviewed in Manchester by Tony Wilson, a man who was already promoting punk sounds on his *So It Goes* television show, George was honest about his wish to appeal to his original fan base, stating: "everybody grows with us" and comparing the early and loud Beatles with the seventies punks, saying: "we had very short hair and we were very mild compared to what's going on [with the punks now]."

Thirty Three And A Third and the subsequent *George Harrison* (1979) both went gold in the U.S. The 1979 album saw Harrison enjoying some of the best reviews since *All Things Must Pass* and employing a few craftsman-like tricks he had used to give variety to earlier albums. "Here Comes The Moon" joined "This Guitar (Can't Keep From Crying)" as a blatant attempt to revisit an earlier song and rework the idea in a different form. "Soft-Hearted Hana" was the kind of deceptive gem George could load onto an album with ease. Apparently a wildly inventive love song this "Soft-Hearted Hana" reveals a different angle entirely if listened to in detail. Verses like

And then somebody old appeared and asked had I come far . . .
And hadn't they just seen me up on Haleakala . . .
I kept on body surfing to pretend I hadn't heard
There was someone there beside me, swimming like Richard III
And I'm still smiling

Are really recounting an hallucinogenic experience eating magic mushrooms on Maui but the light breezy acoustic rock setting of the album is several sonic miles away from the psychedelic twists and turns of the late sixties Beatles visiting the same territory. The spiritual message of the record is also very light, culminating in the closing "If You Believe" which – metaphorically – has its cake and eats it, seeing value in both spiritually focussed prayer and pragmatic self-reliance, and presenting its observations with the sutra-simplicity Harrison achieved so deftly.

Get up - you have all your needs; Pray
Give up - and it all recedes away from you.
If you believe - if you believe in you.

Harrison's intense involvement in the film business followed the *George Harrison* album and his musical fortunes waned. The making of *Somewhere In England* (1981) was a less happy process than the making of the positive and flowing *George Harrison.* George endured the ignominy of his record company demanding the ditching of songs and getting on his case about producing more market friendly material. A number of his peers were suffering similar fates in a period when the music business remained nervous about the earning capabilities of a generation of rock musicians now well into their thirties. Harrison hadn't toured since 1974. His videos and interviews were entertaining but weren't bridging the increasingly wide gap to the younger record buyers of the period. Harrison agreed to drop four songs from the original album and re-shoot the cover, but struck back by writing and recording "Blood From A Clone," his searing indictment of the state of the early eighties music industry. The lyrics are more downbeat than on *George Harrison* and the sound still firmly in the semi-acoustic mainstream of singer songwriter territory. The main talking point of the album – then and now – is "All Those Years Ago," the song George wrote for Ringo but changed and re-recorded, utilising Ringo's original drum track and the vocal contributions of Paul and Linda McCartney. The newer version, in tribute to John Lennon, duly brought George his highest chart position for a single in Britain and America since "Give Me Love (Give Me Peace On Earth)." The song peaked at #2 in the U.S. The album also contained another light gem of a devotional song, in the mould of "Dear One" which could drift past effortlessly in the background, but reveal its true nature on the lyric sheet. "You Are The One" is simple but explicit about its real subject.

You are my friend and when life's through
You are the light in death itself, oh yes are
You are the one

They call you christ, vsnu, buddha, jehovah,
Our lord
You are, govindam, bismillah, creator of all

Gone Troppo (1982) followed eighteen months after but marked a genuine watershed in Harrison's career. A personal and fairly easy going record "Gone Troppo" marked a massive fall off in sales for Harrison. "Wake Up My Love" was the only single that achieved even a modicum of chart action in the U.S. and the album wasn't so much savaged by critics as totally ignored. Musically the album hovers between the lush if gentle singer songwriter work of the three collections preceding it, but also manages some of the less cluttered sound that would make *Cloud Nine* such a winner. *Gone Troppo* has moments, notably in the title track, when Harrison positively celebrates the distance between himself and the rest of the world. It also pulls the same trick seen on much of *Extra Texture...* in which material demoed years previously is finally finished and employed on a record. The closing "Circles" which concerns Hindu notions of reincarnation actually started life when The Beatles visited India. *Gone Troppo* is also less apologetic than any album since *Living In The Material World* about the spiritual element in George's music, "Mystical One" is autobiographical, noting:

I know something so dear to me
Beyond words
Beautiful feeling in my soul
Sounds I've heard
Like humming birds in a dream
(Mmm) That mystical one I knew
Is returned

Gone Troppo is something of a resignation of responsibility for producing anything like commercial music. A more personal and less cynical collection. More the work of a film producer getting involved in music than any attempt to move forward George's career. Harrison's musical career appeared in danger of dying of apathy, and the big HandMade hits like *Mona Lisa* suggested he might have his priorities right. When *Cloud Nine* emerged five years later Harrison was a rejuvenated, positive and more energetic musical act than he had been in living memory. The selection of Jeff Lynne for the crucial co-production role was crucial and *Cloud Nine* could be imagined as a deliberate attempt to produce a commercial sounding Harrison record fit for inclusion in a changing market. It could also be considered as the kind of album the ELO could have made if they hadn't been weighed down by all the classical instruments in the line-up. *Cloud Nine* went platinum, its lead single "Got My Mind Set On You" might have been a cover version but it came with a simple and highly effective video and duly restored George to the top of the American singles charts, and came within a whisker of doing the same in the UK.

The market had changed massively in George's favour during his absence. CDs were soon to become the predominant sales format and their ascendency convinced music companies of the value of acts with a lengthy track record and massive back catalogue. Paul Simon and Fleetwood Mac both posted #1 albums in the UK in that year and the reissued *Sgt Pepper's...* was back at the top end of the charts on CD. A stripped back sound, some deft guitar licks and George's best vocal performance in years ended any arguments about which was his most impressive album since *All Things Must Pass*. A strong romantic streak ran through the lyrics and the reflective passages considered aspects of living in the moment, but the strongest spiritual message came from a little covered direction, the presence of evil in the world. On "Devil's Radio" George addressed the presence of a real devil in all aspects of life.

He's in the clubs and bars
And never turns it down

Talking about what he don't know
On the devil's radio

He's in your TV set
Won't give it a rest
That soul betraying so and so
The devil's radio

A backing vocal refrain of "gossip" pushes the choruses along although some listeners hear a literal battle because the phrasing makes it sound very like "God-sin." But despite digging into the fate of the earth and a few personal demons *Cloud Nine* is as light as the *George Harrison* album, as catchy as George's late Beatle/early solo work and a massive step back into the mainstream. An attempt to record a B-Side led to the founding of The Travelleing Wilburys and two more platinum albums. George more than held his own against the monumental talents who shared composition and performance duties in the five piece act. By the early nineties George had done the unthinkable and set up another serious tour, this time with Eric Clapton's backing band and all the dates in Japan. HandMade Films was sold in 1994 and Harrison saw out the rest of his working life with a few guest musical appearances and the lengthy gestation process of an album that went under various working titles including *Portrait Of A Leg-End* and *Your Planet Is Doomed Volume Three*. He was attacked and stabbed in his own home in 1999 and died of cancer on 21 November 2001, aged 58. No imposters appeared to take his place. The album in the works was finished and released posthumously as *Brainwashed*, earning gold discs and showing a continuation of the *Cloud Nine* sound with some more personal and characterful touches. The instrumental "Marwa Blues" earned a posthumous Grammy award and some of the comical lyrical asides were up there with Harrison's best, particularly a Pythonesque sideswipe at corruption in the Catholic Church in "P2 Vatican Blues (Last Saturday Night)." George turns the senior figures of the Church into comic characters, and slyly addresses hypocrisy

It's quite suspicious to say the least
Even mentioned it to my local priest
One Our Father, three Hail Marys
Each Saturday night

Before – apparently – introducing a guitar solo by guest performer Paul Marcinkus (i.e. an American archbishop at the centre of the running of the Vatican bank). "Marcinkus" throws in some deft licks as George comically urges him on; "Play it Card baby!" The last track on the last official George Harrison album ends with a beautiful rendition of the "Namah Parvati" a prayer dedicated to the Hindu goddess Parvati. George and his son Dhani chant together, in unison and without music to the final silence of the record.

George's final statement on album is as strong a spiritual affirmation as he ever recorded. When he was attacked and in danger of death in 1999 he also chanted "Hare Krishna" and was ready to pass into another reality. George may have died at that moment but Olivia Harrison took the more practical step of grabbing a table lamp and hitting Michael Abram; a 33-year old from Liverpool with a history of mental health problems.

If Claudia Gates was still following Harrison's career as avidly during these final years it may well be that she was convinced her earlier fears were misplaced. Harrison had his moments of losing spiritual focus but his faith kept coming to the fore, and the moment when he faced death in an attack, along with the final moment on the final album suggest that when it really mattered George's spiritual commitment stayed strong and true.

A couple of useful conclusions might be drawn from George's life between the brief eruption of the imposter theory and the 21 November 2001. Firstly, the dismay in Clauda Gates' words over George's desertion of his spiritual message and style of music is wholly misplaced. Biographers and those – like Simon Leng – who have made it their business to chart George's career see progression and some coherence in the themes and styles of his music. George's own detailed account of his song writing which forms a major part of *I Me Mine* is also quite illuminating. For those not minded to read entire books about George Harrison's work there are many very informative Wikipedia pages, presenting a digest of the various studies each devoted to individual Harrison songs. The later albums fare worst with many songs lacking a specific page, but there is enough out there to allow a casual fan to get a strong insight into the particular genius of George Harrison. His spiritual life informed his song writing career from the mid-sixties to the very end, and that is beyond dispute. The second conclusion we might usefully draw looking at Claudia Gates' claims and the truth of George's life from 1976 onwards is that her particular conspiracy theory failed to take off and find a long life because there was little belief in it and little demand for her message. Reading the other chapters in this book and comparing them with the George Harrison story should give you some insight into the incredible imaginative twists fandom can take.

In general terms the elements seen in the George story up to and including the paranormal aspects and the belief of some telepathic contact between artist and dedicated fan are not limited to George Harrison. This book hasn't covered it but you will find online evidence of songs John Lennon wrote after he died. In fact some post-mortem work by a number of dead performers exists in mp3 files online, you might want to hunt down and enjoy *The Elvis Presley Séance* album (Elvis turns up, obviously, they'd never have got a whole album out of the séance if he didn't). You will also see from other stories in this book that there can be lingering belief in a story despite frequent factual evidence that it is wrong. A simple example occurs in the next chapter. Ringo Starr faced a death threat in 1964, because he was believed to be Jewish. He isn't, but that hasn't stopped people finding that story and believing it for over 50 years. The basic facts of Ringo's life are online in many locations, but some people insist on seeing and believing what they want.

Beyond the above I can only speculate. To my knowledge I am the only writer or journalist who bothered to investigate the death rumour relating to George Harrison after 1976. Once the initial joke had died down and those prone to reading the music press had stopped joking about it and searching for their own clues to fuel the jokes, the story simply died. So I can only offer my best guesses for why it failed to take off, and why the internet appears to lack a rabid little enclave in which the credulous and paranoid egg each other on to discover evidence and build a metaphorical mountain out of the initial molehill of rantings. To my mind the superficial evidence for this story is – if anything – stronger than the Paul is dead material. *Living In The Material World* focusses so clearly on the gulf between earthly pleasures and spiritual grace that it has the depth of evidence required to fuel a cult belief, and the change in musical style along with the blatant I'm not what I seem messages of *Dark Horse* create a clear break between one George and the next. If *Sgt Pepper's...* and *Abbey Road* are the bedrock of the Paul is dead theory, the two solo Harrison albums have the same strengths as those Beatle albums. The harder you look the more the clues begin to emerge from familiar sounds and scenery. This way, truly, madness lies. Thankfully, this madness has yet to erupt all over cyberspace. I am aware that the act of reviving this old story might just influence some to pick it up and run with it to the point of pasting it all over a website. Though, if it hasn't taken off so far, I seriously doubt it will get very far even if a few people do place it in the public arena with some suggestion that it has merit.

I almost got the chance to take it well beyond the readership of *Dodge* magazine after I covered it for them in 1992. Around that time George Harrison was enjoying the highest profile he had for some time. In the wake of the *Cloud Nine* album and the success of the Travelling Wilburys he had announced a Japanese Tour. Unlike the highly ambitious jaunt of 1974 this was a limited risk affair with Harrison effectively co-opting Eric Clapton's band, including Clapton himself, and touring a reverent greatest hits selection without any reworked lyrics. "Dark Horse" might still have been in there despite its lack of radio play since the mid-seventies, but that was about as daring as the selections got. The tour would eventually be turned into a double CD. The 1992 General Election in the UK also brought George more publicity when he publicly endorsed the Natural Law Party with their new age philosophy which included the advocating of yogic flying.

George was willing to talk to journalists and one day I got a call at work from *Dodge* who gave me the number of a television researcher who had contacted them in response to the article. When I rang it the girl I spoke to revealed she worked with Jonathan Ross, then an up and coming chat show host on Channel 4. Was I, she asked, willing to go on Ross's show and repeat the Harrison is dead story and the evidence I had presented in the article? That was a no brainer once she told me the rest. The plan, put simply, was to announce the Harrison is dead story ahead of time and get that on the show. But whilst this was being discussed on screen the real George would walk out, rapidly be provided with a chair, and sit down to deny he'd ever died. George, supposedly, was up for it.

It's often the tactic of researchers on television and radio to sell the best possible scenario to a potential guest, and I knew enough about rentagob and guesting work by this time to be slightly wary of what I was being told. But the chance to meet George Harrison was the clincher for me and, clearly, nothing was going to happen without him. So she can't have been lying about that bit.

Another couple of phone calls made it clear this meeting was getting less and less likely and in the end it was confirmed it wasn't going to happen. Harrison had been considering touring beyond Japan but this didn't happen. There were pressures on him to continue the same tour with the same band. Graeme Thompson notes that members of Eric Clapton's band were keen to continue working with George and the interest in the United States was strong enough to suggest a full scale tour over there would have been a financial success. I was called after the bulk of the Japanese tour band, minus Eric Clapton, had played a set in support of the Natural Law Party on 6 April 1992. Despite mixed reviews that gig caused brief rapture when Ringo Starr appeared to play on the final songs. Such as I understood it, the Jonathan Ross appearance was being lined up because Harrison was considering announcing more British dates, including a return to the Albert Hall. In the end it didn't happen. Thompson's discussion of Harrison's live work in 1992 gives some indication why. Discussing Harrison's opening song at the 30th anniversary concert in honour of Bob Dylan that year Thompson notes "he played 'If Not For You' with a look that transmitted sheer, unadulterated, terror." Harrison soon settled into a more relaxed frame of mind to sing "Absolutely Sweet Marie" but he remained ambivalent about working live. The Japanese tour generated good money and Harrison was glad of it at the time. HandMade Films hadn't made a great film since Withnail and 1 in 1987 and business problems, notably a major rift between Harrison and Dennis O'Brien, had derailed the focus and direction of the company.

In the end Harrison ceased his interest in that business by the mid-nineties and drew a line under that part of his life. His work on The Beatles' *Anthology* compilations and documentary series kept his public profile high. He returned to being a studio based musician and the live appearances almost ceased. Despite persistent rumours to the contrary he wasn't a recluse. All of the major biographies on Harrison note his habit of turning up in the most ordinary places like a local pub or chip shop. The serious attempt on his life late in 1999 brought a rethink of his personal security and – according to some of those closest to him – may have been a contributory factor in bringing back the cancer that eventually ended the life of George Harrison; in the material world at least.

Whatever happened to George Harrison after his death, the man's legend continues in his music, in the example of the life he lived and in countless places online where fans meet to keep alive their love of the quiet Beatle. That love is both a love of his music and a genuine affection that for many is a strong feeling of love for Harrison the man. George may lack the massive conspiracy theory of the kind that drives the stranger end of internet activity with regard to John and Paul. However, one thing more obvious online than anywhere else is the depths people find in his work, and the inspiration he has provided to the lives of others. The present book is about Beatle myths and legends, and so the George is dead story from the mid-seventies was the only real contender for this chapter. The notion that George is hugely under-rated and all of his albums contain under-appreciated works is probably true, but it is more open-ended and amorphous. Appreciation is in the ear and mind of the listener. That's a side of George Harrison you will have to explore for yourself, unless you're already one of the converted.

The George is dead legend is useful as a reality check against the other stories. It failed to take off, probably, because nobody felt the need of it. George Harrison spent much of his career appealing to a very devoted fan base and sporadically breaking out to a more general crowd who loved The Beatles or simply came to love a few of his songs or a particular album.

Claudia Gates' story from 1976 – in all probability – tells us something significant about the lengths some fans go to to maintain a sense of ownership over their own beliefs about an artist. In that sense Claudia Gates' tale probably overlaps with the reactions of those who booed Bob Dylan when he went electric. It also, probably, overlaps with the odd fan so lacking in boundaries that they might hide in bushes, go through a garbage bin or build a shrine in a bedroom. I tried unsuccessfully to find Ms Gates, so I can't presume any more than I am suggesting here. If she is still around and still a major follower of George Harrison I would be very interested to know what she made of his career after 1976. It may be that she felt gradually less concerned as the George she had previously loved began appearing again on his better records.

What matters now about this strange tale is that its very failure to take off in the manner of the theories about John and Paul can teach us a lot about the way people are motivated to believe things, and how the lives of music fans and musicians in the pre-internet age were almost perfectly matched to create the strange symbiosis that brought about that letter to Sounds in 1976.

Chapter 4

Ringo Starr: Was in the Right Place at the Right Time, he got Lucky Joining The Beatles and There's Nothing Else Interesting About him.

The first three chapters of this book have trawled well-known and little known Beatle myths, lining up such evidence as is available and often treating the same evidence in different ways depending on the story. So, I'll make no apologies for going somewhere else at the start of this chapter and starting with a rant. If you want to cut straight to the stranger Ringo myths and legends ignore the next section and restart where you see the words Rant Over! If you want to wade through the more general Ringo myth – that he just got lucky to join The Beatles – then, be warned, I'll address it only with my own rant that has no truck with the lucky Ringo theory. Here we go:

The Ringo Rant – by way of Dispelling the "Right Time/Right Place" Ringo Myth
Anyone claiming Ringo is a so-so musician who only got the job because the stand-offish Pete Best wasn't considered Beatle material is missing the point massively. The Beatles tapped up Ringo, stealing him from Rory Storm and the Hurricanes and this act was a practical move on their part to bring in a musician who had already recorded with them in Hamburg and proven his abilities live on stage with his "Starr Time" turns in Rory Storm's band, where he would sing a rock 'n' roll favourite in his solo spot. When John and Paul drove to Butlins in Skegness, on 15 August 1962 and asked Ringo to join The Beatles nobody could have known the life changes it would bring about for the drummer. Both sides of the bargain were based on practicalities. Ringo had quit a job assembling climbing frames for children and committed his future to professional drumming, so good deals and – in particular – decent money were a priority. As one the Liverpool drummers with some star quality he was in demand and Ringo's abilities had already opened a bidding war. Tony Sheridan had briefly snagged him but Ringo was unimpressed with Sheridan's habit of changing the running order of songs without consulting his band. So Ringo had returned to Rory Storm and the Hurricanes and their Butlins residency where the throughput of girls and the chance to perform his solo spots were an attraction. By this time he had already adopted the Ringo Starr moniker, ditching Richard Starkey. He had also filled in with The Beatles on stage when Pete Best was ill. Ringo was the kind of drummer who enhanced a band, and its ability to entertain. His genius at this stage of his career was to offer more than just the rhythm. He was fun offstage too, and in the Liverpool music scene of the time other musicians liked Ringo. Ringo was a laugh, and he fitted into a band to the point that ideas tended to take wings when he was around. Life was

better with him in the line-up even if the money wasn't great and the living and travelling could be grim. By the time John and Paul arrived in Skegness Ringo already knew that Kingsize Taylor was preparing to offer him £20 a week for a stint in Hamburg. The Beatles offered to up that to £25 a week and the deal was done. By this time The Beatles had completed one stint in Hamburg, emerging as a solid rocking band capable of storming the live venues in Liverpool and handling the tough crowds in the hard German city. Ringo also knew that territory. So the deal done in August 1962 involved a band keen to improve their live work and get a proper recording deal hiring a man with the drumming abilities and personal qualities to enhance their image. The drummer, for his part joined a band who had come on massively in a short time and earned an enviable reputation in their home city. They had offered 25% more money than the best offer he had on the table at that time, and they were getting bookings, and were almost seven months into a five year management contract with Brian Epstein. Things could have been going better, but the band were a serious professional outfit, capable of earning money and potentially capable of recording. Ringo and the other three Beatles knew and liked each other. The one conspicuous loser in the situation – Pete Best – was left alone to be fired in due course by Epstein.

Ringo didn't get lucky, he had made his own luck. The Beatles decided to hire him because it made sense. Whatever the personal issues and the moralities of ditching their existing drummer, the band had already seen a better way forward with Rory Storm's drummer and the £25 a week was a risk to them and Epstein, but a risk they were willing to take because they believed in what they were doing.

The success that came the way of the band afterwards pushed their creativity and personal qualities to limits none of them could have imagined. Along the way they discovered song writing abilities that went on to change the history of popular music and created a body of work that may well sit at the creative and commercial pinnacle of popular music for as long as anyone alive today can foresee. Had anyone from the future been able to gate-crash that meeting in Skegness in 1962, and tell the three Beatles how they would be regarded 50 years later, that person would probably have been ushered away amid fears for their sanity. The Beatles are generally accepted as the best-selling musical act of all time, and with physical sales of music having fallen so far from the days when Beatle albums dominated the charts it beggars belief that a competitor would now emerge to challenge that primacy. The band are responsible for some of the most covered and widely recognised popular music ever written by anyone and this ubiquity extends to the point that the music they never intended to be released on single is as well-known as major hits by other acts. People born years after the band had any regular career are familiar with this music, and the basic details of the individuals who made it. Ringo Starr remains a famous and well-loved individual, in demand for work. For most of his working life he has been a solo musical act, actor, personality and – in his own very personable way – an activist for a robust philosophy involving causes and an adherence to peace and understanding. He may have enlisted the help of others, including his former Beatle colleagues in this work, but Ringo works mainly on his own terms and has pretty much done so since the end of the sixties.

With regard to his musical skills and the contribution made to The Beatles it is also easy to under-value and misunderstand Ringo's moments of true genius, and why they helped in the journey from three hopefuls around a table in Skegness to the band listed atop the Wikipedia's list of Best Selling Music Artists. It's also easy to rant at length about why Ringo mattered, and that isn't the point of this chapter. So I'll restrict my contribution to the whole debate to ten points, mainly concerning the time between the meeting in Skegness and the release of the *Let It Be* album. Then we'll get to a few other Ringo myths and legends.

Ten Reasons The Beatles Were Lucky to get Ringo:
He's the best Beatle actor, and this matters because brand Beatles was promoted globally by the first two Beatle movies in particular. Making the *Hard Day's Night* movie was a logical step because in the mid-sixties no band who had gone to world-wide success so quickly had the options available today. Stadium gigs were in their infancy, the video and amplification technology that made the twenty first century stars like One Direction a success in a football stadium was nowhere in sight. The tried and tested means of getting a musical hero to a mass public was the same as had been used by George Formby and Elvis; movies. Without the movies millions around the world would have felt less acquainted with the band and without the success of the first two movies the massive artistic developments and investment in recording that made the late sixties period a watershed in popular music would have been harder to justify. When The Beatles signed for their first movie everyone knew they were expecting to make a quick turn-around cash-in film and the competition – artistic and commercial – in the minds of the production team came from the likes of Cliff Richard and Elvis. In *Hard Day's Night* Ringo is a way better actor than anyone had the right to expect and his scenes, including the solo spot around The Serpentine, bring character and a sense of pathos to the film. Because *Hard Day's Night* achieved these levels The Beatles' film career was safe, and a major plank of their future success was secured. Ringo was also a character who played well around the world meaning that the love and affection felt for his screen persona expanded the band's audience, especially amongst mothers who had taken their children to the film and girls who liked "normal" boys. All of the above was achieved because Ringo has a natural talent in this area that allowed him to perform superbly in the movie despite a lack of preparation and experience.

Ringo is the drummer the band wanted in 1962 and they made a good call. Granted, the fans in Liverpool were particularly negative at first. That reaction owed a lot to the fact they knew and liked the good-looking Pete Best. And, in the cramped Cavern Club Pete was so close to the crowd they could admire those looks as easily as they could admire the other Beatles. But, Ringo was signed for his drumming. All the arguments about his technical abilities are of limited relevance because what he did helped to put the The Beatles into a position to secure a record deal and write and record the songs they imagined they could record in those early years. If the progress between signing Ringo and signing with EMI hadn't occurred, there would have been no Beatles as we know and love them. The other three got what they wanted, a mate who knew their work, played in a sympathetic way to their style and shared many of the same assumptions about how their love of rock 'n' roll could be transformed into a distinctive sound for a beat group, playing well to the audience they already had. Ringo's strengths at this time were his lack of fussiness, his ability to perform and engage with audiences in a small venue and his willingness to endure the accommodation and travel conditions that were the norm in those circumstances.

Ringo is also the drummer the band needed when massive success overwhelmed them and Beatlemania ensued. With all due respects to the band as a live act, the best that can be said during this period is that they stayed tight as a unit and true to the cohesion that had seen them through their second stint in Hamburg and the all-important Cavern gigs that helped to build their British reputation. So, musically, the band needed Ringo to do the things they wanted from him when they first sought to prize him away from Rory Storm. From the moment they appeared on the Ed Sullivan show their musical abilities on stage were secondary to their ability to play recognisable versions of the songs and keep their sanity together as the crowd suggested insanity was the right response. In those circumstances each Beatle needed three fellow Beatles he could trust and Ringo's ability to remain sane and unaffected in these insane times was, if anything, greater than that of his bandmates. His presence on stage and in public brought a down to earth realism to the whole circus. Had – say – Keith Moon been The Beatles' drummer, this period of their career could have been their undoing.

Ringo is also a major part of why The Beatles took Beatlemania through a gradual change from beat group rock 'n' roll through the ground-breaking expansion into creative possibilities on *Rubber Soul* and *Revolver* to the full-blown psychedelia that went on to spawn some of the best and worst excesses of rock music. Much of this music required a deftness of touch that placed all the creative elements in perfect balance. Ringo may not have been the most articulate about what he was doing on cuts like "Tomorrow Never Knows" and "Strawberry Fields Forever" what matters is that he did it. Those moments when he could channel something he'd first heard on a Dave Brubeck record are as influential as the moments when John Lennon channelled things he'd first read in the *Tibetan Book of the Dead*.

Ringo is enough of an everyman that Beatle fans could read meanings into him. When the others developed strong images and areas of interest – John's intellectualism and George's spiritual side – Ringo remained accessible and grounded. Many fans who couldn't make all the shifts their heroes were making would still feel an attachment to the band, because for as long as Ringo was there The Beatles were still The Beatles. For example, the trip to India with the Mahareshi pushed some fans to the limits of their understanding. In the circumstances Ringo's comment comparing the experience to Butlins was marketing genius, not that he was even thinking in terms of marketing. But incidents like that remain the essence of Ringo and they really mattered during the Beatles' most intense periods of creativity and personal exploration.

Ringo's role as the glue in the band is highly important and often under-rated. The best bands often have such a member. Crosby, Stills, Nash and Young have always credited Graham Nash with this role and without him that band, in its various lines ups of CSN/CSNY might have ceased operating when David Crosby's drug addiction got to the point of making him dysfunctional as a working musician. In Ringo's case his role in holding the band together is central to an important element of their history and their legend. When the sessions for *The Beatles* (aka The White Album) got personal, self-indulgent and unproductive the first Beatle to make a formal break and effectively leave the band was Ringo. He informed the others they were simply no fun to work with and took a fortnight's holiday on Peter Sellers' yacht. Various written accounts of the aftermath describe a scene in which Ringo eventually came back to Abbey Road to find his drums covered in flowers and the other Beatles suitably chastened at their actions. Ringo's act brought the band to their senses and promoted an end to their career in which they found a working arrangement acknowledging the pressures that were gradually fracturing them. It didn't always work perfectly but it did produce some great music. Without Ringo's actions during the 1968 sessions the break-up of the band would likely have come earlier and been even more acrimonious. In that reality the world would have been denied *The Beatles* in its final form, *Let It Be* and – perhaps most crucially – *Abbey Road*. The pragmatic arrangement that put aside personal differences to record *Abbey Road* was born of the band's reaction to Ringo's departure in 1968. Of all the late period work *Abbey Road,* which remains the band's biggest selling album in the USA and a perennial high performer in best album of all time style lists, is vital to their legend because of its quality. It's also got some superb performances from Ringo.

Ringo's best drumming is emotional, subtle, crafts-man-like and shows a sympathy for songwriters. He manages these performances repeatedly on the later Beatle albums, notably *Abbey Road.* He is capable of bringing enough character to his work to make it noticeable and enough restraint to support all his fellow Beatles, the differences between his performance on "I Want You (She's so Heavy)" and "Something" are subtle, but part of what makes The Beatles' final recording such a masterpiece. However, Ringo's work on John Lennon's *Plastic Ono Band* collection is – arguably – the stand out performance of his drumming career in support of his fellow Beatles. The range of moods on that album demands an accomplished drumming performance and Ringo is often exposed in a very small combo, his work alongside Lennon's rhythm guitar and Klaus Voormann's bass on tracks like "Hold On" shows an affinity with the emotion of the work. The opening trio of tracks on that album all showcase the Lennon/Voormann/Starr trio and set a mood of intimacy and emotional honesty that has established the album, rightly, as a classic. Lennon rated Ringo's contribution at the time and – as with his trip to Skegness eight years earlier – made a good call. Other honourable Ringo performances showcasing that soulful subtlety, and requiring less listening than a whole album, include "Strawberry Fields Forever" and "Hey Jude." They sound easy, but plenty of drummers in covers bands would attest, making it sound that effortless is hard work.

Ringo is a passionate creative performer in his own right, and he has never lost his focus. His albums may receive mixed reviews – often being praised and lambasted for their continued focus on themes of autobiographical fragments, love and peace and their adherence to a steady pop/rock sound – but Ringo has carved the kind of niche familiar to country artists and other purveyors of little guy/big dilemma fayre. A measure of Ringo's feeling for his material is that he has been more prolific as an albums artist in the 21st century than most of his contemporaries in the business, including Paul McCartney, and EMI re-signed him four decades after letting him go.

Ringo's post Beatles work often did credit to his former band and expanded the audience and respect for The Beatles. When his former colleagues appeared briefly marooned (McCartney pre-*Band On The Run*) or determined to pursue eclectic directions that alienated some fans (*Mind Games* and *Living In The Material World*) Ringo kept it real. His work with Marc Bolan put him firmly back with the kids in the early seventies, so too his superb performance alongside David Essex in *That'll Be The Day*. Ringo's albums more than those of any other Beatle have brought his former bandmates together, indeed the first time they all – sort of – worked together after the break-up of the band was on the *Ringo* album in 1973 (they're all there, just not on the same tracks or in the studio at the same time). Subsequent work, like his voicing of Thomas the Tank Engine stories for television in the eighties meant some of those who went on to investigate The Beatles did so because they took to Ringo and gradually became aware he had a past that was important. Without ever trading purely on his past, Ringo has often used his celebrity skilfully in ways that continue to bring people to him and lead them to The Beatles.

He's a top bloke. Ringo's indiscretions and lowest points are not such disasters that they have greatly alienated Beatle fans or greatly tarnished his star quality. He was the most popular Beatle for many years in the United States and people – quite simply – continue, in large numbers, to love him. For his part Ringo has done a few life-affirming things and been sparing in airing the worst of his dirty laundry. His story is all the more endearing because it rings true and honest. He lost his way badly to the point his drinking led to his relationship with Barbara Bach getting badly violent but in typical Ringo fashion he worked at it and turned things round. He and Barbara have been married since August 1981, making theirs the longest marriage of any Beatle. A real testament to good sense and honesty because relationships between two notable stars with a rehab past are notoriously short-lived. In later life he has come to Transcendental Meditation and continues to perform with his band. His love of music remains transparent and the joy he finds in being surrounded by good musicians remains infectious. All of which means he remains identifiable as the man with whom much of the music loving world fell in love in the sixties.

All told, it was a smart move when The Beatles and their management saw Kingsize Taylor's offer, and upped it by £5 a week.

RANT OVER!

Some Engaging Ringo Myths and Legends

Ringo Is Dead: Apologies, but you probably knew this was coming if you'd read the first chapters of this book. It is unlikely to be a surprise that a highly obscure book and some websites also exist in support of this highly spurious theory. The first and most obvious point to make about the core of the dead Ringo rumour is that much of the evidence is the same as that feeding the Paul is dead story. Indeed the turnmeondeadman website that so comprehensively explores the Paul story also offers a page summarising Azing Moltmaker's

PAUL IS DEAD!!!! OR............ IS RINGO DEAD???? DO YOU WANT TO KNOW THAT SECRET????

You'll gather from the title that this is a highly unofficial effort sprinting at you from the very margins of the publishing world, and battering you with the kind of missionary zeal that fires those for whom a unique discovery has become an all abiding passion. In fact, Moltmaker isn't the only one who has put forward this theory but – as of this writing – the world's main Ringo is Dead site appears to have discontinued itself. In addition to some of the same clues – like the fractured band name on the back of *Abbey Road* – the Ringo is dead rumour trades on the same kind of clues, highlighting instances in which he appears out of step with his fellow Beatles. Three of the band's waxworks sport suits and ties on the *Sgt. Pepper...* cover, only Ringo's waxwork sports a turtleneck (a symbol of death, apparently). Then there's the massive clue that leaves the Paul is dead rumour clunking, as the band finish the opening track of *Sgt. Pepper...* and establish that the ensemble you are hearing are not The Beatles they announce "the one and only Billy Shears" and the next voice you hear is Ringo, or is it Billy doing a superb Ringo impression? Rather conveniently anyone replacing Ringo in the late sixties had no significant song-writing legacy to live up to. Billy Shears, near enough, had an open ended opportunity to write Ringoesque songs and gradually develop a style and a catalogue of compositions. Which – of course – is exactly what the post-Beatles Ringo did, with a little help from his friends. Over the years the most unlikely cult heroes have appeared to endorse this legend with their own observations. The band Negativeland – no strangers to controversy – include a song entitled "Ringo is Dead" on their collection *Over the Edge Vol. 4: Dick Vaughn's Moribund Music of The '70s* and since 2007 one of the finest alternative rock bands from Texas have been channelling much of the best in British indie – Smiths, Cure etc. – into their very own blend of sparky and alternative music, all the while trading under the glorious moniker of Ringo Deathstarr.

Ringo is Jewish: He's not, of course, but no amount of provable evidence to the contrary has stopped people believing him to be so. It is mentioned in a few places – including the gloriously named website Jew or Not Jew? – that Ringo performed in Montreal in on 1964 in spite of an anti-Semitic death threat. This situation arose when Brian Epstein took a call claiming Ringo would be shot at the gig on 7 September. The anti-Semitic caller was, of course, adding insult to threatened injury by ringing the band's Jewish manager. Epstein duly arranged for a detective to crouch beside Starr during the gig and Ringo combined a low crouch over his drums with a raising of his cymbals to decrease his visibility. This didn't exactly help his performance on the night, though the wildly screaming crowd didn't complain.

The half-jokey Jew or Not Jew site is regretful at losing Ringo, finishing his page with the thoughts: "Ringo's only connection to Jews is his wife, the half-Jewish former Bond girl

Barbara Bach. But it doesn't look like he had Jewish heritage, and he definitely did not convert after marriage.

Sad, really. Because we would take Ringo. It's not like we can have John. Or Paul. Or George..."

Ringo has done a few things along the way to inadvertently support this belief. His full beard and long hair around the time he was hanging out with Marc Bolan and directing Bolan's *Born to Boogie* documentary movie give him a very Jewish appearance.

Ringo Didn't Play on "Love Me Do": There are two "hit" versions of the song, recorded on 4 and 11 September 1962. On the first version Ringo plays drums and this take was released with a red Parlophone label in October 1962. The 11 September version features session drummer Andy White on drums and Ringo on tambourine (so he plays on both cuts). This is the version appearing on the black label Parlophone single released early in 1963. The *Please Please Me* album features the Andy White version of the song, and the 1982 reissue which rose to #4 in the UK is also the Andy White version. The common belief for many years was that Ringo's performance was so poor on 4 September 1962 as to leave EMI convinced he needed replacing, though the initial release of the Ringo-drumming version on single suggests otherwise. The one version recorded and generally agreed to be inferior precedes both of these takes and features Pete Best on drums. This was widely believed lost but was rediscovered and eventually saw official release on the first *Anthology* collection. The reasons for rejection of one version over another with regard to release are not simple. The use of session drummers, skilled in studio technique, was standard at the time. This didn't mean the working drummers with bands were poor. It had more to do with the cost of studio time and the practice of setting up and recording quickly. Then, as now, popular music was/is often recorded in a way that means the drum sound is established and the other instruments slotted in around that. George Martin was inexperienced at recording rock 'n' roll bands in 1962, his most notable records at that time being comedy productions including the work of Peter Sellers. Left handed Ringo playing a right handed kit, Martin's inexperience, and the cost of a short session of which little was expected are all likely to have contributed to a situation in which EMI and their house producer thought a rapid re-take the following week might improve matters. The fact they went with the first version having paid for the second and seen it as an opportunity to improve is actually testimony to the fact Ringo did a decent job. Telling the versions apart is – of course – easy, listen for the tambourine. If it's there, you are hearing the 11th September version. But Ringo is definitely on both.

Ringo Came up with the Title for A Hard Day's Night: It's by no means proven that he did, though – in a general way – that is exactly what happened. Alan Clayson and Spencer Liegh's book of debunked Beatle myths *The Walrus Was Ringo* provides a general summary of the situation. It is notable that the Beatles' film and album title bears a strong resemblance to Eartha Kitt's self-penned song "I Had a Hard Day Last Night" which trades on her smouldering sexuality and a reading of the title's word play not appropriated by The Beatles. So, a pragmatic view of the titling of film and album suggests they tweaked an already good pun, thereby avoiding any copyright issues, and knew when they did so it had the kind of jokey word play already known and loved by fans of Beatle wit. It sounded exactly like the kind of thing Ringo would say, and quite close to the off the cuff word wizardry of Lennon in a press conference, so it belonged with The Beatles. George Harrison in particular was assertive in his stated love of Earth Kitt, so they had to be aware of her song.

Ringo said things like "hard day's night" all the time. In fact, Alan Clayson is one of those who notes that Ringo's thoughtful and reflective moments were often mangled into "Ringoisms" and enjoyed by the band, even if they frustrated Ringo sometimes. At his best Ringo had the ability to produce effortlessly comic phrases at will. So much so that his school friends would sometimes amuse themselves simply by involving him in conversation.

Paul McCartney has spoken of the film and album title emerging when the band were sitting around at Twickenham Studios during the filming and thinking up possible titles. At which point they recalled something Ringo had said. Lennon discussed the same point by crediting director Dick Lester with identifying the saying by Ringo, though Lennon also used the phrase in his own prose writing. Whether the recall was totally accurate, came from the band or the film director, or whether it came from the Kitt song can now never be conclusively proven. The most effective Ringoism, in terms of lasting significance, is probably the elliptical "Tomorrow Never Knows" which gives a truly enigmatic quality to the closing track on *Revolver*. The original title, "The Void," was rightly ditched once Ringo came up with this winner.

Ringo's current habit of giving himself time to think when he speaks without notes means he allows himself an "errr" or "umm" often delivered in a perfect nasal twang halfway between Toxteth and California. It may well be that this habit, combined with his adherence to Transcendental Meditation, has finally allowed him to master the mental muddle that prompted the mirth amongst his school friends, but a number of online repositories exist collecting Ringoisms and his best moments of wit, like: "I like Beethoven, especially the poems" and "I think I was nostalgic at birth."

The Beatles Completed a whole Tour Without Ringo: If Pete Best wants consolation when he thinks about what he missed when Ringo replaced him he can always contemplate the up and down story of Jimmy Nicol. Nicol was the drummer drafted in when Ringo had tonsillitis and had to sit out some of the 1964 world tour. Ringo is a noted grafter and he pushed himself to the point of collapse before being persuaded he needed medical help. Incidentally, in the late eighties something similar happened when Ringo, struggling with a drink problem, still put in 15 hour days with producer Chips Moman, and even submitted to vocal coaching from Moman's wife, singer Toni Wine. Dissatisfied with the results Ringo and Moman ended up in court disputing the producer's right to release the music, Moman won. But, with a less willing worker the tapes wouldn't have existed in the first place. We digress.

Jimmy Nicol rehearsed live material with the other Beatles, having qualified for the role with a good performance on a sound alike album of Beatle covers. Paul's observation that Nicol played well but genuine fans would accept no substitute for Ringo at a recording session was probably fair. Most likely Nicol thought less of George's observation that the line-up put together to honour the tour dates was akin to a car with three wheels. In retrospect it was probably a bad idea to squeeze Nicol into one of Ringo's suits, i.e. a suit owned by Ringo. The jacket fit fine, but Nicol's legs were noticeably too long for Ringo's trousers. A more respectful move involved shortening the live show to ten songs by dropping Ringo's solo spot on "I Wanna Be Your Man." It is widely, and erroneously, believed that Nicol completed a full Australian tour. In fact he played live dates in Holland and Hong Kong before filling in four times in Australia, by which time Ringo was back and the band posed for a unique five man publicity shot. From that point, Ringo drummed out the tour.

Nicol was briefly in demand and went on to deputise for Dave Clark in the Dave Clark Five. But, as Bill Harry's *Ringo Starr Encyclopedia* notes "the high-profile image of being a Beatle didn't bring the expected offers and success that Jimmy had imagined. He didn't even get to meet them again." A solo single stiffed and by the end of April 1965 Jimmy was declared bankrupt, with only £50 to his name, over £4000 of debt and only nine months on the calendar since he had last worked with The Beatles. Jimmy's rueful comment, "after the headlines died I died too" sums up the experience. In retrospect he thought he'd been doing better pocketing £30-40 a week for sessions prior to the handful of dates with The Beatles. Things picked up a little when Jimmy was drafted into the Swedish instrumental outfit The Spotniks. Nicol eventually went into the building trade and often shied away from offers to discuss his Beatle past. Ironically, though not surprisingly in the context of the stories discussed in this book, Nicol's increasingly reclusive ways promoted a death rumour that broke in 1988. He has not been a public figure for many years but a few articles and the increasingly eclectic Beatles material on the web do keep tabs on Jimmy's continued existence.

I can't predict Jimmy's future but it seems a certainty that whatever he does, some dedicated Beatles follower will eventually bring news of this to a website. Perhaps more predictable is the observation that anyone so dedicated as to read this book to these final points about Jimmy Nicol might be dedicated enough to read a complete volume dedicated to Jimmy's bittersweet life story. If I've just described you then you may well want to hunt down a copy of *The Beatle Who* Vanished (2013) by Jim Berkenstadt.

Chapter 5

The Beatles Never Acknowledged a Major Part of their Real Output, and they Never Really Split up!

O
r to give the chapter its full and unwieldy title: There is a Vast Archive of Covert Beatles Material Available if you know Where to Look. Much of it Unacknowledged by the Band, one Reason for this is that The Beatles Carried on a Covert Career Recording under Assumed Names and Continued this Long after they had Officially Split

The basis of this rumour is long established and very well recorded in some books and websites. The stories have become better known over time despite the fact that much of the evidence, in the form of the records they supposedly released in secret, lie a long way in the past. The rampant downloading of files and the advent of sites like YouTube have been central to keeping the various rumours alive. Another element keeping these stories alive is the ongoing conflict in accounts regarding unreleased Beatle music. As long ago as 1976 when Parolophone set about reissuing all the band's singles and achieved a brief chart blitz as a result it was widely reported that nothing much of any value remained in the archives. It was reported that a few songs, mainly incomplete, had been considered for additional releases but the range and quality of material was such that this seemed a bad idea. The appeal of outtakes, alternative takes and session material hadn't been proven in the market at this point so it would have been difficult for EMI's A&R chiefs to predict the subsequent success of the *Archives* series. However, the implication that there was very little left unreleased and the sheer scale of the three release *Archives* series highlights the mismatch between some official accounts of what remains to be released and the real situation. Over the years the relentless fact finding of Beatle fanatics has put detailed lists of every possible recording into the public domain. It has also fuelled the belief amongst the more paranoid and fanatical that the failure to release some material or acknowledge the existence of particular tracks amounted to deliberate secrecy on the part of those in a position to issue the material. From this point onwards it is easy to understand how some of the more credulous seekers of rare Beatle sounds could easily be persuaded that a few non-Beatle cuts were really the work of the band.

Alan Clayson and Spencer Leigh's *The Walrus Was Ringo* (2003) devotes four pages to a list of unreleased material, concentrating mainly on tracks known for certain to exist. Whether –

for example – anyone will now see fit to find a release for Rolf Harris using The Beatles as his backing band in a 1963 version of "Tie Me Kangaroo Down Sport" is debateable. That one's for fans dedicated above and beyond the point of enjoying every track, surely. Clayson and Leigh's book barely scratches the surface with regard to live recordings, several of which have been bootlegged and contain very familiar material captured in what would now be deemed poor recording quality. Online sources also explore in some depth the potential for entire new albums of material to be released. Perhaps the greatest prize amongst these is the – alleged – existence of good quality material sufficient to create another *Anthology* style release and culled from early sessions for the White Album held at George Harrison's home, Kinfauns in Esher. Some, but not all of the recordings, have appeared on the final *Anthology* album but the bootlegging of other songs recorded in these sessions suggests there is more available. The bootleg tracks appear to come from mono recordings belonging to John whilst the material used on *Anthology* comes from George's stereo recordings, suggesting that everything, including the material already bootlegged, is available in stereo and a Kinfauns Sessions release is possible in future, perhaps showcasing the longer and unedited versions of these songs and making available Beatle demos of the songs "(I'm Just a) Child of Nature", (the song later reworked as "Jealous Guy") and the Harrison songs "Circles" and "Sour Milk Sea."

Chasing unreleased and alleged Beatle works online is a perplexing business, often bringing you up against the same stories and tracks. The following is a top ten of works occasionally attributed to The Beatles and/or rumoured to exist. This little chart is compiled to showcase the range of reasons spurious Beatle links emerge to material never originated by the band.

The L.S. Bumble Bee
A 1967 single by comedians Peter Cook and Dudley Moore, originally issued on the Decca label. The song has subsequently appeared on Beatle bootlegs. Its failure to snag much airplay or get anywhere near a chart meant it remained largely unknown before it began to be claimed by bootleggers as a genuine Beatle cut. The production is highly professional with a harmony chorus – obviously performed by session singers – and erupting sound effects including a crying baby. So, the notion of this as a head-on collision between a cheery McCartney tune, some off-the-wall Lennon sound effects and the knock about Beatle humour of all the boys isn't such a stretch. In the less than reputable world of rampant bootlegging the temptation to pass this off as the genuine article also makes sense. A close listen to the well- produced vocals is enough to convince most Beatle fanatics this isn't the band, though the sheer quality of the work suggests it is the kind of thing they would have attempted. The fairly obvious spoof on psychedelia is so well handled that the track manages to satirise and celebrate the whole scene. Cook's disdainful vocal is a brilliant comic turn and Dudley's music expertly parodies psyche-pop. In 1981 Dudley Moore commented on the record: "Regarding 'The L.S. Bumble Bee', Peter Cook and I recorded that song about the time when there was so much fuss about L.S.D., and when everybody thought that 'Lucy In The Sky With Diamonds' was a reference to drugs. The exciting alternative offered to the world was L.S.B! and I wrote the music to, in some ways, satirize the Beach Boys rather than the Beatles. But I'm grateful if some small part of the world thinks that it may have been them, rather than us!"

"Have You Heard The Word"

Arguably the most celebrated of all the alleged recordings. This one is so convincing Yoko went as far as to claim and copyright it as her late husband's work. It isn't. But the blatant John Lennon impersonation on the record is good enough to fool many who have given it a cursory listen. The song's regular appearance on Beatle bootlegs is also a source of common belief that it is a late sixties session outtake by the boys. "Have You Heard The Word" packs an insistent chorus and a big cluttered sound. Opening on a Lennonesque strumming of acoustic guitar and a reedy bass that bursts out and clogs the sound the song soon morphs into chunky piano and a Lennonesque snarl intoning a cynical/hopeful questioning of whether the listener has ever heard the word. Just past the two minute mark a bridge brings in a blast of insanity and the lead vocal hits a fleeting half scream in true Lennon style before the original tune and arrangement returns to a shambolic fade out with some obvious humour and a final Lennonesque spoken "so you've heard the word, then?" The reply in a comic scouse accent from someone pretending – apparently – to be George Harrison is much less convincing, but at this point the record is almost over. The lead vocal takes on Lennon's style and mimics it expertly. The compression on the vocal gives a slightly low-fi feel and the ending in which the song falls apart rather than concluding gives it a session quality of something being tried out. So, all in all, it sounds like a plausible stab at a demoing late Beatle album track, or run through for something Lennon would use on a solo album.

Four of the five piece line up of The Fut – for whom this is the one and only official single release – are known, but it's anyone's guess who is drumming. This is in fact a quietly issued recording by one genuine high-profile sixties hero, but this time we're acknowledging the singular talent of Maurice Gibb. It's the Bee Gee channelling the Lennon style so well and balancing the cynical and inspirational to such effect. Rumours of it being a Beatle cut were well enough known during Lennon's lifetime for him to be asked about it and to go on record denying it, but Yoko, prompted by its appearance on bootlegs, claimed it for Lenono Music in 1985. In reality it is composed by Steve Groves and Steve Kipner who both appear on the track. Some claim has also been made for a composition credit for Billie Lawrie (brother of singer Lulu), who sings backing vocals and was at that time Maurice Gibb's brother-in-law. The song is compiled on the awesome *Love, Poetry & Revolution* a monster 3CD trawl of the best of the British psychedelic underground, where it more than holds its own with an explosion of creative talent.

"The Girl That I Love"

1965 single credited to The Beatles and – basically – nothing to do with them. It's an old-school rock 'n' roll number with a swooping "ooh ooh" doo wop falsetto part and a gleefully gormless refrain of "dong dong diddley." The lead singer heaps praise on the subject of his infatuation. The girl is such a stunner "you'd have to see her for yourself" to get the scale of her attractiveness etc. etc. All standard fifties stuff and perfectly honed to sit next to the likes of Danny and the Juniors on a jukebox. But from the blatant American accents to its backward looking sound and style this is NOT Liverpool's inspired and forward looking Fab Four of the same era. Available for your delight online in the kind of places you'd expect to find it.

"I'm Waking (All Alone)"
1965 single credited to John and Paul, a pair who may – just – be mistaken for the two main song-writing Beatles. As with "The Girl That I Love." Its main claim to be Beatle-related product ends once you've gone past the name of the act and sampled what's on offer. In this case the London Records release is a muscular and fairly simple piece of standard sixties ballad pop with few surprises once you've sussed that the singer is walking alone because the object of his affections has dumped him. The simplest lyrical rhymes and the blatant American accent make it clear this isn't anything to do with The Beatles and the one notable element in an otherwise unremarkable outing comes with a few spirited licks on an organ. Since there is only one singer it's a fair assumption that whichever one of the duo – John or Paul – is not singing must be the organ licker! Oddly this cut has seen action on Beatle bootlegs. One rumour – which presumably helped it remain active in that area – is that this cut is very early Beatle work and Pete Best is the singer, not so!

"Sing This All Together"
The argument here is that a Beatle recording has remained hidden in plain sight for years. It hasn't, but at least it's a more credible suggestion than those expecting people to believe the "John and Paul" single above had anything to do with the band. This track from the Rolling Stones' *Their Satanic Majesties Request* album leaks *Sgt Pepper's...* influences, as does the front cover of the album where the Stones sit resplendent surrounded by enough enigmatic artwork and frippery to beg fans to study the cover. The London party scene at the time made the Stones and Beatles familiar acquaintances so it wasn't much of an imaginative stretch to picture The Beatles gathered in the studio to contribute to the big crowd of vocalists who intrude between the opening trumpets and piano noodling and the fade out. It's a stoned and slightly debauched sing-along simply made for loading your loaded mates in the studio and getting them involved. It's a nice thought, and completely plausible that The Beatles could have done this, their distinctive voices lost because the crowd stay behind Jagger and are miked up as one, but years of rumour are wrong, there are no Beatles here. It's a decent bit of psychedelia though.

"Lies"
As with "Have You Heard The Word" this work has seen action on Beatle bootlegs because its sheer quality and similarity to legit Beatles releases suggests it belongs there. Unlike anything else on this top ten its qualities have also been its main strength in ensuring a decades long affection and collectability for the song. It long ago outgrew its rumoured association with The Beatles and became known for the mini-masterpiece it undoubtedly is. "Lies" boasts an improbably simple vocal refrain built around the title, a cascade of clichéd lyrics so expertly handled you know the writers are having fun with the form because they have talent to burn, and a deft little guitar lick that – just – about – qualifies as a riff. The mass vocal chorus repeating the title is pure Beatles as is the muscular guitar sound. If there's an instant give away that this is someone other than the Fab Four it's the harder, rockier, less Ringoesque drumming that impels this corker of a cut. The band responsible – Knickerbockers – are rightly celebrated amongst the greatest there and gone garage guitar bands of the sixties and

"Lies" has long been a standout in the embarrassment of compiled riches available on various versions of the classic *Nuggets* compilations. These albums brought belated recognition to the bands spawned in America between the British invasion and the last moments of first wave psychedelia. "Lies" just about straddles all of those styles, though it is first and foremost a garage band at the height of their powers.

"Magical Misery Tour"
A spoof so blatant, accurate and expertly realised that most of those encountering it on the National Lampoon's *Radio Dinner* album were reduced rapidly to giggles and got the joke. Tony Hendra's Lennon impersonation is nasal, cutting and rabidly sarcastic as he emotes a catalogue of pain and loneliness. The massive "Magical Misery Tour" joke is that this is Lennon, caught in the throes of recording the *Plastic Ono Band* album having a load off at – like – everyone, bar Yoko, of course. His fellow Beatles are misguided, for example George with his "fookin' Hari Krishna," the band's rivals are useless and Mick Jagger "with his stupid faggot dancing" can't touch Beatle achievements. In addition Lennon's Aunt Mimi has been in his bad books since she threw his childhood drawings away and Lennon has – therefore - endured a lifetime of painful under-appreciation. So now he's getting even by channelling the whole effort into one monumental piano song with accompanying primal screams. The tirade concludes with screams, assertions that "genius is pain" and a rant that breaks out of the singing, leaving the song to fade and fall apart at the same time. Few better parodies take on and celebrate artistic integrity with such skill, though The National Lampoon probably deserve some credit for getting almost as close with their Neil Young-alike "Southern California Brings Me Down." A few Beatle scholars have rightly acknowledged that a smattering of the highly credulous have mistaken Beatle parodies for genuine Beatles' work, putting "Magical Misery Tour" up there with the work of The Rutles (a skilful Beatle parody act with Neil Innes as their main creative force) and one-off joke records like Kenny Everett's "Bye Bye Bye." "Magical Misery Tour" is the least convincing of the parodies, but edges the mention in this chapter because – assuming you haven't heard it – it's a corker and worth a few minutes of your time to seek out and enjoy.

"Season of the Witch"
In their chronicle of Beatle product *All Together Now* Harry Castleman and Walter J. Podrazik cite the parent album of this track as "The only album to be recorded after it was reviewed!" "Season of the Witch" is what you think, the Donovan psych-folk standard. The confusion here regards who you might be listening to. The singer is – apparently – Bob Dylan but he's doing the unthinkable and covering Donovan, complete with a fairly accurate appropriation of Donvan's vocal style. So, this is a complete about turn from the public sarcasm heaped on the hippie troubadour by Dylan in the *Don't Look Back* documentary. "Season of the Witch" nestles on the one and only album by The Masked Marauders. The album came about after a spurious article written under a pseudonym by journalist Greil Marcus discussed the existence of a taped jam featuring what would have passed as the ultimate late sixties/early seventies supergroup. Marcus was poking fun at the fashion for supergroups and the targets of his fun were the likes of Crosby, Stills, Nash and Young and Blind Faith but his article cited Dylan, along with various Stones and Beatles as the participants. Predictably tapes duly surfaced,

earning radio play and a record deal, at which point sales of 100,000 copies ensued. But this was always a cult item, little prone to turning up in second hand bins. So once the furore had died down the album remained an in-joke to those nerdish enough to buy it and get the consistent and generally funny gags on offer. Those too young to register the original story were unlikely to chance upon the treasured album in second hand bins because few owners were prone to parting with it. These younger and more unwary types might hear some of the cuts and be fooled into thinking it was the real thing. Like the dead Beatle legends one part of this process might involve an older person deliberately misleading a younger one into falling for the hoax. In this regard "Season of the Witch" is one of the better Beatle hoaxes because it doesn't attempt to pass off a Beatle vocal. However, the bass guitar and piano work that push the track along for over ten minutes suggest Paul McCartney may, indeed, be in attendance on one of those instruments. It's gloriously loose and very much like a bunch of top musicians getting into the vibe. There's a combination of precision, confidence and inventive lines on the bass that is very McCartneyesque. When albums like *Super Session* were allowing the likes of Al Kooper – who is involved with The Masked Marauders – Steve Stills and Mike Bloomfield to spin out the rock songs of their generation into supergroup self-indulgence The Masked Marauders hoax didn't sound out of place at all.

"Peace of Mind (The Candle Burns)"
AKA "Peace of Mind" this is a glorious piece of late sixties weirdness opening with a long vocal section before a pop song breaks out in scratchy low-fi with tape hiss and a vocal distorted by crude production effects. The off-key twanging in the background can't decide if it's an out of tune guitar or the perfunctory efforts of an enthusiastic but unfocussed sitar player. Lyrically it's a wonderful deep and meaningless exploration of inner space with the lead singer being joined by others now and again. So, a few Beatle tricks are there, and there's even a backward section to enjoy. The Beatle angle claims this as a White Album demo/outtake picked from a rubbish bin at Apple HQ, hence the provisional quality of the performance and poor sound quality. A hard listen to the vocals betrays a spirited attempt at Lennon impersonation, but the sharpness and distinction of the great man's voice is absent. If anything, this is an actor giving us a very stagey Lennon. The meandering sitar, suggesting George in a state of slight disrepair desperately trying to keep up with proceedings as they run through the song is probably the real delight here, because – if the whole thing is a wind up – this is a damn good joke and probably worth the effort of hunting it down on YouTube. Another, faintly plausible, twist on the same track suggests the retrieval from the dustbin story is true but the song is the work of some hopeful bunch of unknowns offering a demo tape to Apple Records. If that's the case the anonymous band in question have never come forward to claim the moment of cult stardom which would surely follow once the various internet homes of Beatle bootleg discussion were alerted.

"Pink Litmus Paper Shirt"
At this point let's bow to the power of shared wisdom online and simply quote the Wikipedia on Beatle bootlegs, because "Pink Litmus Paper" shirt has grown wings. Wikipedia notes: "In 1971, humorist Martin Lewis compiled a Beatles bootleg discography for Disc magazine, inserting four song titles he'd simply made up: the John Lennon polemic "Left Is Right (And

Right Is Wrong)," George Harrison's "Pink Litmus Paper Shirt," a Paul McCartney vaudeville-style number "Deck Chair," and another supposed Lennon track, "Colliding Circles". These spurious tunes were then picked up by other compilers who have continued to propagate them ever since, despite the complete lack of any evidence for their existence. Outsider musician R. Stevie Moore has since written and recorded tunes entitled "Pink Litmus Paper Shirt" and "Colliding Circles", making them real songs—just not real Beatles songs."

What Wikipedia hadn't got round to noting as this research was done, but I'll point out here, is that the band Strange Turn have also recorded a song called "Pink Litmus Paper Shirt." The point of my rant being that history has proven that taking on board a Beatle hoax and turning it into genuine music can easily lead to the unwary and befuddled someday discovering your work and mistaking it for the real deal. A twee piece of psychedelia rejoicing in the title of "Pink Litmus Paper Shirt" sounds like the kind of concoction George Harrison would produce alongside "It's All Too Much," "Blue Jay Way" and "Only a Northern Song." Strange Turn explore the simple rhymes and knowing sentiments of those tracks from the outset rhyming "strange things are happening to me" with "Salvador Dali." Go George! This is a catchy and muscular piece of psych-pop with a strident guitar chord opening, and a gradual ratcheting up of the weirdness. For all that it remains a tale of an individual looking at confused circumstances and trying to make sense of it all whilst wearing a pink litmus paper shirt. With its little oasis of clear focus amidst the insanity it's all very George Harrison, all the more so because the simple melody and the concentration of the lyrics on how the singer feels suggest that Harrisonesque quality of reflection and the ability to channel the experience for others to understand. There's some agreeable weirdness, including sampled Shakespearean dialogue (from Act 1, scene 1 of *Hamlet* if you want to be pedantic) at the end, not something George usually went in for. But, then, the genius here is that nobody is likely to mistake this for a genuine George recording. They might just believe this a cover version of a George song unreleased by The Beatles. If you ever see that claim online, remember where you read it first. Or, if you are a wind-up merchant yourself, gather some mates, record a song called "Left Is Right (And Right Is Wrong)," "Pink Litmus Paper Shirt" or "Deck Chair," give yourselves an enigmatic name, and put the results on Bandcamp with little in the way of information about who you are…

So it goes.

The reasons the songs above found their way into Beatle rumour show the main routes to this ongoing and ever-expanding archive. The internet has not necessarily been The Beatles' friend in this battle. It may have helped to identify and present information on the real membership of a highly obscure act like The Fut but as fast as a definitive solution to this mystery is offered other mysteries appear. The widespread ripping and sharing of music files means most people now hear their new music divorced from any details of a parent album, or even much information about the performers. Music is music and it's freely available, so people hear first and investigate later. Often they hear first, and assume they know. One song provably believed by some to be a Beatle tune is "Mr Blue Sky" by the ELO. "Gladstone" posting on Cracked.com adds it in a list of half a dozen songs widely believed to be by artists who never recorded them. Gladstone even links in to other evidence posted on that site where people have linked it with The Beatles. Incidentally, the #1 in his chart shows that many people believe Bob Marley sang "Don't Worry Be Happy." The late-sixties Beatles were clearly a massive influence on the ELO, and The Move who preceded the ELO. But "Mr Blue Sky" is surely too much of a seventies production to fool too many people.

When the sounds are so similar it is possible to fool a lot of people at once. Such is the case with the parody-Beatle songs of The Rutles. "Cheese and Onions" in particular has the power to mislead those with a casual acquaintance with The Beatles. The funny mockumentary made by George Harrison's friend Eric Idle, and featuring George and Mick Jagger is available on DVD but seldom gets an airing in front of a large television audience, leaving the recorded works free to roam around the internet and mug the unwary. "Cheese and Onions" even has its own video ripping off the style of *Yellow Submarine.* So, the presence of the track on some Beatle bootlegs isn't so surprising, though Yoko has yet to be fooled into copyrighting this one. Similarly, Badfinger's "Come and Get It" sounds very like The Beatles because it was recorded under the direction of Paul McCartney, who instructed the band to copy the demo of the song he had written. McCartney had a contract to provide three songs for the movie *The Magic Christian* starring Ringo and Peter Sellers and the open-ended lyrics to "Come and Get It" make a lot more sense in the context of the movie's story about a wealthy prankster, fond of using his financial power to show the absurdities of capitalism. More songs have been briefly mistaken for The Beatles than can be usefully listed here. In the countless Beatle bootleg recordings on offer a number of these songs have been compiled, perhaps as an innocent mistake but more likely as a cynical ploy to put some sales on a bootleg by convincing the buyer there was at least one genuine rarity on offer. The round up below would not have been possible without Doug Sulpy's *The 910's Guide to the Beatles Outtakes.* A few of the other regular candidates in the tracks mistaken for genuine Beatle cuts include works by artists sharing a name with the band, like John Lennon and the Bleechers "Ram you Hard" (sexually explicit reggae with genuine west Indian accent from "John Lennon" but nothing like The Beatles). A few other groups of the Beatles' era and afterwards managed the same uncanny overlapping of sounds that made Knickerbockers' "Lies" such a ringer for The Beatles. Perennial performers in this area in terms of bootleg inclusion include The Fourmost's "I Love You Too" (a harmonious slice of beat-ballad with a lively bongo rhythm), The End's "Shades of Orange/ Loving Sacred Loving" (choppy hippie pop with a hint of the lighter end of *Sgt. Pepper* – actually culled from a highly collectable album produced by Bill Wyman), "We are the Moles" by The Moles (Lennonesque weirdness in the "Magical Mystery Tour" style and actually recorded by Simon Dupree and the Big Sound), "I Wonder" by The Gants (cheery beat group fodder with a fuzz guitar and McCartneyesque chorus), Smyle's "It's Gonna be Alright" (blatant Beatle sound-alike pop from canny Dutch style-copyists) and Campbell's Lavender Circus' "N. Bourbaki's Multicoloured Jam" (B-Side of a single so obscure it didn't offer itself anywhere online during the research for this book, rumoured to be the work of an Arkansas garage band, also the subject of much online discussion debating its very existence), "That Thing You Do" by The Oneders/ Wonders (a unsurprising inclusion from the movie of the same name starring Tom Hanks as the manager of a one-hit wonder U.S. band), and "I'm Sad The Goat Just Died Today" by The Frogs (one and a quarter minutes of low-fi piano driven nonsense and morose musing, in a comic style). Regarding The Frogs it should be noted that "I'm Sad The Goat Just Died Today" appears on *My Daughter The Broad*

(1996) by the Milwaukee mavericks where it shares the playlist with delights like "Grandma's Sitting on the Corner with a Penis in Her Hand Going 'No, No, No, No, No.'" You get the impression John Lennon would have loved these guys. A few other items also make the spurious bootleg list, notably a very short fragment known as "Carnival of Light" which contains speeded up guitars and feedback and a range of production effects. "Carnival of Light" exists in short and long forms, a near 15 minute version widely available online sounds like what it is claimed to be; a monumental experiment recorded around the time of the *Sgt Pepper's...* album. The one major stumbling block here is the obvious point that *Anthology 3* didn't belatedly claim this avant-garde wonder. The drumming isn't exactly typical Ringo either. "Oh, I Need You" sometimes known as "Oh, I Want You" is another low-fi cut that sounds for all the world like a demo. Chunky piano and drums battling along and begging for a decent production sound. There and gone just past one minute and 41 seconds this one stays just long enough to reveal the Beatles' style isn't matched by Beatle vocals. A few bootleg watchers online believe it to be an Abbey Road recording and put it in with the likes of Badfinger by crediting it to the band Mortimer (a band of Beatle protégés who were once signed to Apple).

Beyond the individual tracks above there are several albums which have – however briefly or erroneously – been credited to The Beatles. Probably the most celebrated such rumour briefly identified the eponymous debut by Canadian band Klaatu (1976). Klaatu's own official site still celebrates the various strands of evidence that raised the rumour in the first place. Superficially they have some merit, but they also show the desperate levels some fans would go to to prove a Beatles reunion had finally occurred. Klaatu, incidentally, is the name of a humanoid alien played by actor Michael Rennie in *The Day The Earth Stood Still.* The cover of Ringo's *Goodnight Vienna* is a recreation of a still from that movie with Ringo as Klaatu, see point nine below.

The band Klaatu's website credits Steve Smith, a reporter with The Providence Rhode Island Journal with starting the rumour by writing a piece making the initial suggestion. The rumour overlaps with the Paul is dead story but in this little offshoot the Klaatu record is a lost Beatle album between *Revolver* and *Sgt Pepper's...* It doesn't take much of a listen to *Klaatu* to spot seventies production trickery, or the fact the band don't sound like The Beatles in the vocals or harmonies. Never-the-less the official Klaatu site highlights a series of numbered clues that fuelled the story once it got going, clues 19 onwards relate to other Klaatu albums so only those linking the first – eponymous - album and its alleged link to The Beatles are copied below. As an aside, the first Klaatu album wasn't eponymous in their native Canada where it was titled *3:47 EST.* Capitol Records were unimpressed with the enigmatic title and resolved to use the band's name to try and sell the album in the U.S. But we digress again. Those clues, celebrated on Klaatu's website:

1. The record was on Capitol records, the American record company that had released most of the Beatles' records in the US.
2. The record had no names of band members listed on it anywhere.
3. The record had no producer name on it anywhere. It simply said, "Produced by Klaatu."

4.   The record had no songwriter credits other than simply, "All selections composed by Klaatu."
5.   The record has a mysterious publisher listed. It says, "All selections published by Klaatu ASCAP/CAPAC." (The US re-issue in 1981 says the songs are published by Welbeck Music Corp/ASCAP and MCA Music/ASCAP)
6.   CAPAC (see clue number 5) is the Canadian equivalent of America's ASCAP and Britain's BMI and John Lennon had recently been rumored to be moving to Toronto Canada since the US was trying to deport him.
7.   The record had no pictures of band members on it anywhere.
8.   On a couple of songs (Calling Occupants, Sub-Rosa Subway) the vocals sound like Paul McCartney & John Lennon.
9.   The name Klaatu is taken from the movie "The Day The Earth Stood Still" in which the alien named Klaatu tells his robot Gort to stop hurting people with the command, "Klaatu barada niktu!" On Ringo Starr's Goodnight Vienna album Ringo is seen coming out of the spaceship from that movie and is standing next to Gort.
10. When Sgt. Pepper had been released, the inner sleeve showed Paul McCartney with a patch on his uniform which read O.P.D. Although many interpretations of this have come and gone, one of them was used in the Paul is dead myth, "Officially Presumed Dead". During the song Sir Bodsworth Rugglesby III on their first album, the lyrics state, "Officially Presumed Is Dead." Thanks to the outtakes of the Sgt. Pepper picture that are included with the CD we can now see that the patch says O.P.P. which stands for Ontario Provincial Police. Since John Lennon had been rumoured to be moving to Ontario, this fits the rumour that Klaatu was the Beatles quite nicely.
11. Capitol Records USA messed up a song title [does this surprise us?] on the original release, listing it as Sir Bodsworth Rubblesby III. This mistake carried onto their subsequent reissues until the first CD issue on Capitol which finally corrected this error. Says Crazy Ray, of WDRC (*see below*) in Waterbury, CT, "If you were to define Bods, Worth, Rubbles, and By, it would mean 'persons of importance born of quarry.' The Beatles were first known as the Quarrymen."
12. Beetles are heard to be chirping and buzzing at the start of Calling Occupants. (Sounds more like Crickets and some birds to me.....)
13. The song title, Sub-Rosa Subway was thought to be a take off on Paul's Red Rose Speedway.
14. In Sir Bodsworth Rugglesby III there is the line, "he's the only man who's ever been to hell and come back alive." Some people thought that this was a reference to the Paul is Dead rumor which states that Paul died in 1966 in a car crash and was replaced with a look-alike making it seem like he had come back alive.
15. While there are 8 trees pictured right at the very bottom of the front cover of the band's first album, only 7 have their roots showing. There are 7 letters in the name Beatles.
16. On the back cover of the first album is a two colored planet. Some took this to be an allusion to Paul's album, "Venus and Mars".
17. On Abbey Road the Beatles sing about the "Sun King". The Klaatu album covers all have a picture of the sun on them.

18. The initials for the Beatles last album, Abbey Road, are AR. If spelled backwards that becomes RA which is the name of the Egyptian god of the sun. See number 17 for the "sun" connection.

(source klaatu.org)

There isn't a strong suggestion that Klaatu set out to mislead anyone into thinking they were a reunited Beatles. Their celebration online of the alleged link is more a bemused recounting of the evidence. In reality the band were an accomplished if slightly nerdy bunch taking advantage of studio trickery to produce an album of varied sounds and styles. They don't sound much like Boston (who also emerged at the time) but share a similar vision of unleashing a debut album with only the band name (or a highly enigmatic title) out front and letting the music find a following on FM radio and amongst dedicated record buyers.

A slightly more cynical linking of a little-known band with an allegedly reformed Beatles also took place in 1976. Ironically this started with the type of good natured hippie ideals that had fuelled some of the most creative ideas of the late sixties. As the website popgeekheaven.com notes: "In the early '70s, Ronan O'Rahilly, the founder of British pirate radio station Radio Caroline began to use the radio station to promote an pseudo-Eastern philosophy called Loving Awareness. This philosophy promoted social and personal change through the awareness and encouragement of loving feelings. Disc jockeys, especially Tony Allan, interspersed their programs with Loving Awareness adages and jingles."

Ronan O'Rahilly followed up on the announcements with the funding of an eponymous album recorded by a band called Loving Awareness. The various band members were seasoned pros who had been there or thereabouts in the British music scene of the late sixties onwards. Keyboardist Mick Gallagher and guitarist John Turnbull had been together through the bands Skip Bifferty and Arc. Bassist Norman Watt-Roy and drummer Charley Charles had done the rounds as well. All four would later get some moments of glory in Ian Dury's Blockheads. Once the album was released a publicity campaign invoked the name of The Beatles repeatedly, once again I'm indebted to popgeekheaven; "Promotion for the resulting album… explicitly drew the connection of the band to the heritage of the Beatles. At a press conference announcing the release of the album, an open letter to the Beatles was read, which asked for permission to use the Beatles' name to promote the Loving Awareness cause as well as the album. A placard behind the band at the press conference stated plainly, 'Meet the Beatles.' This connection was also an important theme on the inside gatefold for the album. On a chalkboard next to the band, a one word question appears—"Beatles?"—along with the phrases "A is for apple" and "B is for Beatles." On a cupboard behind the band, four 8×10 portraits of the members of the Loving Awareness band are placed directly below the photos of the individual Beatles that were included with the White Album."

Those watching the press conference proceedings with interest were likely appalled at what they saw. But, these days the strongest suit in the album's torrid existence on the edge of rumoured Beatle product is its very obscurity. A combination of poor distribution and lack of interest beyond the initial press conference meant the sales of the album appear to have topped out somewhere just beyond 10,000. Radio Caroline of course gave it heavy play and the announcements ahead of many plays invoked The Beatles' name in some way. So unwary listeners, and those perusing the gatefold albums in record shops were often brought up short by product associated with the name. To many the use of The Beatles' name suggested the album must have some official connection with the band. That confusion led many to investigate the music. Musically the record is a strong slice of lengthy and accomplished mid-seventies pop/rock. If you encountered an announcement on Radio Caroline and stopped to listen once you heard the Beatle name, or found yourself looking an album cover with "Loving Awareness" on an otherwise blank front and "Beatles" written inside, your first reality check would be to investigate how the band sounded. Whichever track you heard from this point might just intrigue you. *Loving Awareness* and the band of the same name knew exactly what had to be done. The album imagines The Beatles who last convened on *Abbey Road* as if they had reformed, given the likes of 10cc and ELO a listen and then rolled up their sleeves to show these chancers how to craft the most listenable and credible radio friendly music of the mid-seventies. The album is musically ambitious, dripping Beatlesque vocals, happy to throw in some backward masks and unafraid of the big issues in the lyrics. "Existence" is a near eight-minute epic linking romance with the entire point of human existence, and boasting a sparingly plinked sitar in the mix. That cut exposes the vocals to the point it clearly isn't the reunited Beatles, but catchier cuts like "Love You To Know" are so heavy on the sixties vocals and Beatle tricks they might just pass muster if heard in the background whilst others talked. The one jarring feature of the record is its reliance on a mystical strand in the lyrics that even the older guard of the mainstream music world was ditching by 1976. Well, that and the way the drumming gets a bit showy and ahead of the beat, bringing a strident efficiency in but losing any link to Ringo's typically characterful performances.

Less convoluted and simpler to explain is the (non) Beatle *Lord Sitar* album. The record is what you might expect. The 1969 album wasn't the first time Big Jim Sullivan (Lord Sitar) had picked up the Indian instrument. Indeed, the UK's top session guitarist had been in very heavy demand for his sitar skills ever since the pop world went mad for the instrument and many lead guitarists struggled themselves to a standstill attempting to carve out licks fit to add to the albums of their bands. Jim was something of a go to guy to rescue the situation and his abilities led to a series of solo outings. Before *Lord Sitar* his solo output also included *Sitar Beat* and *Sounds Of India*. *Lord Sitar* simply captured the imagination more widely, and even boasted a tasteful version of "Blue Jay Way." Elsewhere it was an infectious collision of old stagey sounds like "If I Were A Rich Man" and reworked rock and pop including "I Can See For Miles" and "Daydream Believer." The album boasts three Beatle tunes in all, leading a credulous few to think it was an uncredited solo George Harrison album, possibly with his fellow Beatles in support. At the time this didn't seem such a stretch given that the most exotic solo Beatle releases during the band's last years were George's *Wonderwall Music* and *Electronic Sound*. Lennon may have shaded it in terms of avant-garde solo music, but George clearly had an enjoyment of esoteric musical sounds and possibilities and *Lord Sitar* sounds fairly mainstream next to his first solo releases. So the idea that the album is George in action is a pleasant little notion but not one supported by the facts or the sweet exotica of the final results. These days the album finds many friends amongst collectors of exotic music. The odd burst of airplay on shows like *Stuart Maconie's Freak Zone* or Jeremy Smith's and my own *Strange Fruit* continues to propel public interest. Apart from any other reason to play it the collection offers so many options to change the mood of a radio show in an instant that it remains a gem amongst a sea of cash-in product from the same era. Sullivan (1941 – 2012) was such a ubiquitous figure in UK music circles that he may, just, have managed to pass a Beatle in a corridor once or twice and found time to discuss covering their songs with his sitar.

By contrast to both of the above the brief suggestion that The Residents were The Beatles pretty much ran its course with debates regarding the cover of *Meet The Residents* (1974) and its obvious parody of the *Meet The Beatles* front cover. The Residents' cover was soon changed when Capitol Records saw it and rang their lawyers, since when the art collective have carved out an insanely prolific career built mainly around musical works and multimedia output. The anonymity of the various members – who typically appear in pictures and on stage sporting huge eyeball helmets to cover their individual heads – also gave some fleeting momentum to the Residents/Beatles rumour. But if this was The Beatles they had truly done the unthinkable and surrendered all artistic direction to Yoko! The Residents' most accessible albums are typically those in which they take on and reimagine the works of well-known composers and stylists of popular music. Their take on James Brown is one such recording; offering a particularly explosive mix of two rabidly creative forces. It should also be noted in the context of this argument that "The Residents" and "accessible" are words which seldom appear in the same sentence, so the one above is an anomaly. The single "The Residents Play The Beatles and the Beatles Play The Residents" probably owes something to The Residents' own enjoyment of the brief Residents/Beatles rumour. The A' side is a sound collage incorporating Beatles clips and a snatch of John Lennon's "God." Along with easily identified song clips it features a sample from a The Beatles' third Christmas record. The other side of the Residents' single is a cover of "Flying" which suggests The Residents have always loved the track. The Residents are all over the slow psychedelic melody of "Flying" with doomy vocal harmonies and a single doleful drum before the inevitable explosion of Residents' creativity brings in a demonic chuckle and their trademark horror-movie chic production to bring a sinister element to an often overlooked Beatle winner. The Residents may not be The Beatles but they are amongst a select few who can rightfully claim to have covered The Beatles and matched the original for quality.

The rumours of a full blown Beatles reunion under an assumed name – more or less – died in the late seventies, though some of the tracks widely mistaken for Beatle work – like the work of the ELO – come from slightly later. For as long as John Lennon was alive the band did tend to congregate around Ringo's solo output. *Stop And Smell The Roses* was well underway when Lennon was killed. John had already offered Ringo the song "Life Begins at 40" and was planning to work with him on "Nobody Told Me" in January 1981. Ironically, Lennon's death brought about a full reunion of the other three on record. George's song "All Those Years Ago" had already been offered to Ringo for *Stop And Smell The Roses* but the high register vocals didn't suit Ringo and he recorded another George Harrison song, "Wrack my Brain," instead. "All Those Years Ago" was a tribute to Lennon. Harrison's version, released in 1981 included contributions from Ringo, and Paul and Linda McCartney. In the nineties two new singles "Free as a Bird" and "Real Love" did count as genuine Beatle work, boasting the band's name and contributions from all four of the Fabs. To date these represent the most recent full Beatle reunions.

Beatle business, including the managing of the band's catalogue and various ongoing business interests, has never gone away and – nominally at least – the band still exists, it's just that these days it includes the rhythm section and two widows. This quartet continue to make business decisions and help manage a catalogue that places the band amongst the top performers of record selling acts annually, to this day. The Beatles place as the biggest selling music act of all time, therefore, looks secure long into the future.

One other source of spurious Beatle product is so blatant it often remains hidden in plain sight. Official releases have caused some confusion because the odd mistake in titling or understanding the nature of a release has spawned rumours. Where there are rumours there is also the potential for bootleggers to make a quick profit. Perhaps the most celebrated Beatle album in terms of demonstrating this rumour-belief-product route is *The Beatles In Italy*. The official release sold poorly and was soon pulled from sale. The album comprised a compilation culled from other official releases, its unique selling point relied on it featuring the songs the band had played on their 1965 tour of Italy; numbers that went back to "Rock 'n' Roll Music" and "Twist and Shout" but came up to "Ticket to Ride." Harry Castleman and Walter J. Podrazik as far back as 1975 were warning that anyone believing *The Beatles In Italy* to be anything other than a compilation was in for a disappointment. Confusion arose about whether the collection was a genuine live album of the tour because John Lennon appeared to believe that it was, he responded to an interview question with a remark that clearly indicated he thought a live tape had been turned into an album. After which the scarce vinyl became highly collectible and people paid massive sums only to be massively disappointed when they slapped their rarities on the turntable. Decades later the number of Beatle bootlegs is sufficient to prompt people to write books on the subject, and openly admit there may be more product than anyone can ever chronicle accurately. Such a situation means now that you may find a *Beatles In Italy* bootleg offered and discover it is a live recording, or the studio cuts. If it is a live recording it may not have come from the country claimed. So the hunt for honest bootlegs, and rare Beatle recordings goes on, but rumours can start for the most innocent of reasons, and when they do, they fuel misunderstandings that are hard to clear up. Ironically, in preparing this book I tried a few friends, including some major Beatle fans with another Beatle track to test their reactions. "Cry for a Shadow" is an instrumental, clocking in a few seconds short of two and a half minutes. It's highly unusual in The Beatles' canon by being an instrumental, and it is unique as the only Harrison/Lennon composition officially released by the band. The recording dates from their Hamburg days and was originally planned as the B-Side of "Why" with Tony Sheridan on lead vocal. It was dropped from that record but eventually saw release in 1964, with "Why" relegated to the B-Side as Polydor saw the commercial potential in the few Beatle tracks they owned. Online write ups tend to cite the tune as a parody of The Shadows, but a more pragmatic view suggests The Beatles – including Pete Best on drums at this point – wouldn't have refused if someone discovered their talents and offered to record them as a competitor to The Shadows. "Cry for a Shadow" dates from 1961 when Cliff Richard's backing band could do very little wrong chart-wise. I struggled to convince some of those who heard the track they were listening to The Beatles. Lacking the distinctive voices the track is atypical of the band. But the examples above show how confusion becomes fact. If genuine Beatles music can confuse long-term fans, an individual Beatle can make a mistake when interviewed that sends collectors off in search of albums they believe to be something different to what they really are then any sounds, within reason, might pass muster. The point of my inflicting "Cry for a Shadow" on a few Beatle fans was more than curiosity about whether they would spot it. I was told in the compiling of this chapter, but couldn't source or prove, that over the years a few other anonymous low-fi instrumentals have been offered up online and via bootleg purporting to be the Harrison/Lennon track. All the clips I found on YouTube were the genuine Beatles cut, but YouTube and other forums are open to anyone who wants to post material. Some of the cuts mentioned in this chapter and wrongly believed to be genuine Beatle work appear on YouTube with tags suggesting they are the real thing. As a final twist in this strange meander it is worth noting that some Beatle work amounts to little more than a marginal contribution by one of the band, but a few gems exist in this area. The one unattainable item in this regard is a prime quality version of the single Frank Sinatra cut for the Apple label. "The Lady Is A Tramp" was re-recorded with new lyrics including: "She married Ringo, and she could have had Paul/That's why the lady is a champ." The whole effort was produced in honour of Maureen Starkey's 22nd birthday, given a catalogue number, pressed onto a precious few records and then consigned to collectability when the master tapes were destroyed. Poor quality versions have been bootlegged, but that may be all we get of a massive romantic gesture from Ringo.

There will never be complete clarity in these muddy waters. If this chapter has proven one thing beyond doubt it is that the demand for any Beatle work, especially rare Beatle work, will not go away. So the uncertainty about where the margins of the real work are will keep fuelling misunderstandings. The internet is both your friend and tormentor in this world, the present chapter is simply a crude map of what you might find in that labyrinth.

And finally...

The website that claims The Beatles never existed, or to be more specific: "The Beatles were always sets of multiples since their inception, and were not just four individual young men "from Liverpool", as we've been led to believe. Not particularly hard to find, or understand once you are on the site, the basic claim – supported by photographic evidence – is that the band's incredible work rate and achievements are more easily understood once you realise there was a team of look-aliky young men involved. They may have fooled most of the people most of the time when they were turning up on stage and cranking out albums but a detailed look at photographs and other material from back in the day reveals individual look-alikes were slightly different heights to their counterparts, sported slightly different teeth, you get the idea. thebeatlesneverexisted.com seeks to convince you.

Assuming you're the kind of dedicated reader who would consume the present book to the final words, this may be an online nugget capable of bemusing you, despite the mad meandering you've already enjoyed in this book.

Bibliography

A brief round-up of the most used and useful books in the writing of the present work:

Astucia, Salvadore - Rethinking John Lennon's Assassination: The FBI's War on Rock Stars – Ravening Wolf (2004)

Barratt, Colin - Ringo Starr in the News – Lulu.com (2015)

Bresler, Fenton – Who Killed John Lennon? - St Martin's Press (1989)

Castleman, Harry and Podrazik, Walter J. - All together now : the first complete Beatles discography - Ballantine Books (1975)

Clayson, Alan - The Quiet One: A Life of George Harrison – Sanctuary Music Publishing (1997)

Clayson, Alan - Ringo Starr: Straight Man or Joker? – Sanctuary Music Publishing (1997)

Clayson, Alan and Leigh, Spencer - The Walrus Was Ringo: 101 "Beatles" Myths Debunked – Chrome Dreams (2003)

Coleman, Ray – Lennon: The Definitive Biography – Harper Perennial (1999)

Constantine, Alex – The Covert War Against Rock – Feral House (2000)

Dailey, Forrest - The Fifth Magician: The Great Beatles Impostor Theory - 1st Book Library (2003)

Fawcett, Anthony – John Lennon: One Day at a Time: A Personal Biography of the Seventies – Grove Press (1980) (Note: Mark Chapman read the 1976 edition, now very hard to find, the 1980 edition was published after Lennon's death and is more readily available)

Goldman, Albert - The Lives of John Lennon - William Morrow & Co (1988)

Greene, Joshua M. - Here Comes the Sun: The Spiritual & Musical Journey of George Harrison – Bantam (2006)

Guiliano, Geoffrey - Dark Horse: The Life And Art Of George Harrison – Da Capo Press (1997)

Harrison, George and Harrison Olivia (introduction) – I, Me Mine – Phoenix (2004)

Harry, Bill - The George Harrison Encyclopedia – Virgin (2003)

Harry, Bill - The Ringo Starr Encyclopedia – Virgin (2004)

Jones, Jack - Let Me Take You Down: Inside the Mind of Mark David Chapman – Man Who Shot John Lennon – Virgin (1994)

Keith, Jim – Mind Control, World Control - Adventures Unlimited Press (1997)

Leng, Simon and Halberry, Dave - While My Guitar Gently Weeps: The Music Of George Harrison – Firefly (2002)

Lewis, Jon E. - Cover-Ups – Robinson (2008)

Lewisohn, Mark - The Beatles Day by Day: A Chronology 1962-1989 – Harmony Books

(1990)

MacDonald, Ian - Revolution in the Head: The Beatles' Records and the Sixties – Vintage (2008)

Moltmaker, Azing - PAUL IS DEAD!!!! OR............ IS RINGO DEAD???? DO YOU WANT TO KNOW THAT SECRET???? - From http://www.7inchrecords.com/books.Asp (2014)

Niezgoda, Joseph - The Lennon Prophecy: A New Examination of the Death Clues of the Beatles – New Chapter Press (2008)

Pang, May – Loving John – Corgi (1983)

Patterson, R. Gary - The Great Beatle Death Clues – Robson (1998)

Patterson, R. Gary - Take a Walk on the Dark Side: Rock and Roll Myths, Legends, and Curses – Simon and Schuster (2004)

Reeve, Andru J. - Turn Me On, Dead Man: The Beatles and the "Paul Is Dead" Hoax – AuthorHouse (2004)

Rolling Stone, Editors of and Harrison, Olivia (foreward) – George Harrison – Simon and Schuster (2002)

Shapiro, Mark - All Things Must Pass: The Life of George Harrison – St Martin's Press (2002)/ Virgin (2005)

Sounes, Howard - Fab: An Intimate Life of Paul McCartney – Harper Collins (2011)

Spizer, Bruce - The Beatles Solo on Apple Records – Four Ninety Eight Productions (2005)

Strongman, Phil and Parker, Alan - John Lennon and the FBI Files - Sanctuary Publishing (2003)

Sulpy, Doug - The 910's Guide to the Beatles Outtakes – 910 (1999) 3rd Edition

Thompson, Graeme - George Harrison: Behind The Locked Door – Omnibus (2013)

Weiner, Jon - Come Together: John Lennon in his Own Time – Faber and Faber (1984)

Willis, Paul – Profane Culture – Routledge (1978)

Woofinden, Bob - The Beatles Apart (1967-1980) - Proteus Rocks (1981)

About the Author

Neil Nixon

Neil Nixon has been writing for publication since he was a student. Much of his output as an author and journalist has revolved around the paranormal in its various forms and popular music, so the collision of legend and popular music legends in this book is well within his comfort zone. His previous books for Gonzo Multimedia are *500 Albums You Won't Believe...Until You Hear Them* (co-authored with Thom Nixon) and *The Devil's Jukebox* (co-authored with Owen Wilson). Neil also alternates presentation of the radio show *Strange Fruit* which focusses on the obscure and generally strange, and presents every *Strange Harvest* (a monthly round up of new music fit for the *Strange Fruit* audience). Both shows are syndicated via the web radio page of Gonzo Multimedia. When not writing for a living Neil can be found teaching undergraduates to do the same thing, running a course in Professional Writing based in Dartford. A brief insight into Neil's various activities is available at his website www.neilnixon.com. He can be contacted through this site and is generally amenable to paid gigs which involve turning up and discussing his various strange interests, including myths and legends concerning The Beatles.

PHOTO: Neil Nixon photographed at a workshop/gig in Bucharest, November 2014.

Gonzo Books

There is still such a
thing as alternative
Publishing

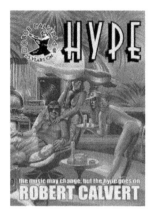

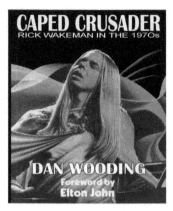

Robert Newton Calvert: Born 9 March 1945, Died 14 August 1988 after suffering a heart attack. Contributed poetry, lyrics and vocals to legendary space rock band Hawkwind intermittently on five of their most critically acclaimed albums, including Space Ritual (1973), Quark, Strangeness & Charm (1977) and Hawklords (1978). He also recorded a number of solo albums in the mid 1970s. CENTIGRADE 232 was Robert Calvert's first collection of poems.

Hype   'And now, for all you speeding street smarties out there, the one you've all been waiting for, the one that'll pierce your laid back ears, decoke your sinuses, cut clean thru the schlock rock, MOR/crossover, techno flash mind mush. It's the new Number One with a bullet ... with a bullet ... It's Tom, Supernova, Mahler with a pan galactic biggie ...' And the Hype goes on. And on. Hype, an amphetamine hit of a story by Hawkwind collaborator Robert Calvert. Who's been there and made it back again. The debriefing session starts here.

Rick Wakeman is the world's most unusual rock star, a genius who has pushed back the barriers of electronic rock. He has had some of the world's top orchestras perform his music, has owned eight Rolls Royces at one time, and has broken all the rules of composing and horrified his tutors at the Royal College of Music. Yet he has delighted his millions of fans. This frank book, authorised by Wakeman himself, tells the moving tale of his larger than life career.

"So many books, so little time."
Frank Zappa

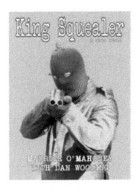

There are nine Henrys, pur
ported to be the world's
first cloned cartoon charac
ter. They live in a strange
lo fi domestic surrealist
world peopled by talking
rock buns and elephants on
wobbly stilts.

They mooch around in their
minimalist universe suffer
ing from an existential
crisis with some genetically
modified humour thrown in.

Marty Wilde on Terry Dene: "Whatever
happened to Terry becomes a great deal
more comprehensible as you read of the
callous way in which he was treated by
people who should have known better
many of whom, frankly, will never know
better of the sad little shadows of
the past who eased themselves into
Terry's life, took everything they
could get and, when it seemed that all
was lost, quietly left him ... Dan Wood
ing's book tells it all."

Rick Wakeman: "There have
always been certain 'careers'
that have fascinated the
public, newspapers, and the
media in general. Such
include musicians, actors,
sportsmen, police, and not
surprisingly, the people who
give the police their employ
ment: The criminal. For the
man in the street, all these
careers have one thing in
common: they are seemingly
beyond both his reach and,
in many cases, understanding
and as such, his only associ
ation can be through the
media of newspapers or tele
vision. The police, however,
will always require the ser
vices of the grass, the
squealer, the snitch, (call
him what you will), in order
to assist in their investiga
tions and arrests; and amaz
ingly, this is the area that
seldom gets written about."

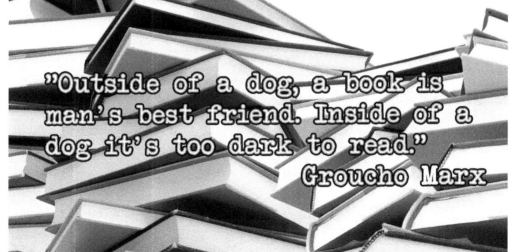

"Outside of a dog, a book is man's best friend. Inside of a dog it's too dark to read." Groucho Marx

Bill Harkleroad joined Captain Beef heart's Magic Band at a time when they were changing from a straight ahead blues band into something completely different. Through the vision of Don Van Vliet (Captain Beefheart) they created a new form of music which many at the time considered atonal and difficult, but which over the years has continued to exert a powerful influence. Beefheart re christened Harkleroad as Zoot Horn Rollo, and they embarked on recording one of the classic rock albums of all time Trout Mask Replica - a work of unequalled daring and inventiveness.

Politics, paganism and ... Vlad the Impaler. Selected stories from CJ Stone from 2003 to the present. Meet Ivor Coles, a British Tommy killed in action in September 1915, lost, and then found again. Visit Mothers Club in Erdington, the best psyche delic music club in the UK in the '60s. Celebrate Robin Hood's Day and find out what a huckle duckle is. Travel to Stonehenge at the Summer Solstice and carouse with the hippies. Find out what a Ranter is, and why CJ Stone thinks that he's one. Take LSD with Dr Lilly, the psychedelic scientist. Meet a headless soldier or the ghost of Elvis Presley in Gabalfa, Cardiff. Journey to Whitstable, to New York, to Malta and to Transylvania, and to many other places, real and imagined, polit ical and spiritual, transcendent and mundane. As The Independent says, Chris is "The best guide to the underground since Charon ferried dead souls across the Styx."

This is is the first in the highly acclaimed vampire novels of the late Mick Farren. Victor Renquist, a surprisingly urbane and likable leader of a colony of vampires which has existed for centuries in New York is faced with both admin istrative and emotional prob lems. And when you are a vampire, administration is not a thing which one takes lightly.

"The person, be it gentleman or lady, who has not pleasure in a good novel, must be intolerably stupid."

Jane Austen

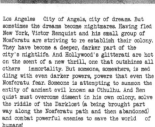

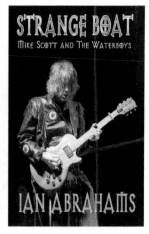

Los Angeles City of Angels, city of dreams. But sometimes the dreams become nightmares. Having fled New York, Victor Renquist and his small group of Nosferatu are striving to re establish their colony. They have become a deeper, darker part of the city's nightlife. And Hollywood's glitterati are hot on the scent of a new thrill, one that outshines all others immortality. But someone, somewhere, is med dling with even darker powers, powers that even the Nosferatu fear. Someone is attempting to summon the entity of ancient evil known as Cthulhu. And Ren quist must overcome dissent in his own colony, solve the riddle of the Darklost (a being brought part way along the Nosferatu path and then abandoned) and combat powerful enemies to save the world of humans!

Canadian born Corky Laing is probably best known as the drummer with Mountain. Corky joined the band shortly after Mountain played at the famous Woodstock Festival, although he did receive a gold disc for sales of the soundtrack album after over dubbing drums on Ten Years After's performance. Whilst with Mountain Corky Laing recorded three studio albums with them before the band split. Follow ing the split Corky, along with Mountain gui tarist Leslie West, formed a rock three piece with former Cream bassist Jack Bruce. West, Bruce and Laing recorded two studio albums and a live album before West and Laing re formed Mountain, along with Felix Pappalardi. Since 1974 Corky and Leslie have led Mountain through various line ups and recordings, and continue to record and perform today at numer ous concerts across the world. In addition to his work with Mountain, Corky Laing has recorded one solo album and formed the band Cork with former Spin Doctors guitarist Eric Shenkman, and recorded a further two studio albums with the band, which has also featured former Jimi Hendrix bassist Noel Redding. The stories are told in an incredibly frank, engaging and amusing manner, and will appeal also to those people who may not necessarily be fans of

To me there's no difference between Mike Scott and The Waterboys; they both mean the same thing. They mean myself and whoever are my current travel ling musical companions" Mike Scott Strange Boat charts the twisting and meandering journey of Mike Scott, describing the literary and spiritual references that inform his songwriting and explor ing the multitude of locations and cultures in which The Waterboys have assembled and reflected in their recordings. From his early forays into the music scene in Scotland at the end of the 1970s, to his creation of a 'Big Music' that peaked with the hit single 'The Whole of the Moon' and onto the Irish adventure which spawned the classic Fisher man's Blues, his constantly restless creativity has led him through a myriad of changes. With his revolving cast of troubadours at his side, he's created some of the most era defining records of the 1980s, reeled and jigged across the Celtic heartlands, reinvented himself as an electric rocker in New York, and sought out personal renewal in the spiritual calm of Findhorn's Scot tish highland retreat Mike Scott's life has been a tale of continual musical exploration entwined with an ever evolving spirituality. "An intriguing portrait of a modern musician" (Record Collector).

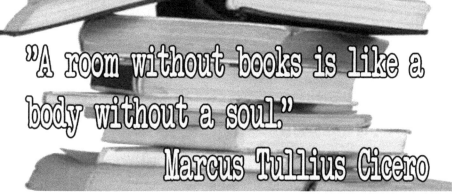

"A room without books is like a body without a soul."
Marcus Tullius Cicero

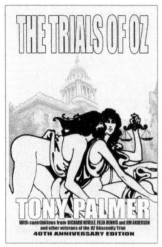

The OZ trial was the longest obscenity trial in history. It was also one of the worst reported. With minor exceptions, the Press chose to rewrite what had occurred, presumably to fit in with what seemed to them the acceptable prejudices of the times. Perhaps this was inevitable. The proceedings dragged on for nearly six weeks in the hot summer of 1971 when there were, no doubt, a great many other events more worthy of attention. Against the background of murder in Ulster, for example, the OZ affair probably fades into its proper insignifi cance. Even so, after the trial, when some newspapers realised that maybe something important had hap pened, it became more and more apparent that what was essential was for anyone who wished to be able to read what had actually been said. Trial and judgment by a badly informed press became the order of the day. This 40th Anniversary edition includes new material by all three of the original defendants, the prosecuting barrister, one of the OZ schoolkids, and even the daughters of the judge. There are also many illustrations including unseen material from Felix Dennis' own collection…

Merrell Fankhauser has led one of the most diverse and interesting careers in music. He was born in Louisville, Kentucky, and moved to California when he was 13 years old. Merrell went on to become one of the innovators of surf music and psychedelic folk rock. His travels from Hollywood to his 15 year jungle experience on the island of Maui have been documented in numerous music books and magazines in the United States and Europe. Merrell has gained legendary international status throughout the field of rock music; his credits include over 250 songs published and released. He is a multi talented singer/songwriter and unique guitar player whose sound has delighted listeners for over 35 years. This extraordi nary book tells a unique story of one of the founding fathers of surf rock, who went on to play in a succession of progressive and psychedelic bands and to meet some of the greatest names in the business, including Captain Beefheart, Randy California, The Beach Boys, Jan and Dean… and there is even a run in with the notorious Manson family.

On September 19, 1985, Frank Zappa testified before the United States Senate Commerce, Technology, and Transportation committee, attacking the Parents Music Resource Center or PMRC, a music organization co founded by Tipper Gore, wife of then senator Al Gore. The PMRC consisted of many wives of politi cians, including the wives of five members of the committee, and was founded to address the issue of song lyrics with sexual or satanic content. Zappa saw their activities as on a path towards censor shipand called their proposal for voluntary labelling of records with explicit content "extor tion" of the music industry. This is what happened.

"Good friends, good books, and a sleepy conscience: this is the ideal life." Mark Twain